CHASING THE
MOUNTAIN OF LIGHT

By the same author

Eating the Flowers of Paradise:
A Journey through the Drug Fields of Ethiopia and Yemen

CHASING THE
MOUNTAIN OF LIGHT

Across India on the
Trail of the Koh-i-Noor Diamond

KEVIN RUSHBY

ISBN 0-312-22813-9

Library of Congress Cataloging-in-Publication Data

Rushby, Kevin.
    Chasing the mountain of light : across India on the trail of the
    Koh-i-Noor Diamond / Kevin Rushby.
        p. cm.
    Includes bibliographical references and index.
    ISBN 0-312-22813-9
    1. India—Description and travel. 2. Koh-i-Noor (Diamond)
    3. Rushby, Kevin—Journeys—India. I. Title.
    DS414.2.R87   1999
    915.404'52—dc21   99-36877
                                                                     CIP

First published in Great Britain in 1999 by Constable and Company Limited
First published in the United States in 2000 by St. Martin's Press

10 9 8 7 6 5 4 3 2 1 0

In memory of my father,

GEOFFREY WILLIAM RUSHBY

CONTENTS

AUTHOR'S NOTE

Without the hospitality and assistance of many people in India, I could not have completed this journey. In Hyderabad I am grateful to Narendra Luther and the staff at the Andhra Pradesh State Tourism Office; in Bombay to Harshad Mehta and his family; in Gujarat to Shambhubhai Desai, Mahendra Bilkha and the people of the wonderful village of Bilkha, and in Delhi to Dr Yunus Jaffery for his insight into Mughal history. As a result of events described in the book I am particularly indebted to various individuals in the Punjab, notably Mehtab Singh and Professor Sher Singh 'Sher' in Chandigarh. In England I was given an invaluable start on the diamond trail by Lesley Coldham at the Diamond Information Service and the late Howard Vaughan. In addition my researches would not have been complete without the help of Harbinder Singh of the Maharaja Dulip Singh Memorial Trust and Eric Bruton. I am also grateful to my agent, Carolyn Whitaker, my editor at Constable, Carol O'Brien, Maggie Body and my wife, Judith, for their various invaluable comments and suggestions on the text.

The transliteration of names used here is based purely on familiarity and readability for English speakers; hence, Bombay rather than Mumbai, and Alauddin rather than 'Ala'u'd-Din.

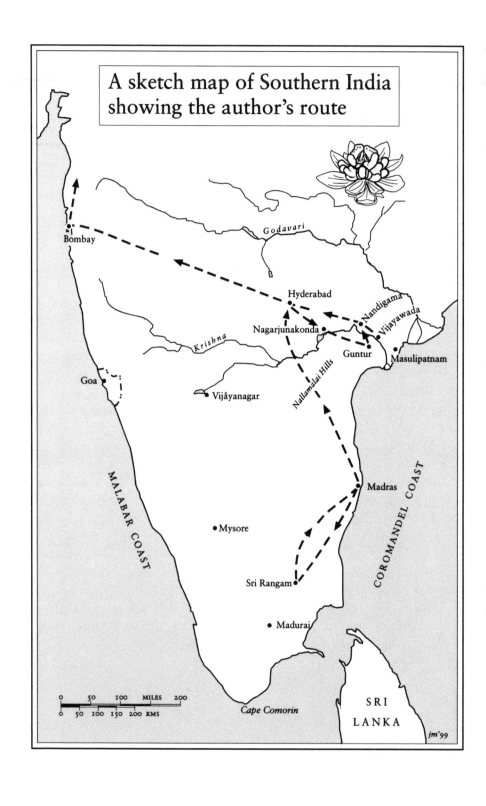

A sketch map of Southern India showing the author's route

Godavari

Bombay

Hyderabad

Nandigama

Vijayawada

Nagarjunakonda

Guntur

Krishna

Masulipatnam

Goa

Nallamalai Hills

Vijáyanagar

MALABAR COAST

Madras

Mysore

COROMANDEL COAST

Sri Rangam

Madurai

0   50   100   MILES   200
0   50   100   150   200   KMS

Cape Comorin

SRI
LANKA

jm'99

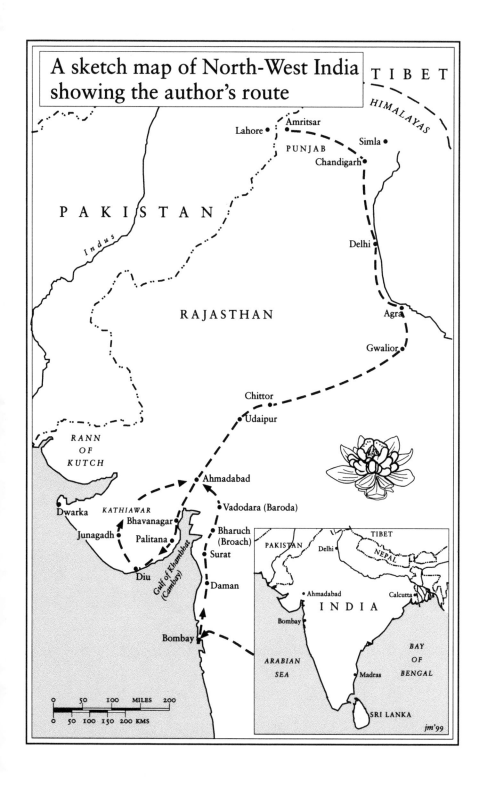

A sketch map of North-West India showing the author's route

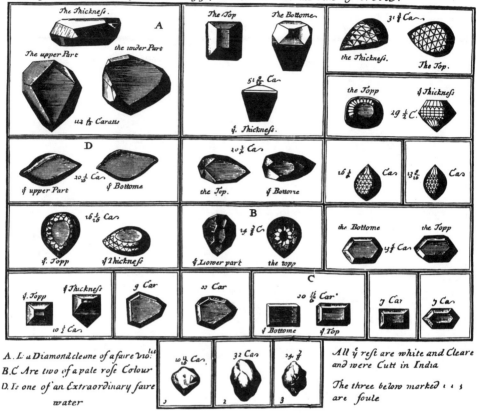

A Representation of 200 of the fairest Diamonds Chosen out among all those which Monsieur Tavernier sold to the King at his last return from the Indies, upon which Consideration, and for severall services done the Kingdome His Majesty honored him with the Title of Noble.

A. L: a Diamond cleane of a faire Violet.
B.C Are two of a pale rose Colour
D. Is one of an Extraordinary faire water

All the rest are white and Cleare and were Cutt in India

The three below marked ι ι ʒ are foule

PROLOGUE

I was living a life of unexampled pleasure when, one day,
the old desire entered my head to visit far countries and
strange people, to voyage among the isles and curiously
regard things hitherto unknown to me.

The second voyage of Sindbad the Sailor.

'IN the beginning God was creating His earth with eighty-four gem
stones,' said the Indian gentleman in the grey cardigan, leaning
forward so that his hands appeared in the light of the desk lamp.
He was holding a square white envelope. 'That is not by chance – each
one was put here for a reason and a purpose, each has its properties
and its importance.'

He did not play with the paper, turn it or fold the corners: his finger-
tips were very still, and carefully manicured. On the first finger of his
left hand was a ring of yellow sapphire in a gold setting, on the third
coral, and the fourth an emerald.

He opened the envelope and poured out a shimmering cascade of
pale yellow jewels onto his blotter. With the light catching the stones
it appeared liquid, almost alive.

'Yellow sapphire is the stone of Jupiter. It brings calm and tranquillity to the higher meditational levels. That is important, for this
world is a troubled place.'

He poured them back into the paper scrip and leaned down to take
a handful of others from a low drawer. As his head came back up, I
saw his face clearly for the first time, smooth-skinned with strangely
lifeless dark eyes; there was a small scar next to his left eye. He began
to pour stones from the packets; his movements were rhythmic,
meditational, and I watched each cascade from each new envelope,
sudden beauty that was gone, then repeated, and gone.

'These stones are from Sri Lanka, from mines run by the Liberation

Tigers of Tamil Eelam, sold so they can buy guns, but this is the stone of peace and meditational power. What use is fighting?'

There was a rustle behind me and I turned to see a tea tray on the floor in front of a curtained archway. In the space between cloth and floor, just for an instant, was a brown-skinned foot, toenails painted scarlet and a silver ankle chain hung with talismans.

The gemologist got up and brought the tray to his desk: there were two bone china cups and saucers and a plate of Rich Tea biscuits on a picture of the Tower of London. He placed a cup in front of me, then went back through the archway.

What I could see of the darkened room was fascinating. On my right, next to the door, was a glass case containing a large figure of the Hindu elephant god, Ganesh. At his feet were half a dozen everlasting incense sticks – a trickle of electricity maintaining the glow – and roll upon roll of banknotes neatly secured with elastic bands.

Down both sides of the room were large posters, also of Ganesh, brilliant with sky blue, scarlet and saffron, then across the shuttered window was a Chinese carved wooden screen hung with pictures of holy men – among them, the guru Sai Baba and Jesus Christ. Every frame had a necklace of coral, rubies and wizened rudraksh seeds; in front of each was more everlasting incense.

The curtain swished back and the man in the grey cardigan returned, carrying a clutch of smoking incense sticks.

'Breathe,' he said, allowing the smoke to pother up in front of me. His manner was precise and calm, like a counsellor, his English gently accented with Indian. He offered the sticks to each and every image before finally setting them up in a pot at Ganesh's feet, then he sat down and pressed his fingertips together thoughtfully. 'I live simply,' he said. 'I charge a hundred rupees for an astrological consultation and I put that money in front of Lord Ganesh. That is for charity. The gemstones, of course, people must purchase if they wish.' He sighed. 'This is a very large topic – for twenty-three years I have been studying it. My father and grandfather started here in Bombay and I have followed, finding yet more knowledge.

'In your country – countries like Britain, Germany and the United States – they have cars, electronics, computers, new this, new that. People have reached saturation point and are disillusioned: they want only peace and calm. The world is a troubled place. The world needs peace and calm.'

He reached behind him to a shelf and fetched a large computer printout. 'You see this lady's chart. Here is the twelfth house, here the fifth. She is a German lady and came to me because everything she did was not successful. Everything she did fell to pieces. Every project she had was a mistake, nothing succeeded. Actually, this lady was totally buggered.'

He began the rhythmic pouring of stone again, the yellow stream sparkling and moving.

'I recommended yellow sapphire and within forty-eight hours – only forty-eight hours – she had some benefit.'

He showed me more stones. 'You are a writer and so I would recommend emerald – perhaps a ring on the fourth finger. Each finger has its stone and each stone its planet.'

'What about diamond?'

He smiled. 'That is a most powerful stone. It is white. It unifies the cosmic rays and so is the symbol of divinity – the king of stones and the stone of kings. The first diamond was the Syamantaka which the Sun god, Surya, gave to Sattrajit as reward for worshipping him. When this magical gem disappeared, the people accused our god Krishna of stealing it and he fought terrible battles to return it to man.'

He reached down to a low drawer and I heard a key turn in a lock. When his hands came up, he was holding a red square box.

'That stone passed down so many generations to Babur, the first Mughal, then others and others till your Maharani, Victoria, stole it away to the Towers of London. Now the House of Windsor is having hard times due to the malevolent aspect of that great jewel – the Koh-i-Noor, the Mountain of Light!'

'Is it always a bad force?'

His hands stroked the velvet cover of the box. 'Not always. According to scripture – our Puranas – the Syamantaka jewel will do good for a good man, and bad for the bad man.'

He opened the box and held it out for me to see. 'This will be for my daughter.'

There were nine white silk beds set in a square and nestled in each was a sparkling gemstone. His fingertip followed the edge of the box.

'This is emerald, this ruby. Here is cat's eye and topaz. Next is blue sapphire, pearl, coral and moonstone.' His finger went to the centre. 'And this is diamond.'

I noticed that he did not touch the stone.

'This is without flaws,' he said. 'To carry any diamond that has flaws is to invite disaster.'

My hand went to my pocket and fingered the ring I kept there. I never liked wearing rings and this one I had bought as a cheap souvenir: nine chips of coloured stone in a silver band.

'Nine stones together,' I said. 'Is that significant?'

'The nine heavenly bodies rule our destinies – Sun, Moon, Mercury, Venus, Mars, Saturn and Jupiter are seven. Then there are the dragon's head and the dragon's tail – rahu and ketu. Those are the empty spaces in the heavens, the black spaces. Each of these channels its cosmic energies through the stones. The nine stones together, we call that navaratna.'

'And it brings good luck?' I was actually more interested in getting his professional opinion as a gemstone dealer. The ring had come very cheaply in Hyderabad, but there was always a chance I had made a good deal.

'Not always,' he said. 'Sometimes the opposite. I have a letter from a lady in New York. She bought a navaratna ring in India – not from me – and it was stolen recently. So she wrote asking for another.'

'Did you send one?'

He looked away from me. 'You see the stones will move on. There is no point to ask why or to try to prevent it. She will not understand, but the navaratna has left her for a good reason – to replace it would be a mistake.'

'Could it have been a flawed stone?'

'Of course. I never sell imperfect stones but others do – it is a danger – very grave danger. If so, she is better without it.'

I turned the ring over and left it in my pocket. Perhaps, I decided, it was better not to know.

CHAPTER 1

The Agra diamond, reputed to have glinted on the
turban of the 16th century Mogul emperor Babur, sold
for £4.07 million at Christie's last night.

The Times, 21 June 1990

Mere carbon, my good friend, after all.

Mr Godfrey in *The Moonstone* by Wilkie Collins

IT was Cedric who made me think about diamonds. We had met by
chance in Ethiopia and travelled down to Djibouti, that sweaty
little crack in the backside of Africa. Cedric, or Gordon, or Arthur,
or one of half a dozen pseudonyms, wanted to recover a car he had
abandoned in haste four years before. I was looking for a dhow to take
me to Yemen. When I finally escaped Cedric's clutches I understood
that he smuggled diamonds in secret compartments inside cars. He
had told me how he travelled to the Angola-Zaire border and, through
contacts with Jonas Savimbi's rebels, bought stones to smuggle across
Africa. Once he had driven across Africa and left from the east coast
ports, he would deliver them to Antwerp, Tel Aviv, India or the far
east.

'Diamonds are tellin' no tales,' he said. 'They are small and light
and no one can know where they are comin' from. The diamond has
no memory.'

It was the germ of an idea: to find those markets on the border and
travel east with the diamond men, picking up stories and characters,
perhaps heading out to a grand finale in the docks of Antwerp or the

skyscrapers of Taiwan. Then, quite unexpectedly, Zaire disappeared. One moment there was President Seseko Mobutu, conniving in a diamond trade that kept the Angolan rebels supplied with bullets, then he was gone, replaced by Laurent Kabile who had the support of the Angolan government. Not only that but the Angolan government overran the diamond mines. When the telephone rang to tell me that De Beers in London had agreed that I could visit their headquarters, I had almost given the diamond idea up. Cedric had been right. No tales.

It was a summer's day in London: a thin cold drizzle tickling the pavements. In Smithfield Market a meat porter with a beef carcass on his shoulder was chatting on a mobile phone. Almost opposite, in Charterhouse Street, was the building through which three-quarters of the world's annual diamond production passes, and where jewels worth five billion dollars are stored at any one time. There are no signs to announce the fact, nor any other facts, the building is anonymous, discreetly unidentifiable. Only the plethora of security cameras, both outside and in, suggest anything other than a large insurance company, or a particularly dull branch of government.

I was taken up through the fortified building to a comfortable reception room where a video introduced me to the world of De Beers; another video watched me, watching them. I was allowed to admire the trays of twinkling cut stones, all neatly laid out on black velvet beneath the spotlights. I heard how they sold their production in monthly 'sights', held in the same building. I learnt that diamonds was a business, an industry dedicated to sharpening the world's drill bits and making brides happy. And I was despairing of finding anything of interest.

Then the public relations lady took me to a side cabinet. 'These are carob seeds,' she said, pointing to a pile of reddish bean-shaped objects. 'They are very regular in weight and so in ancient times they used them as measures – what we know as the carat.' She had another object in her hand. 'Two hundred and ninety-seven of those make this.'

It was a yellowish stone, the size of a goose egg. The shape was roughly octohedronal and the surface looked strangely smooth with tiny curving striations. With the light behind it, bringing it closer to my eye – 'You hold the magnifying glass like this,' she demonstrated

– I was drawn into the complexities inside the crystal, the yellow and gold of hidden worlds within, slanting and whirling chaotically, leading the eye ever onward, as though vast distances could be seen and what was a few millimetres could be mile upon mile. When it was too close to focus any longer I pressed it to my cheek and the chill of its touch was like steel.

It was flawed: presumably that was why it had remained as an uncut showpiece rather than becoming a hundred tiny sterile specks of perfectly formed light. But it was the very imperfection that fascinated me. Somewhere deep in its centre, light seemed to be generated, and yet that centre, like the heart of distant nebula, was hidden. Here, I decided, was a stone worthy of an idol's eye, a Moonstone that could entice men to evil deeds and then curse them for it.

'There was an Indian lady here the other day,' said the lady when I mentioned the Moonstone. 'She was saying that she would never accept a flawed diamond as a gift – it would bring very bad luck.'

I moved the diamond away from my eye. 'Do they have many superstitions?'

She shook her head. 'I don't know.'

We were running out of things to say. If only I could be interested in the statistics, the production methods, the global enterprise with its thousands of workers and strong profits. But I could only think of the three Indian fakirs whose malevolent presence brings the first shiver of fear in Wilkie Collins' novel.

'Is there much of an Indian connection?'

'They cut and polish eighty per cent of the world's stones. Over 750,000 people are employed.'

'Do they mine them?'

'The ancient mines are disused now – but once India was the only source of diamonds.'

'So all those famous stones – like the Koh-i-Noor – they are all Indian?'

She nodded and going to a cupboard took out a leather-bound volume.

'Would you like to see Jean-Baptiste Tavernier's book? We have a first English edition – 1678. He was the first European to leave a detailed account.'

I reluctantly replaced the diamond on its tray and went and sat at the coffee table, leafing carefully through the old book. There was a slip of paper marking the page where Tavernier visited the diamond mines, and I read his description of the rites performed before the digging begins: 'he brings along with him some little Image of the God that they adore; which being plac'd upright upon the ground, they all prostrate themselves three times before it, while their Priest says a certain prayer. The prayer being ended, he marks the forehead of every one with a kind of Glue, made of Saffron and Gum, to such a compass as will hold seven or eight Grains of Rice, which he sticks upon it.'

I read more, about the diamond dealers sitting in the trees waiting for buyers and how the poor miners would swallow stones to smuggle them out and, as I did, I forgot about Africa where the diamonds told no tales. India was the source, both of ancient stones and ancient stories.

Diamonds were certainly being recognised and used as gems as early as the second century BC. A Greek statue from that time has two uncut specimens as eyes. Legend has credited Alexander the Great with discovery of the remote Indian valley where the diamonds originated, a place so deep and inaccessible that the only method of retrieving the stones was bizarre in the extreme. Raw meat was dropped over the cliffs and the diamonds would stick to it. Passing eagles, spotting this free lunch, would then take the meat to their nests where the enterprising diamond collector could retrieve the jewels at leisure. Marco Polo repeats this tale, as do the *Arabian Nights*; Sindbad's second voyage takes him to a remote valley filled with deadly snakes who lick the diamonds and make them poisonous – another enduring myth. Curiously, however, diamonds do adhere to meat and though not strictly poisonous, they can kill – by lacerating the intestines. Crushed diamond has long been a favourite in the Indian royal poisons cabinet.

Where the earliest diamonds were found can be narrowed down to only a few possibilities. In Tavernier's day the one non-Indian origin was Borneo, but it was a minor source compared to the mines of Golconda, a kingdom in the central Deccan centred on the capital of Hyderabad. The diamonds were found close to the banks of two rivers, the Krishna and Godavari, which both rise in the Eastern Ghats and flow east, right across the sub-continent.

Bengal did produce some diamonds in Tavernier's time and there were other mines further south, but the Krishna-Godavari was the main area for mines. And, although individual diggings came and went, the region probably always had been known for diamonds: Tavernier records that Kollur, an important mine, was discovered by a 'Countryman, who digging in a piece of ground to sow Millet, found therein a pointed Stone that weigh'd above twenty-five Carats'.

What intrigued me was the possiblity that the legendary valley of Sindbad, Marco Polo and Alexander might be that of the River Krishna: my map showed it cutting through a vast gorge to the south of Hyderabad. Such a place might be the source of the greatest diamond of them all, a stone that had come from the southern mines and traced a course of destruction northwards as it passed from hand to hand. It was the stone some Indians believe to have been Krishna's Syamantaka jewel, a diamond in whose depths were mingled the massive forces of creation and destruction, waiting to be controlled or unbalanced according to the nature of the stone's possessor. For centuries it rested in the treasure vaults of Rajput princes before the Mughals invaded and claimed it. Babur, founder of the dynasty, gave it to his son Humayun who promptly lost the kingdom and found himself wandering in Rajasthan, pestered by a diamond merchant to sell his greatest asset.

'Such precious gems,' he told the man, 'cannot be bought. Either they fall to one by the arbitrament of the flashing sword, which is an expression of divine will, or else they come through the grace of mighty monarchs as an honourable gift.'

It was the flashing sword that generally prevailed: it had been looted by the Persian Nadir Shah, stolen by the Afghans, reclaimed by Maharaja Ranjit Singh for the Sikh kingdom of the Punjab, then lost to the English and Queen Victoria. It sits now in the Tower of London, temporarily becalmed, planning its next move. The great rulers of three thousand years had looted, loved and lost it. This jewel was the Koh-i-Noor.

So it was that the most ancient diamond suggested a route across India, from the southern coastal city of Madras to the nearby fabled mines of Golconda, then north into the Punjab, through all the places where it had exerted its malign influence to the place where its ownership remains a contentious issue. The track of the Koh-i-Noor not only spans the landscape of India but it weaves through the history, turning up like Blind Pew's Black Spot in every cursed hand. And there is no doubt that its history is not over yet, though the Jewel House at the Tower of London looks so solid and enduring.

The more I read of the modern world of diamonds, the more I felt that buried beneath the mountains of cash, the auction catalogues and the business jargon lay a darker corner of the human psyche – one that those industry executives and millionaire collectors might not care to admit to – where the spirit of something greater haunted the stones they worshipped. And the place where that spirit was strongest was in India.

CHAPTER 2

Asleep and naked as an Indian lay,
An honest factor stole a gem away;
He pledged it to the Knight, the Knight had wit,
So kept the diamond and the rogue was bit.

Alexander Pope, 'Epistle to Bathhurst'.

THE deluge began two hours after my train pulled into Madras. There was a movement of air, like a drawn-out sigh, then the bruised yellow sky seemed to swell. Black umbrellas blossomed in the hands of passers-by and the rain started to fall in relentless columns. I pressed myself against an arched wooden door set deep in a stone wall; opposite me were crumbling colonial shop-houses, trees sprouting from gutterings and algal stains under the shutters like the shadows of sleeplessness.

Within a minute the road was full of muddy water: those who had not taken cover gave up weaving between puddles and began to wade. A large white cow stood still, blinking slowly at the downpour, while a fat man with five hands of bananas on his head fed it green grass. When the cow had finished, the man turned and came along the street with the corners of his lunghi loincloth daintily held between thumb and forefinger, rainwater coursing down his face.

'Are you from London?' he asked as he passed, raising his voice to be heard above the roaring static of the rain.

'Yes.'

'Proper London?'

'Er . . . No. Not really, the north of England.'

[23]

'Proper England?'

The ancient door behind me creaked as I pressed back further, the iron ring between my shoulder blades.

'Yes, proper England.' I felt the door give a little more.

'I saw your Maharani,' he said, smiling. 'She was here a few months back.'

'Elizabeth?' I stepped back onto the stone lintel and half-turning my head could see a dark stone tunnel with a courtyard beyond.

'She was not wearing a crown,' the fat man continued, quite happy to chat amiably while a cloud emptied over him and his bananas. 'A proper Maharani wears a crown.'

'Too dangerous,' I said. 'Someone might steal it.'

He nodded glumly. 'Pinching of perquisites is definitely a possibility – but then most probably that crown belongs to India. This Koh-i-Noor diamond, for example. Miscreants were stealing it – but those ruffians were your own people, not ours.'

'She rarely wears that diamond,' I said. 'The kings and princes never do – superstition.'

The rain was stopping, as though a faulty tap had been turned off, leaving a few drips.

'They should return stolen properties immediately,' said the fat man, unwilling to be diverted. I stepped back into the dark tunnel.

'I'll ask – next time I see her.'

He laughed as I turned away. Ahead of me was a cool stone tunnel leading to an archway where, a hand's width inside the wet mark of the rain, an old woman and a black dog lay stretched out fast asleep beside a wire cage of yellow ducklings. Beyond them was a lovely tree-lined courtyard filled with plants in terracotta pots. On the far side of this, standing beside the buttermilk walls of the church itself, was a tall belltower of stout but elegant symmetry.

I stepped gently over the woman, keeping my eye on the dog. On my right a colonnade led away to various rooms, on my left was a small office in the archway. It was empty. On the wall was a pencil drawing of a church, entitled, 'The Cathedral of Holy Etchmiadzin, 303 AD'.

The courtyard was paved with gravestones: each larger pair surrounded by pitifully small stones, some no more than eight inches long – the children who had predeceased their parents, a macabre hopscotch of death all the way to the foot of the belltower. Some of the gravestones were incised with a skull and crossbones, others had protractors, scissors, or a pair of scales. There were dates going back to the eighteenth century and, though I could not read the script, I recognised it as Armenian.

There was quiet after the hullaballoo of the street, a delicate perfume of frangipani came from a tree by a well where luxuriant arrow-shaped leaves sprang from between the stones. There were mango trees, guava, banana, almond and Indian curry-leaf – the tiny aromatic foliage that seems to turn up in all South Indian cooking – and gliding gently between them all, large black and red birdwing butterflies.

I walked past the well and under the dripping trees, enjoying the peace disturbed only by the gurgle of drains. I was two weeks into my journey and back where I had started, in Madras, in the rain, the city pungent with rotten fruit and urine. The coastal strip had been flooded and newspapers had put the death toll at 162. My enquiries into diamonds seemed to be pitted against a tide of scummy, rubbish-laden water. Everywhere I went I had to wade or seek shelter or turn back. A local historian, his backyard awash and front room dark and humid, had sent me to Coral Merchant Street where, he claimed, Jewish diamond merchants had once traded.

I found some fine houses, none more than a century old, and a coffee shop where the proprietor told me that a huge diamond had been stolen from the eye of an idol at the temple of Sri Rangam. So I went there, a four-day journey that culminated in meeting one of the Brahmin priests who assured me it was a false story. Then back through the floods, Madras station flooded, families camped on piles of baggage. Given directions to an aged priest, I found him in his shuttered room at the Jesuit College, the air thick with moisture and the foetid breath of banana trees. He toyed with a magnifying glass and talked of Princess Diana and the ordination of women, anything but diamonds, then gave me a sealed envelope and said goodbye. Opening the envelope, I found an invitation to meet Sai Baba, the guru, savant and charlatan (depending on your view) at a hospice for the blind. I went but could not find the hospice.

Madras had never promised much, either to me or the early settlers.

A scrubby strip of land trapped between river and sea, it had been given in 1639 to the East India Company whose servants complained bitterly about the place from the start. As a port it was a disaster waiting to happen and captains soon learnt to put out to sea when storms approached, preferring to risk the open water rather than face certain ruin on the beach. The attraction for the English merchants, or factors, was only partly the possibility of trade with the rich inland states of Arcot and the Carnatic which were, and still are, renowned for their cloth. More important to them, at least early on, was that Madras looked east and was well-positioned to allow English infiltration of existing trade routes to Sumatra, the Spice Islands and China. They had needed someone to open their eyes to the fact that the kingdom of Golconda was three hundred miles to the north-west, home to almost all the known sources of diamonds and a market where they were traded. I knew where the ruins of that once-thriving city lay, but it was not enough to follow the dead roads that history books could point me along: I wanted to hear it from the living, I wanted to see what diamonds meant to them.

I had searched through southern India for two weeks without success: no one knew anything about diamonds, no one had heard of any famous diamonds, no one worked with diamonds, collected, sold or stole diamonds. In Tiruchipalli market, a dealer offered me a sparkling ring: 'Diamond rings made in America,' he whispered. 'Even experts may be fooled, such is the imperishable quality of these items.'

'You mean it's not actually a diamond?' My hopes of a useful contact took another downturn.

'It is not strictly speaking a diamond, but even world-famous experts cannot be sure.'

'It's a fake.'

He frowned at my lack of subtlety, 'Yes, my brother, you may say that.' He cast around for the right words, then took my hand. 'You may say it is fake – but this is a genuine fake.'

Such were the frustrations, the inability to find any trace of an ancient trade or a modern one. But it came, eventually, in the Armenian churchyard.

As I reached the church door, a charpoy creaked from under the belltower and a man appeared.

'We are closed now,' he said. 'Lunchtime.'

He led me back towards the entrance. The old lady and black dog had mysteriously vanished, but the ducklings remained. 'Are there any Armenians left in Madras?' I asked.

He nodded. 'I myself am half-Armenian, but the last true Armenian is Mr Gregory – he is the only one.'

'Can you read the gravestones?'

'No. Only Mr Gregory can read this language.'

We stood in the cool behind the great old wooden doors. I would have liked Mr Gregory to read the gravestones to me. 'Is he here? Does he live here – in the churchyard?'

He nodded. 'Yes, he lives here, but you cannot meet him. He is very old.'

'Perhaps another day?'

'No.'

'Perhaps you could ask him if he wants to meet me?'

'That will not be possible.'

'Why?'

He jangled his keys and smiled secretively. 'He is not easy. Things can irritate him. He can frighten people. And his health is not good these days.'

'Does he speak English?'

'Oh yes, very well. He worked in London in the 1950s at a famous restaurant – Claridges, is it?' He saw that this had only further aroused my interest and made a move for the door. I did not follow him.

'Is he here now?'

'No, he went out.'

'When will he be back?'

'It is not known.'

He stood with one hand on the gate, waiting for me to move past him, but I did not. There was a long silence.

'He may not come today at all,' he said. 'If he comes he will go immediately to his room and see no one.' But he stopped, a shout from the street had distracted him; he gave me a worried glance and went outside. I waited.

The street noise was of water in gutters, the sudden rasp of an auto-rickshaw engine, bicycle bells and the calls of children. But above that

[27]

I could hear the caretaker, insistent and persuading. Suddenly there was an enormous crash, the whole gate juddered and I took a step back.

'Tell him I'm dead!' came a ferocious old voice. 'Tell him I'm six feet under the ground. Show him bones! Get rid of the man!'

A tip of a walking stick appeared and felt for the ground. Then came a foot in a stout leather shoe and the rest of the stick, clasped in a vast hand, gnarled with arthritis and age. The man appeared: a long intelligent face with brilliant yellow-grey eyes burning feverishly from under shaggy white eyebrows. He was dressed in a dark suit and black beret.

I smiled but got no return. Instead he began to fall forwards, his other foot caught on the sill of the door. His frown suddenly became a look of concern as he toppled. Then one hand shot out towards me with a long wrinkled finger raised: 'Hold my finger!' he bellowed. I seized the digit. It was cool and hard, like the root of some ancient forest giant. I felt the last joint curling over my hand and gripping. He steadied himself and disentangled his foot. Now the fearsome leonine face pushed up close to mine, not six inches away.

'You young puppy!' He roared. 'With your pink cheeks fit for eating – what are you? Not twenty-four, I reckon.'

He shuffled around me to get my face in the light. 'From London, are ye?'

'Yes – proper London.'

His face broke into a radiant smile. 'I loved that woman for six years and she loved me back. D'ye love her too? D'ye love that sweet woman?' He began to sing. ' "Maybe its because I'm a Londoner . . ." '

We shuffled, like a tired ballroom couple on a last waltz, into the colonnade opposite the office. 'Y're not lettin' me go, are ye? I'm ready for Jesus, but you won't let him have me, will ye? Look at this,' His stick swept up and pointed to the church. 'This holy place, full of 'em that came before me – all dead and gone and me the last to go. I won't move out. They'll not get me out. I'll die here and they can put me down and walk all over me like the rest!'

Saying this he turned to glare at the caretaker who was following behind us; the man gave a hopeless shrug. 'The Armenian community have a nice home in Calcutta for old folks. You get a nice room to yourself and a television.'

'Pah! Television! Calcutta!'

The caretaker shrugged and retreated into his office. Mr Gregory forgot his anger. 'London, eh?' A dreamy look stole over his face. 'A fella asks me in Trafalgar Square, "How many eyes has Lord Horatio Nelson got?" So I says to him, "Why don't you look for yourself?" And when he did a pigeon dropped something in his face! Ha!' He hooted with laughter. 'I had a family there in London – wife and children. Never seen them in forty years.'

'Were you born in London?'

His brilliant yellow eyes regarded me with interest. 'It's the whole story you want is it, you young pup? But it's too long to tell.' He sighed. 'And they're all dead.'

We stood in thoughtful silence and the black dog reappeared, wagging its tail at him. 'Pedro – I saved him from the street.' He pulled his hand loose from mine to pat the animal.

'What do you want, my dear? Why have you come to see me?'

It was a second before I realised he was speaking to me, not the dog. 'I'm interested in the history of the place,' I said.

He frowned. 'History is it?'

'Especially gemstones – diamonds, in fact.'

'Diamonds?' He began to laugh, thumping the stick up and down on the flagstones with pleasure. Pedro licked him. 'Diamonds? Big diamonds fit for a king?' From under his shaggy eyebrows, he shot me a look of devilish amusement. 'Why if it's diamonds you want, my dear, you're standing on them.'

He gripped my arm and began tracing out the lines on the gravestone under our feet with his stick.

'Can't you see it?' He hissed conspiratorially. 'The weights and scales? This one was a jeweller – an Armenian jeweller dealing in diamonds.'

He pointed out some more graves. 'These were jewel merchants, too: the Agah Shameer, his wife and seven sons. Look at the poor babies, all dead and in their graves. They say he made his fortune from the Nawab of Arcot.'

We moved on to another gravestone. 'This is Petrus Voskan: he got so rich he had the streets draped in silk for the Nawab's visit. When he died they found seven lakhs of rupees in cash – for you it would be like finding a room full of hundred dollar bills.'

He tapped the carved skull and crossbones. 'My dear, many of them traded diamonds, the mines were all on the Krishna River up near Hyderabad, so naturally they came this way. Golconda was the place for buying. It's thirty years since I saw it – near Hyderabad.'

'And the British bought diamonds?'

'All of 'em wanted to. Thomas Pitt bought the biggest of the lot. The Armenians and British were thick as thieves,' he said. 'We'd been here as traders but when the British came, we joined 'em and did well. Look at these two – interpreters at the courts of justice.'

He shuffled over to them, his toes were painfully twisted by arthritis. 'They say the Pitt diamond came from Parteal on the Krishna River – a lost mine somewhere. It was we Armenians who were the middlemen, the merchants, bringing the stones down from Golconda, then selling to the East India Company people.'

I felt a jolt of adrenaline at this. The end of the thread was in my hand, the fragile link between this place and Golconda, preserved in these flagstones and the memory of the last Armenian in Madras. I wanted to hug him, but we were already holding hands.

'When did your ancestors come from Armenia?' I asked.

He shook his head. 'I'm telling you, the whole story is too long to tell and there is no time left for me to tell it.'

We stood silently, then I said. 'If you won't tell the story, nobody else can.'

He grunted and tapped his stick. 'They were all from Persia – like myself. I was born in the city of Shiraz.' His stick swept in an arc over the graves. 'Armenians and all from Persia. My father worked for the Anglo-Persian oil company, but when the First War came we had to run. We rode camels into Afghanistan and six years later we reached Bombay.' He fell silent again and we both looked at the churchyard: a faint fragment of rainbow had formed over the belltower. When I looked back at his face, I saw he was weeping, the tears rolling down his withered cheeks.

'My father died,' he said after some time. 'And we don't even know where he was buried. I've never seen his grave. All I want is to be buried in my own church.'

He looked up, and following his gaze I saw that the rainbow's colours had grown more vivid.

'Look at that sign,' he said, shaking his stick again. 'When these children of Madras see such things they say, "Pretty colours!"'

With alarming speed, he flung himself into a rage. 'The Devil's work! Pretty colours! God sent the Flood, the end of the world is coming. Look at it. I went in a bank this morning and found women working there – women! Boys will be girls and girls will be boys. Their heads are full of shopping lists: air-conditioners, cars, televisions, refrigerators.' He was roaring again and the caretaker appeared at his office door with a worried frown on his face. Mr Gregory's eyes were flashing, spittle shot from his lips like hot shrapnel, and tears were rolling down his cheeks.

'I say this: that the end is coming and man will do it. God won't destroy his world, man will do it. Look at the rain – this isn't our normal rain. I can barely walk but I'm burning up. Give me wings and I'll fly. Sweet Jesus. Never even seen the grave!'

The caretaker came hurrying over and gently took his hand from mine. 'Come, come, Mr Gregory. Lie down in your room.'

I said goodbye but he did not hear me. His voice was echoing down the colonnade as I stepped outside. 'Sweet Jesus is here. I tell them He is here, but no one will listen. The Flood is coming and they've all gone shopping!'

Walking out of his church gate, I took off my shoes to cross the swirling milky brown waters and tied the laces around my neck. Observe, I told myself, the clues are here: the symbols on the gravestone that I had blithely passed over were easily deciphered. The cacophony of modern India could all too readily drown the small voices I needed to hear.

On Bose Street where naked children were jumping in the grey frothy bow-waves of buses, just like any child playing in the surf on a sandy beach, I put my shoes back on and decided to revisit Fort St George.

Modern Madras bypasses the fort almost completely and, with the rampant vegetation threatening to engulf it, the largest edifice left to the world by the East India Company is easy to miss. Built over many years and by successive governors, the walls prickle with bastions and redoubts. I walked in through a tunneled entrance, the original gates still there, though long since unused. Some boys were driving in a herd

of big-humped zebu cattle to graze on the dripping grass, while soldiers ambled towards barracks. Most of the buildings were either in
army hands or else government offices: their modern defences were
bits of barbed wire hung on fences, the vast cannonball-proof walls
reduced to public urinals and sun-terraces for lizards.

Within this compound the English factors were required to live. The
Black Town around Armenian Street was for Indian merchants, servants and Europeans not attached to the Company. Life was meted out
in mean little doses: daily prayers and two Sunday sermons, plus
access to a library almost entirely consisting of books on divinity.
When more active pastimes and hobbies were needed, there were two
billiard tables and several garden strolls. Most, however, chose to
drink themselves into oblivion. Life was usually short, brutal and
redeemed by one tiny glimmer of hope – wealth.

The East India Company expected its men to get rich, or at least to
try very hard before expiring. There was no pretence in its miserly
wages that anyone was working solely for the benefit of the share-
holders: mutual enrichment was the order of the day. As to methods,
Sir Josiah Child, Governor of the Company in the 1680s reprimanded
one officer who questioned the legality of an order, writing angrily
that he expected his orders 'should be obeyed as statutes, and that they
were to be his [the officer's] rule and not the laws of England, which
were a heap of nonsense compiled by a few ignorant country gentlemen, who hardly knew how to make laws for the guidance of their
own private families much less for the regulating of companies and
foreign commerce'.

For the overseas agent, the favoured method was to engage in a little
country trade: transactions started and finished in the east, far from
London's gaze. Quite often, the Company's capital would come in
handy to finance such deals and the experience gained on official business could always be turned to extra advantage on private terms. Little
wonder that Head Office back in Leadenhall Street employed its own
spies and was constantly engaged in replacing officers, prosecuting
and imprisoning others. The atmosphere was one of almost perma-
nent intrigue and accusation.

The claustrophobia is there even today in Fort St George. The
featureless grey walls slant and angle across one another, too high to

look over. Many gateways are locked, with piles of refuse or vegetation building up against them. The air seems mouldy and rotten. I sat on a wall watching clerks stroll past, their shirts glued to their backs with the humidity. In this climate, wooden gateposts sprout and grow branches, puddles lie like poleaxed clouds and the sun, hidden by the grey sky, has no power to lift them. The ships that were the lifeblood of the place would often desert at such times, lifting anchor and departing for the safety of Ceylon – anywhere but the treacherous Coromandel Coast.

There is a small museum in the fort; it looks out across the wall to where the treacherous sea once was. Land reclamation projects have pushed the ocean eastwards, making room for a wide road where the black and yellow autorickshaws buzz piratically. A few cannons aim from the wall at the thorn trees. I found the museum-keepers keen to point out the 'No Photography' signs before offering exemption at ten rupees a shot. I declined.

There was relatively little to show for the long British occupation: a handful of portraits of haughty notables, some porcelain and various prints done by Thomas and William Daniell between 1784 and 1794. Perhaps it was difficult for the Indian authorities to tactfully display the true life of the English – rooms full of empty bottles.

Madras was never a plum posting for the Company men: Bengal suited the real hard cases, ready to get rich quick and damn the methods; Surat and later Bombay were for the diplomats and strategists as they had links with the Mughal capital at Agra. China, Burma, Thailand, Java and Japan were all promising theatres for rising entrepreneurs. Madras was steady and unspectacular which could seem unendurable to the young hopefuls who stepped inside the walls, many never to emerge. Even the young Robert Clive, yet to achieve fame and glory as Clive of India, found it too much and tried suicide.

But it was another man, one whose fame has faded, who realised that Madras had more potential. I searched for him through the museum, past the Rajas with their pearl strings and the various forgotten governors, but it was without success. In the end, giving up hope of a portrait, I spotted his name on a map, a plan of the town drawn 'By Order of the Late Governor Tho. Pitt Esq'. That was all that remained of the man who had built Madras to new heights of prosperity and, as Mr Gregory had reminded me, had lined his own pocket with the largest diamond in the world.

Though he ended his days a Member of Parliament with his son a lord and grandson soon to be Prime Minister, Pitt had begun humbly, born to the wife of a Dorsetshire clergyman on 5th July, 1653. Having shown early signs of sound common sense, resolute courage and a foul temper, he was encouraged to go to sea, something he did at twenty, sailing east on the Indiaman, *Lancaster*. When the ship returned to England three years later, his family learned that the headstrong young lad had jumped ship in Bengal and set himself up as a trader. Like many of his contemporaries, Pitt thought little of royal charters and trading monopolies. It was an age when kings' wings were being clipped and, in the eyes of renegade merchants at least, an Englishman could do business where he bloody well liked – even if some die-hard traditionalists called it piracy.

Pitt's gamble paid off: after a tough four-year apprenticeship, he began to make large amounts of money. On his second visit to England he was allowed to join the Company and eventually, in 1697, secured the appointment of governor to Fort St George. The pirate had become a pillar of the establishment.

Quite why Pitt accepted the post is a mystery. He was rich, held a seat in parliament and owned two country estates. His own letters state that he wanted to found a county family, but that scarcely required a dangerous voyage and hazardous life in Madras. Dalton, his biographer, suggests patriotism, a modern opinion might be mid-life crisis, but greed seems the most likely motive: Pitt knew that he had never failed to make money on Indian enterprises and this was the biggest of them all. Not only that, but he was certainly aware of the added ingredient which Madras could offer – diamonds.

Gemstones, along with spices and silks, had been moving west from India long before Europeans reached its shores. Knowledge of this lucrative trade had been brought back by a motley selection of pilgrims, spies, fearless merchants and downright liars. Among them, Marco Polo is best known today, but in the fourteenth century it was an Englishman who created the greatest stir. *The Travels of Sir John Mandeville* was written in French around 1350 and became the first book to be printed in any language other than Latin. By 1500 it had been translated into every major European language, including Czech and Irish. Leonardo da Vinci read it, so did Columbus and Prince Henry the Navigator. Mandeville was arguably the most influential traveller of the age, inspiring and educating explorers for more than two centuries. He was, however, almost certainly a fraud.

The real identity of the writer is lost, but whoever did pose as a well-travelled English knight knew his audience, serving up all the outlandish monsters they wanted. People with ears down to their knees, headless men with eyes on their shoulders, self-sacrificing fish, men with one foot who used it as a sunshade – 'It is a marvel to see them,' Sir John wrote. But though curiosities and freaks were an interest, his real passion was diamonds: 'They grow together, male and female, and are fed with the dew of Heaven. And according to their nature they engender and conceive small children . . . I have many times tested and seen that if a man takes with them a little of the rock they grow on, provided they are taken up by their roots and watered with the dew of May, each year they grow visibly.'

India was the source of good diamonds, he reported, though potential purchasers should beware of imitations which might not have the useful properties of the original. 'The diamond gives to the man who carries it boldness (if it is freely given to him) and keeps his limbs healthy. It gives him grace to overcome his enemies, if his cause is righteous, in both war and law.'

Like the rest of his book, this was inspired nonsense containing enough truth to hook the unsuspecting. Mandeville probably had travelled to Jerusalem – further at least than his local library (the suggestion of one debunker) – then embroidered experience and hearsay with liberal helpings of other texts. It scarcely matters now if it were true or not; what counts is that people believed it. The thirst for the east, and for diamonds, had been whetted.

Inspired by such tales, the Portuguese discovered the route around the Cape of Good Hope and in 1498 Vasco da Gama reached India. There was no subtlety to their conquest: appalling acts of savagery tore apart the quiet Indian Ocean mercantile life of free trade; defenceless Muslim ships were plundered and sunk, the crews butchered, towns that refused to capitulate immediately were peppered with

the heads and limbs of captives blasted from the cannons. The ferocious Portuguese burst upon the scene like pit bulls into a poodle
parlour. By 1510 Goa had fallen to the invaders and, helped by vicious
repression of other ports, soon had developed a flourishing market in
gemstones.

The first eyewitness account of the diamond region of Golconda
came from an English adventurer, Ralph Fitch, who had set out in 1583
with the expressed intention of buying jewels. Fitch was a resourceful
and sturdy character: captured by the Portuguese and imprisoned at
Goa, he escaped and headed for the unknown interior, finally reaching the Deccan kingdom of Golconda after considerable hardships.

He was quick to notice the abundance of gems: 'There is a great
market kept of diamants, rubies, saphires, and many other soft
stones.' Eight years after setting out, Fitch arrived back in London to
find himself presumed dead and his will already executed.
Nevertheless, his lively account of 'diamants of the olde water'
undoubtedly had an enormous impact on the hopeful young bloods
eager for a share of the eastern trade.

A century later, Pitt had more to go on than Fitch's picaresque adven-
tures. In 1620 William Methwold, a factor based in Masulipatnam, had
made it to the mines which, he declared, were 'situated at the foot of a
great mountain not farre from a river called Christena'. Later came
more precise information: in the library of divinity texts at Fort St
George there was at least one unusual addition – Jean-Baptiste
Tavernier's accounts of his visits to the diamond mines in 1642, 1645
and 1651. The book appeared in English in 1678 and from Pitt's letters
it is clear that he consulted it carefully as a buyer's guide. Initially this
was without much luck: in one transaction he was cheated by Indian
merchants, in another the Indiaman, *Bedford*, went down on its way
home, taking a fifty-eight-and-a-half-carat stone with it.

These early disasters did not deter him: Pitt first heard of the huge
diamond in 1701, when the fort at Madras was under siege by the
army of the Mughals. A local merchant 'Ramchund' brought it in for
him to see. By tradition, large stones were offered to the Moghul, so
this one must have been smuggled out of the mines.

It was not unusual to be contemplating such a purchase at such a
risky moment – quite the opposite. Diamonds had long been consid-

ered the perfect method of remitting a fortune back home. They were small, easily carried, and commanded vastly inflated prices in Europe (a trade secret kept from the local merchants for many years).

Various ugly rumours as to Pitt's methods of purchase began to circulate soon after he completed the deal. One had him personally digging it from a hole in the leg of a miner who had used this painful method to conceal it. Another was that a French sailor had stolen it from an idol, then sold it to Pitt – the same tale that had sent me on a wild goose chase to Sri Rangam temple. The truth, probably, was more mundane. Pitt haggled. The price fell from £80,000 to £20,000 – still a vast sum in the days when company factors earned £20 per year, but a useful measure of Pitt's previous success as a merchant. With the siege lifted, Pitt despatched the jewel home and waited to become one of the richest men in England. His confident expectation was a clean profit of a staggering £430,000.

It was not to be. Pitt's fortunes, far from improving, took a downward turn. At home in England, his wife began to spend recklessly and was scandalously associated with a notorious roué. The diamond, though safely arrived, was brutally cut down from 426 carats to 140 – but still no one in Europe could afford it. Finally, in one of those arbitrary and sudden reversals the Company seemed to favour, he was dismissed.

Back in London in 1709, with his diamond in his pocket, Pitt was alarmed to discover its existence common knowledge. Terrified for its safety, he never slept two nights under the same roof. It was not until June 1717 that the jewel was finally sold to Louis XIV, the 'Sun King', for £135,000. Even then, only £40,000 was paid immediately and Pitt spent the last nine years of his life trying to get the balance and prevent his family squandering what else was left: 'What hellish planet is it that influences you all?' he wrote to his son Robert. 'Did ever mother, brother and sisters study one another's ruine and destruction more than my unfortunate and cursed family have done?' There were those in India and at home who were only too ready to ascribe such curses to the infamous diamond.

If any evil did attach to the stone, then it travelled with it to the execution of the French royal family in 1793. By the close of the century the great jewel had been stolen, recovered, then pawned.

Napoleon redeemed it for his coronation, before plunging Europe into another round of wars. His great foe in England at the time was none other than William Pitt the Younger, Thomas Pitt's great grandson.

The Regent or Pitt diamond (which is still in the possession of the French government) was said to have come from the Parteal mine on the Krishna River. From this deposit and others nearby had also come the Koh-i-Noor and dozens of others: the Orlov, the Great Moghul, the Great Table, the Darya Nur and so on. Each had their own story, some had disappeared, some even appeared in different guises, confounding experts. Was the first Mughal Emperor Babur's great diamond the same as the Koh-i-Noor? Was the Orlov really the Great Moghul? My desire to trace the history of the Koh-i-Noor and the Indian diamond trade had to tackle the murky ambiguities of several histories, and I could think of no better place to begin than the mines – if I could locate them.

Golconda, now on the edge of the city of Hyderabad, is often cited as the ancient source, but it was only a trading centre, the mines were to the south. However, eager to leave the semi-submerged city of Madras behind me, I waded down to the railway station and took the night train north.

After the stench of flooded Madras, Hyderabad came like a fresh draught of attar of roses, beckoning from the perfumier's counter. On my first evening in the city, I strolled down a sweeping boulevard to the River Musi and saw a mysterious pink palace hovering in the haze. No matter that the palace was the law courts, built by the British, and the haze was pollution, the effect was exquisitely beautiful. And the bazaars were full with perfumiers, pearl dealers and silk merchants. There was a colour and exuberance that I had not expected: girls on motor scooters in shalwar kameez with wisps of scarves trailing behind them, ephemeral as a delicate fragrance; a cow stealing the snake-skinned chiku fruits from a barrow; the click of glass bangles on slim brown wrists and the jangle of silver anklets; boys running under the arches to the shops with glasses of cardamom-scented tea, and the glint of golden threads in the bolts of silk hung out on the street by the shopkeepers.

I had first heard of Hyderabad from an elderly Yemeni in Aden who had been born there.

'My father was in the personal bodyguard of the Nizam,' he explained. 'All his closest soldiers were Yemenis.' He leaned closer, so the other men in the Aden teashop would not hear. 'I remember it as a . . .' He struggled for a word. 'In English you say "sexy". It is sexy: all perfumes and pearls and beautiful clothes.' His voice fell to a whisper. 'You know, as Muslims we are forbidden to do it, but my father told me it was true: the Nizam's son, he wore silk underpants.'

I remembered that elderly Yemeni as I passed the shoe shops. Muslim ladies swathed in black were trying silver spangled slippers on their hennaed feet – one finger delicately caressing a strap over the heel. There were Aladdin's magic shoes with curled toes and frivolous bits of frothy lace and latticed leather that looked like the pastry chef's party pieces rather than footwear.

Close to the Char Minar, a curious four-towered triumphal gate in the heart of the old bazaars, I took off my cumbersome boots and climbed the short wooden ladder into a pearl dealer's shop. Customers from Oman were lazing on the cushioned floor with a white bolster under one elbow and a low table laden with tea beside the other. The dealers sat cross-legged before them, hauling great ropes of shimmering pearls from aluminium suitcases like hanks of some rare and wonderful seaweed, still gleaming with the brine.

'Every pearl in the world passes through Hyderabad at least once in its life,' boasted the dealer, who was dressed all in black as part of forty days religious penitence.

Why, I asked. Diamonds I could have understood: the mines had once been relatively close. But pearls?

'The kings who built the city were Turkish slaves called the Quli Qutbs,' he explained. 'And they felt threatened by the Mughal Empire to the north, so they encouraged the Persians to come. They brought pearls with them from Basra and the trade started.'

That had been in the sixteenth century when Muhammad Quli Qutb Shah had come to the throne and moved his capital from the grim battlements of Golconda Fort to a new site seven miles away by the river. Appropriately for a famous lover, he is credited with choosing the site for romantic reasons and ever since, the city has been irredeemably racy, nestled in the dry calloused limbs of the Deccan hills, as gaudy and decadent as a pair of silk drawers on a dervish.

'Would you like some tea?' asked the shopkeeper, despatching a man at the door with a wave of the hand. The Omanis were disappearing behind mountains of pearls.

'Do the Basra pearls still exist?' I asked.

He shook his head. 'No, my father used to see them but everything is cultivated now – most of it in China.'

The tea came in a chipped and stained cup and saucer. I drank the slops from the saucer and he smiled approvingly – tea is rarely drunk from the cup in the south.

'Do you sell diamonds?' I asked.

'You want diamonds? Better to buy in Bombay.'

'I thought perhaps you might have local diamonds.'

He pursed his lips. 'I can get you diamonds, American diamonds, much better. Give me a few days and I'll arrange it. What do you want? Ring stones? I'm sorry but I never heard of local diamonds in Hyderabad.'

'Parteal? Have you heard of a place called Parteal, or another one called Kollur?'

'That was a long time ago – hundreds of years – it's all finished now.'

'But where is it?'

He shrugged. 'I don't know.'

I sat sipping my tea from the saucer and suffering, for the first time, serious misgivings. From faraway England, with only the haziest idea of the place, it had been easy to imagine some fabulous Rider Haggard vision of lost mines still being worked in secret. But now I was only a couple of hundred miles away and the trail was cold.

The man called to his father who came over and stroked his white beard reflectively. 'Parteal and Kollur? Yes, the names are correct, but where they were is forgotten. You must ask at the mining corporation headquarters – there may be someone who will know.'

Before I left he pushed a silver ring into my hand. 'Here, you take this – very good price – a lucky ring.' It had nine different coloured stones set in a square, and though none of them looked like anything but glass, the effect was quite attractive.

I paid what he asked and left, walking back towards the river through the narrow lanes. Most of them were almost impassable with silk merchants' wares spilling out in displays of deep green, crimson and orange. In one shop men were hammering silver leaf between blocks, a monotonous xylophonic clipclop of mallets on wood; their bodies reduced to no more than automata, arms forever going up and down while their faces smiled and chatted.

At the bridge that Muhammad Quli Qutb Shah's father had built, I stood staring down into the thin wriggle of black water. This road had once led through the diamond cutting and polishing centre of the world, a place that had thrown up vast wealth for those with the cunning to lay their hands on it: Mir Jumla, a Persian adventurer who rose to be Prime Minister under the Sultan of Golconda, was so wealthy he kept his diamonds in buckets. Tavernier had come here and bought many fine specimens to sell to the French nobility. But all that was long gone: the only visible reminder of the past was a small, rundown workshop called, Koh-i-Noor. On closer inspection I found it sold irrigation equipment.

The following day was a Sunday and I walked to Golconda, now a ruined fort on a hill with a military camp at its foot. Crenellated walls ring the entire town but most of that area is unvisited, the few tourists and many local picnickers preferring to wander up the crags to the palace complex. This impressive ruin is set amongst vast pink boulders, but when I reached it I found the main durbar hall was closed. 'They are looking for something,' a young student whispered to me. 'A huge diamond is buried inside.'

Intrigued, I crept around the side and climbed up a wall to get a better look. Some workmen were mixing cement and carrying it inside to reinforce a wall; they did not appear to be looking for anything, but the treasure-hunting instinct is never far from the surface in such places.

Squirrels skittered across the dusty tracks, a gardener snoozed in the shade of a thorn tree, and I explored the overgrown backrooms of the zenana, the women's quarters. Here were archways and vaults, traces of hammams and dazzling turquoise tiles that once covered the walls. In this fabulous gilded cage, the king of Golconda kept four wives and a thousand concubines in a fort more sumptuous than any other in India.

The great diamonds had come through here but they had all moved on eventually. It was the constant hope of ambitious Muslim invaders that they would conquer the Deccan and establish an Indian empire. The vast wealth of the area must have seemed to them like a magic Guinness bottle to a drinker – always filling itself up. From the first Muslim adventurer to reach south, Alauddin Khilji, in 1296, to the Mughal Aurangzeb four centuries later, the Deccan was plundered and despoiled. In 1565, Muslim Golconda sacked the great Hindu empire of Vijayanagar, taking unprecedented quantities of loot. Then Golconda itself was plundered by the Mughals who, in turn, were plundered by the Persians who paid off the expansionist Russians. Vast riches heading northwards towards Delhi were repeatedly grabbed and dispersed, west into Persia and from there to Europe. At the centre of this was Golconda, the diamond in the Indian lotus, the only source of those mysterious stones. Trade certainly did exist and relations with Persia were strong, but that road heading north and west was a highway of stolen goods, the glittering spoils of war and tribute. If there was any trace of those days, it was not to be found here.

I left the mysterious labyrinth of the zenana and strolled out of the citadel into the modern village of Golconda. Beyond that were the outer defensive walls where boys were flying home-made kites from the crumbling bastions.

The tombs of the Quli Qutb dynasty were a kilometre further, built along Mughal lines with a square base forming a terrace from which rises a square turreted block and full dome over the sarcophagus. By late afternoon, when the sun was stumbling through the day's dust, a dozen cricket matches were in progress in the shadow of the coconut palms and pomegranate trees. The other boys were watching the girls stroll by in their dazzling silks or else having fortunes told by card-sharp parrots in cages.

Muhammad Quli Qutb Shah's tomb had a short poetic eulogy at its base which ended:

Each new year the bulbuls sing,
Their songs of Your renascent loves,
Your beauty wakens with the spring
To kindle these pomegranate groves.

The elegance and balance of the building was reflected in its easy combination of both Muslim and Hindu motifs: the five-arched sides of the central mausoleum representing the five holy figures of Shi'ism – the Prophet Muhammad, Hassan, Hussein, Ali and Fatima – then the bud of the dome rising from lotus petals.

One gang of lads showed me the catacombs beneath the tomb. 'Here brother,' they said, leading me to a stone grave lit by a shaft of golden sunlight from above. 'This is the real place. The one up there is for showing only.'

We stood gazing at the stone until one sighed and said, 'Ninety-nine wives! It is almost something unbelievable.'

The others grunted and one, searching for the right words, gripped my arm. 'Brother, this king, he was the most prodigious fucker – really, most prominent in that field of activity.'

'He was a great king, not like our politicians now,' said the youngest of them, clearly rather disapproving of his friend's crudity. 'He was being kind to poor folk; he was an artist, a poet, a romantic and a plumber.'

The others did not know what a plumber was. 'He constructed so many good streams and fountains and lakes and all,' the youth explained. 'He delivered water and that is the kindest gift. Look at our politicians now – they are bringing us nothing.'

The others giggled. 'He is a Naxa!'

The charge brought an instant response. 'Why not? They are good men and women – like Robin Hoods.'

Some of them murmured in agreement. The rampant corruption and venality of state politics in Andhra Pradesh has the peculiar distinction of encouraging a Maoist guerrilla war, just as the rest of the world had abandoned such things to history. Outside the apparent calm of the city the police were locked in combat with the Naxalites or People's War Group, shadowy leftists dedicated to freeing the land from the grip of tyrannical feudal landlords.

In the gloom of the arched tunnels was the sound of a laugh and the

[43]

brief shimmer of pale blue silk disappearing into the darkness. One of the youths changed the subject.

'Under this stone is a big diamond,' he said, and seeing me respond with interest, added, 'Yes, it is called the Koh-i-Noor!'

The others scoffed. 'The Koh-i-Noor is in the possession of the British Queen. How can it be here?' But they agreed that treasure was buried in the gardens.

'One night we shall come with digging equipment and climb the wall, then retrieve our forefathers' treasure.'

The magical attraction of treasure! The dusty side pockets of my bag were filled with things I had stumbled across: a cowrie shell and a nugget of 'dragon's blood' from the island of Socotra, various seeds from a Bornean rainforest, and the handle of a Roman amphora from a Turkish seabed. The man who first stumbled over a strange, glittering stone on the banks of the River Krishna must have picked it up and kept it, not for any value, but for it being different, beautiful, curious and, perhaps, somehow a confirmation that he had travelled wisely, that the stone had chosen him and he had not wasted his footsteps.

'I'll come with you!' I declared. 'Seriously, why not?'

They shifted their feet uncertainly, glancing at one another till one said: 'Because you are Britisher.'

'So?'

Then the youngest burst out. 'It is not pukka!' And the others muttered their agreement. We began to move outside, back into the light and, our discussion at an end, they went off to look for a cricket match to join.

Across the gardens was a small museum whose sorry collection gave little indication of the wealth once enjoyed by the kingdom – a Turkic shield, some terracotta lamps and shards of Chinese porcelain. The truth was, the real treasure, the diamonds and gems, they always moved on. No matter how hard people tried to hoard or entomb them, the stones would search out new masters, leaving behind the failed and the dead.

The NMDC – National Mining Development Corporation – was on the edge of town and had guards who searched my bag. Once inside the building, however, there appeared to be no one around and my hopeful, 'Hello!' echoed unanswered through the open-plan offices, across the stacks of dusty paper and deserted desks.

On the fourth floor at the back corner, there were small offices, no more than cubicles, separated from each other by glass partitions. One was occupied by a small, portly man in a knitted waistcoat with a clipped grey moustache and blackened hair.

'I'm looking for Mr Kimothi,' I said and he nodded.

'It is I.'

His office was just large enough for the two of us to sit down on either side of a desk.

'I spoke to Mr Choudary in the Mines Department,' I explained, hoping that this gave me some sort of official status. 'He thought you might be able to help with my search for the ancient diamond mines – places like Kollur and Parteal?'

Mr Kimothi had a pleasant lined face which cracked into a smile. 'How long are you in Hyderabad?' he asked, looking at a pile of old field maps in the corner. 'It may take some time.'

'I wanted to leave tomorrow.'

He began to go through the pile, tutting to himself. 'So dusty! We are not called on to examine these papers very often.'

A wadge of maps was deposited in front of me, raising a cloud of dust. Mr Kimothi began to read them. 'Madhya Pradesh . . . mmm.' He traced with his finger over the colours marking various rock formations. 'I was twelve years at Panna – you know it? They take 3 or 4,000 carats per year which is very little. It's India's only modern mine – of no interest to you.' Another map was overlaid. 'Ah! Uttar Pradesh, Himalayas, also I was there. Field geology you know. Camp life, no facilities, too much sun and wind. How old do you think I am?'

I would have guessed mid-sixties but I said fifty-eight.

He looked unhappy. 'I'm fifty-two. Field geology, you see.'

'Did you ever find diamonds?'

He looked up sharply. 'That is a matter of personal integrity. Of course, what you find is government property. I could not keep for myself!'

'Oh, I didn't mean . . . of course not. Only villagers must occasionally talk of them – legends and so on.'

[45]

'That is not science.' He turned to another map. 'I cannot pass on stories which I cannot prove – I am a scientist. How old are you? Thirty-seven?'

'Yes.'

His face was kindly, even if his manner was abrupt. 'Don't be surprised. I can judge a stone, why not a man? What is this – Krishna River? But no . . .' The map was whipped away. 'That is upper reaches. Maybe you could return in a few days and by that time I will have found something.' I made no move to leave and he continued going through the pile. 'Which institution did you say you were from?'

I shuffled uneasily. 'Was geology always your interest?'

He squatted down and rummaged out another pile of files and papers. 'In India we marry a woman who is a stranger and in time we learn to love her. It is the same with employment. I studied geology because prospects were good after Independence.' Another batch of curled dusty papers were dropped on the table. 'Actually it would be better to spend some days looking.'

'Don't you miss the outdoor life? The camp fire? The chance of finding gold or diamonds – for the government of course.'

'No. I am too old for field geology. I'm very happy here in the office.'

The maps were upside down for me, and not easy to make out with all the colours of various strata, but the next one was clearly cut by the bend of a big river.

'Is that the Krishna?'

He squinted at the key. 'Mmm . . . could be.'

I could see patches of yellow, like sandbanks on the inner bank and a few inches away were the grey patches of settlements.

His finger dabbed at the yellow. 'Diamondiferous gravel. That's the stuff you are looking for.'

The shape of the grey patches suggested a large scale: individual plots were marked and a name written in tiny neat handwriting. Mr Kimothi was bent over it, attempting to read.

'Parteal. Was that a name you were after?'

'Yes!' I almost ripped the map from his hands, turning it to see. 'Yes. Parteal was one name.' I realised now that I was looking at part of the great loop in the Krishna, the long detour it takes through its own flood plain before straightening out and heading for the coast. About

[46]

fifty miles upstream the river is now dammed but previously it came spilling from a long narrow gorge, only to be forced northwards by some low hills. This loop must have slowed the water and caused silt and debris to deposit on the inner curves. It was these deposits, Mr Kimothi's yellow patches, that had held the alluvial diamonds. By some trick of nature, some particular movement or freak of the turbulence, the stones had accumulated in certain patches but not others.

'It's amazing,' I said, excited by the discovery of some solid information at long last. 'Parteal – one of the old mines – still there as a village name.'

'We never found very much,' he said. 'But there is a camp, close to that village you are interested in. It's not active now but there is a geologist.' He scribbled down a name on a scrap of paper. 'You can ask there, but better you talk to the villagers. They are the fellows who know best.'

I took my own map from my bag and tried to relate it to Kimothi's. About ninety miles due south of Hyderabad the Krishna River entered the Nallamalai mountain range where it scoured a deep gorge and emerged at the point where the ancient city of Nagarjunakonda had been built. That settlement had been flooded after the building of a huge dam where I would be able to cross the river. About fifty miles downstream the watercourse turned north on a long loop to avoid a low spur of hills. Kimothi's map was clearly of the final bend as the river turned to take up its westward course once again. Somehow, I decided, I would approach from the south, trusting to luck for crossing the river but rather hoping I would have no need: Tavernier's account clearly spoke of mines on the southern bank. If, as I now suspected, all the ancient mines had been ranged along this large loop in the river, I would have my pick of them on whichever side I chose. My optimism had yet to be tempered with experience at that point.

'Don't forget,' Kimothi said as I left, 'talk to the local people – they are the ones who know.'

CHAPTER 3

Only God can make a diamond.

Sir Ernest Oppenheimer in 1950

[Two years later Swedish scientists manufactured diamonds.]

THE bus had a shrine on the dashboard: three devotional sticks of electric incense forever glowing red in front of a plastic god, garlanded with marigolds and tinsel. The sign above the windscreen was in Telugu: no more city languages, the landlords' fancy Persianised Urdu, the northerners' Sanskritised Hindi. Here even the numbers were in Telugu, the language of the landless.

I had bought a paperback phrasebook and hoped to make a start during the journey. Useful sentences included: 'Water is for drinking', 'The ears of the elephant are like winnowing baskets' and, appropriately, 'I will learn Telugu tomorrow.' The script appeared to be a lavish series of curvaceous buttocks festooned with nipples and tongues – every sentence an orgy. Although no manuscript survives, some scholars say that Muhammad Quli Qutb Shah wrote poetry in Telugu and one can well believe it of that great sensualist.

The young man next to me brushed aside my hesitant first steps in his native tongue. 'I intend to practise the English on you,' he said ominously. He was a cadaverous youth, spine bent with lugging textbooks, his eyes lifeless and hair lank with coconut oil. 'How many cinema halls are there per square kilometre in your home town?'

He perked up when I did not know. 'In urban India there are ten.'

Outside, we had left the city behind and were rattling southwards across a dry dusty plateau, scarred at intervals with liverish outcrops of red boulders. The only other traffic was ox carts, which the driver harried relentlessly with his klaxon. Clouds of fine dust came streaming through the open windows and all the old men promptly took out their white hankerchiefs and tied them cowboy-style over their mouths. There was something both comical and sinister about it: a coach party of retired Roy Rogers impersonators out for a day's lynching.

'Cigarettes are not smoken by eighty per cent of Indian nationals,' announced my neighbour. 'Liquors are drunken by fifty-six per cent.'

'Men and women?'

He frowned. 'Good heavens, no. Women are entirely excluded from that domain.'

'Even your girlfriends?'

A nervous giggle escaped him and his eyes flickered anxiously to the nearest passengers, none of whom were showing the slightest interest. 'Sir, we used to have girlfriends, but now I am entirely desisting from the vice. Also I do not accept liquor or tobacco. Have you had a vasectomy?'

Without waiting for an answer, he continued: '"We 2, Our 2" – do you know the slogan? This is what we are adopting in India.'

'I have three children.'

He snorted. 'In China they would shoot you!'

'Here you have Naxalites to do that.'

That stopped him. He drew closer. 'What do you know about Naxas?'

'They kill people,' I whispered. Only that morning, the newspaper reported a landmine found on a road outside Hyderabad. In Bihar, the other corruption-ridden state where the Maoists operate, sixty-one villagers had been hacked to death by landlords' henchmen. Their alleged crime was Naxalite sympathies.

'No, no,' the young man said under his breath, glancing around like a stage conspirator. 'They are like your Robin Hood. Many are educated. Engineers, teachers, doctors – seventy-two per cent are having qualifications. What you see in Andhra Pradesh is a traditional place: there was one case where a Dalit accidentally touched a Brahmin with his foot.' Dalit is the name given to the caste once known as

[49]

Untouchables. 'The Brahmins killed that Dalit and seven others. This is what the Naxalites are against.'

'Have you met any of them?'

I thought he was going to ignore the question, but after a pause he whispered, 'I attended some meetings once. They wish for the land to be given to those who work on it – is that a bad thing?'

I wobbled my head – nodding is a northern gesture in India.

'Land is for people to work on,' said the youth, watching me closely and curiously.

'That's right.'

The land under discussion had now become greener and more fertile. Between the low ridges of boulders were areas of padi where white egrets stood watching the ox ploughs turn the rich thick earth. Buffaloes lazed in tumbledown hayricks and kingfishers watched from the telegraph wires. It was almost midday and quite hot, but people were out there working: men struggling with the ox teams and women, whiplash thin, barefoot in the mud, glancing up at the bus, laughing to each other, their wordly wealth glinting on their golden ears and noses.

It was hard to imagine a fanatical leftist guerrilla movement running a Robin Hood operation in such apparently peaceful sur- roundings. I began to mutter a nervous little ditty to myself:

> The Naxalites are men in tights,
> Their great chum is Mao-Tse-Tung.

A few miles further on we stopped in a small town for lunch. The Statistics-Wallah said goodbye and wandered away down the high street. I went and drank a cup of milky tea in the shade of a tree where a white Ambassador car was parked. The driver wound his window down and ordered a bottle of mineral water to be brought out to him. He was a middle-aged man in a high-collared Nehru jacket and white cap; his portly wife next to him in a white sari looking very unhappy that he had stopped.

'Good afternoon,' he said when our eyes met. 'Are you going to Hyderabad?' His wife shifted uneasily and wrapped her white sari tighter; the rolls of fat at her midriff and neck wobbled: brown against white. She looked like an iced bun oozing chocolate cream.

'To Nagarjunakonda,' I said. 'On the river. Have you come from there?'

He shook his head. 'We have been to see some fields of ours. Our home is in Hyderabad.'

'What do you grow?'

'There are some tenants, you know, they grow rice but that is only for their eating, you see – there is no money in it, either for us or for them. We want to improve the land but there are some problems.'

'Naxalites?'

He gave me a cool look, eyebrows raised. 'They are dacoits!' he said forcefully. 'Criminals to be hired by anyone for assassinations and robberies.'

'Someone told me they were Robin Hood characters – stealing from the rich, giving to the poor – that sort of thing.'

He snorted derisively. 'Such people spread lies and rumours and should be punished. Perhaps they had ideals in the past; now they are simply gangsters.'

A lad handed the water to him and, without another word, he wound the window up and drove off.

Our own stop was more protracted but eventually we got moving again, this time entering a drier, less-populated landscape. To the south and west were the rounded massifs of the Nallamalai range. As the road curled up onto the ridge we caught glimpses of a vast sheet of blue water surrounded by scrubby desert hills, then we descended to a small leafy township built on the hillside overlooking the dam itself.

The government resthouse was a well-kept block of shady verandas and airy rooms. As the only guest I had about forty staff to watch over me: at dinner there were three waiters and a man to turn the television on and watch it for me. If I glanced up from my food someone would leap forward with a cauldron of curry or an aluminium bowl: 'Yes, sahib. More chutney?'

After my meal, one of the staff took me to visit his family. We sat in a parlour chewing betel leaves that he kept in a flap of damp hessian while his aged mother shifted and groaned on her bed in the porch. Into each leaf he popped half an areca nut and a dab of limepaste. The bell-shaped nut is extremely hard and usually pre-crushed, but the

[51]

advantage of this tooth-shattering method was in the effects: within a minute the whole left side of my face had been completely anaesthetised, dulling any pain from the tooth damage. The drug has a number of names and types, including paan, supari, chunam and betelnut – the latter being a misnomer as the betel is the leaf and the non-active ingredient. Areca contains various alkaloids which react with the lime to cause nervous stimulation, plus copious quantities of red saliva. In traditional Indian society it was one of the eight cardinal pleasures (the others being: food, music, flowers, incense, women, bed and unguents).

Fortunately, my friend seemed happy to talk as I could only make vague gurgling noises. His father, he told me, had been a tailor who made the high-collared achkan frock coats for local royalty, but in the late 1950s a shortage of monarchs precipitated a change: he had abandoned coatmaking in favour of constructing hydroelectric power plants.

'Oigal, oigal,' I said, like an appreciative imbecile. Perhaps, paan does have some mental effects because at the time, this surprising career move struck me as perfectly logical.

Various children were now paraded in front of me and loudly recited the greetings that their mother had whispered to them around the corner only seconds before. 'Welcome, uncle,' said one delightful child, dressed in pristine white party dress. 'How do you do?'

'Oigal, oigal,' I said cryptically, my anaesthetised mouth now brimming with scarlet fluid which I didn't want to swallow as everyone in India obviously spat it out. Perhaps it's poisonous, I thought. The child fled in horror.

Hydroelectric construction had brought the family relative prosperity: they had a small stone-built house with a garden full of orange trees, a television (carefully protected with a crocheted dust cover) and walls decorated with pictures of Hanuman, the monkey god, and Sai Baba.

'Up the river is a wild place,' my host told me. 'There are Nagas living there who worship snakes and Naxalites who worship nothing.' He shuffled over to the door and let rip a beautiful jet of rich red fluid over the bushes. 'Sometimes I've seen tigers drinking from the river in the early morning.'

I gurgled approvingly, then nonchalantly got up and shuffled next to him. My jet of rich red fluid did not reach quite so well and ended with a limp glug, depositing the last bit down my chin and shirt. We sat down again.

'And diamonds?' I asked. 'Do the people search for diamonds?'

He thought a long time before answering, then said: 'It may be true.'

I felt a sudden lift of excitement: they were here, and people were looking for them. I could see it in his face. The mention of snakes was intriguing too; of all the myths and legends surrounding diamonds, the one connecting them with snakes was the most enduring. Perhaps the earliest source of gems had been the Naga people and their superstitions had impressed those who had come to trade.

A small boy was now ushered in. He kept out of arm's reach. 'Welcome, uncle,' he said. I smiled and held out my hand. The boy bolted. It was only understandable: my mouth was scarlet and my shirt front splattered in gore – he probably thought I had eaten the last child.

'Are there diamonds here?'

'We believe it is a most powerful stone,' my host said, avoiding the question. 'There are nine heavenly bodies and nine stones on the earth. Each stone brings the heavenly power of that planet to help anyone who wears it. Kings, of course, may wear them all – the navaratna, we call it. A poor man can buy only small stones, perhaps only one. Then we ask an astrologer to advise us.'

I pulled the nine-stoned ring that I had bought in the pearl dealer's shop from my pocket. He looked at it, smiling, and passed it back. 'That is navaratna.'

He began to roll another betel leaf, putting powdered tobacco in with the lime and areca. 'Diamond is the rarest and most valuable – even in the darkness, even in your pocket, it will shine. That is the heavenly power passing through it. It is a most useful protection.'

I wobbled my head encouragingly. 'And local stones are the best?'

'There is a man . . .' Standing up, he went to the door and shouted out into the darkened street in Telugu. An answering voice came back and there was a brief conversation. I waited, trying to appear nonchalant, but conscious that I might be on the brink of an important meeting.

[53]

The conversation was short, and when he turned I knew my luck was not good. 'I am sorry,' he said. 'The man who knows about such things is not here. If you stay one week you may meet him.'

He knew perfectly well that I would not do that. 'Here – take your paan.' He handed me another wad.

'This man sells local diamonds?'

He moved his hands in a vague gesture. 'Will you visit the island tomorrow?'

The topic was closed and he would not be drawn on it again, but I felt sure, for the first time, that there was more than dead gravel pans along the Krishna River. We walked back to the resthouse and he encouraged me to visit next day the ruins of Nagarjunakonda which had been rescued from the lake and sited on an island. I spent the evening on the veranda, fighting off mosquitoes and waiting for some feeling to return to my jaw.

The launch did not fill me with confidence. It was largely constructed from rust and lashed to an equally suspect barge. My fellow passengers were a threesome of retired teachers from Calcutta and a party of about fifty Young Communists wearing hammer and sickle tee-shirts. The Indian government of K.J. Gujral had fallen two days previously and they were full of optimism about election prospects, waving red flags enthusiastically. I made the mistake of referring to them as 'The Communist Party of India' which drew howls of protest: 'We are the Communist Party of India – Marxist,' they said. 'The CPI are splitters.'

The launch chugged onwards, leaning alarmingly to port where all the Communists had gone to watch the barren cliffs that rose from the shoreline. The dam is over 400 feet high and I was trying to imagine the depth and steepness of the river valley before the flood. In the legends, the valley of diamonds is too steep to climb down or up, thus necessitating Sindbad's clever escape plan of lashing himself to a side of meat and awaiting the giant eagle – his pockets stuffed with diamonds, of course. The cliffs we were passing were certainly a plausible barrier, even more so had their true height been revealed. One could well imagine devious locals swearing to travellers that the crags were unscaleable and the valley floor infested with deadly serpents.

Like my betel-chewing friend of the previous evening, unwilling for whatever reasons to introduce the diamond dealer, it was always sensible to protect yourself.

The Communists were getting rather excitable, throwing hammer and sickle baseball caps at each other and generally showing off for the benefit of one comrade, a particularly beautiful girl with hair down to her waist. I sat with the retired teachers and one of them, Mr Das, told me about Nagarjuna.

'He was one of the six jewels of Buddhism,' he said. 'And founder of the Mahayana branch in the second century AD.'

Another splitter, I thought.

He gestured to the water. 'Under here was the old bank of the river where a large city developed. People came from as far as China and Tibet to visit the centre of learning. Nagarjuna had a laboratory and conducted experiments to discover amrit.'

Amrit was the nectar of immortality, a few drops of which had fallen on India when the gods fought over a pitcher containing it. Mr Das had visited all the sites and was now exploring the lesser places associated with the myth of immortality, plus the temples that house the holy phalluses, a small project to keep him and his friends busy in their twilight years.

'They were scientists,' he told me. 'There is nothing the ancients did not know. We rediscover atomic theory or electricity but the concepts were familiar to them.'

There is no direct evidence that the city knew of the diamonds, yet it seems self-evident that such a thriving and intelligent people would discover the treasure under its feet. Traces here and downstream at Amaravati prove that contacts between the area and Rome existed, and wealthy Romans of the period certainly wore diamond rings.

Whether Nagarjuna, the Buddhist scholar, was an alchemist is not known; some scholars believe there were two Nagarjunas and it was the second of them who conducted the experiments to manufacture the water of life in medieval times. The city was certainly a thriving and cosmopolitan place with temples, a citadel and an amphitheatre; most of this was lost when the dam was built. Only a tiny proportion of the ruins were moved to the top of Nagarjuna Hill where they were safe from the reservoir.

[55]

After landing on the island, I found the museum contained a few carved lintels, pillars and statues which gave tantalising clues to the nature of the society. On one a Scythian was shown worshipping a stupa, on another is an inscription recording the success of missionaries sent to Kashmir and Gandhara, now northern Pakistan. The Gandharan culture had been influenced by Greeks following Alexander's conquest. That Hellenic influence obviously reached all the way down to the banks of the Krishna, with Buddha statues clothed in flowing robes.

The city's heyday was brief: in the middle of the fourth century the ruling dynasty was toppled and the valley passed through the hands of various rulers before becoming part of the Kakatiya kingdom. These monarchs were based in Warangal, eighty miles north-east of modern Hyderabad and in some accounts the Koh-i-Noor diamond was theirs, passing into the hands of the Muslim raider Alauddin Khilji when his forces attacked the fort at Warangal in 1309.

Alauddin's people had come from eastern Afghanistan and conquered Bengal in the early thirteenth century. In 1296 he came to power in Delhi after assassinating his uncle, Sultan Jalaladin, then set about conquering the Deccan and establishing an empire. His early years were precarious. The Mongol hordes repeatedly invaded and were thrown back. But between these crises, Alauddin took the opportunity to sack the rich Hindu kingdoms of Gujarat and the Deccan. The sheer scale of looting from the great southern temples must have been staggering. At Madurai they took 512 elephants, 5,000 horses and mountains of gold and jewels. At Warangal the army forced a surrender and relieved the Raja of 20,000 highly bred horses, one hundred elephants and enormous quantities of gold.

The chronicles record that 'the diamonds would have penetrated into an iron heart like an arrow of steel' and the defeated Raja's ambassadors declare: 'Each of these jewels is of a kind of which no man can calculate the value and among them is a jewel unparalleled in the whole world, though according to perfect philosophers such a substance cannot exist.'

Such slender evidence is all that we now have that this was the great diamond, the jewel of Krishna and later the Mughals. Two centuries would pass before the first mughal, Babur, declared the diamond captured at Agra in 1525 to be that which Alauddin had once owned; perhaps any further evidence is lying in 300 feet of water.

On the return journey from the island, my Communist companions were quick to claim Nagarjunakonda as a marvel of archaeological engineering, comparable with saving the treasures of the Nile from the Aswan High Dam. This was nonsense, but I could see why they had come: the largest dam in India had a kind of 1950s Great Leap Forward mentality which appealed to them. They cared nothing for the actual ruins nor for Nagarjuna – to practise any kind of religion risked expulsion from their party – what they had come to see was large quantities of water held back by large quantities of concrete. It was almost better for having drowned a Buddhist monument.

'The dam is 409 feet high and 15,956 feet wide,' said one, quoting from a pamphlet and almost dewy-eyed at the figures. 'You British built nothing like this. You were here two hundred years and built only railways – and that was so you could get our resources out faster!'

This jibe provoked laughter and, for reasons not entirely clear to me, they began to sing 'Happy birthday to you. Happy birthday, Dear Comrade, happy birthday to you!'

From Nagarjunakonda I took a bus east to the town of Guntur, a few miles south of the Krishna. My plan was to search the southern bank, then cross to Mr Kimothi's mining camp. This lay on the last bend of a huge loop which took the east-flowing river on a forty-mile detour to the north and back. Kimothi's map had suggested that it was on the inner curves of river bends that the deposits of diamondiferous gravel lay, giving me three possible sites along this loop. Quite probably all of them had been mined, but Tavernier had placed the mines on the southern bank within a short distance of the main Golconda to Masulipatnam road. That would suggest they were inside the eye of the loop.

His account is precise and detailed: 'Seven days journey from Golconda Eastward there is another Diamond Mine, call'd in the language of the Country Gani, in the Persian tongue Coulour . . . From Golconda to the Mine of Coulour or Gani, is reckon'd thirteen Gos and three quarters.' He goes on to give a detailed route march,

[57]

beginning: 'From Golconda to Almaspinda, three Gos and a half.' And ending: 'At Ponocour you only cross the River to Coulour.'

None of the towns and villages he mentions have survived, but Tavernier is authoritative and exhaustive, loading us with numbers and measurements, leaving nothing to chance. He is determined to shed light and dispel ignorance. With the assured arrogance of the Rational Man, he discounts previous writers who filled the roads to the mines with 'Lions, Tigers, and Cruel People', then dismisses those patronising and vulgar visitors who think to fob off locals with 'Spices, Tobacco, Looking Glasses, and such trifles to truck for Diamonds . . . I can assure ye, these people will not only have Gold, but Gold of the best sort too.'

Tavernier reads like a guidebook. His purpose is quite plainly to get you to the mines and assist with the opening of trade routes to the mutual pecuniary advantage of all concerned. As a representative of the European mercantile classes in the seventeenth century, he is exemplary. No obfuscation, no tall tales, no vague hearsay, just straightforward scientific numbers and measurements – in 'gos'.

I could not find any reference to the gos in *Hobson-Jobson*, the invaluable nineteenth-century dictionary of Anglo-Indian terms, but there was the 'Coss – The most usual popular measure of distance in India. In the Pali vocabulary called *Abhidhanappadipika*, which is of the 12th century, the word appears in the form *koss*; and nearly this, *kos*, is the ordinary Hindi. It is a notable circumstance that, according to Wrangell, the Yakuts of N.Siberia reckon distance by *kiosses*. With them this measure is "indicated by the time necessary to cook a piece of meat".'

None of this was helping me to put my cross on the map. *Hobson-Jobson* continues: '*Kioss* is equal to about 5 *versts*, or 1⅔ miles, in hilly or marshy country, but on plain ground to 7 *versts*, or 2⅓ miles . . . The *kos* as laid down in the *Ain* was of 5000 *gaz* [see GUDGE].' (The *Ain* is the *Ain-i-Akbar* or chronicles of Emperor Akbar, written by Abu Fasl.)

So I began a paperchase, flicking backwards and forwards through *Hobson-Jobson*.

Page 400. **Gudge**. 'A Persian yard measure or thereabouts; but in India applied to measures of very varying lengths . . . the determination of its value was a subject of much importance when the revenue surveys were undertaken about 1824. The results of enquiry were very discrepant, however, and finally an arbitrary value of 33 inches was assumed. The *bigha* [see BEEGAH] [is] based on this.'

Page 79. **Beegah.** 'The most common Hindu measure of land-area, and varying much in different parts of India, whilst in every part that has a *bigha* there is also certain to be a *pucka beegah* and a *kutcha beegah* (vide CUTCHA and PUCKA).'

Page 287. **Cutcha.** 'A cutcha brick is a sun-dried brick. A cutcha appointment is acting or temporary. A cutcha estimate is one which is rough, superficial and untrustworthy. A cutcha maund or seer is the smaller, where two weights are in use, as often happens. A cutcha Major is a brevet or local Major. A cutcha pice generally means one of those amorphous coppers, current in up-country bazaars at varying rates of value. A cutcha scoundrel, a limp and fatuous knave. A Cutcha Coss – see analogy under Maund above.'

Having reached the point where I began, I returned to Tavernier and found that elsewhere he helpfully writes: 'the road being measur'd by Gos, which is four French-leagues.'

A league is roughly three miles, giving a credible 165 miles for the Golconda-Coulour (or Kollur) distance. Taking this as a radius and drawing an arc on the map, I found it touched the River Krishna very precisely at the tip of the loop. The problem I now had was my map was empty: no names, no villages or towns to ask for, no route to follow.

Guntur appeared to be filled with religious fanatics: the couple in the next room discussed the Resurrection between sex. There would be a frenzied assault of the headboard on the wall, then silence and she would ask a question: 'So Mister John is saying that Armageddon is coming?' Her partner's voice was just a low murmur. On the way downstairs to fetch a bottle of drinking water, I was stopped by a middle-aged man.

'British? Why you come here? They are all idol-worshippers, you know.'

He had no time for my explanations of historical interest. 'Ancient places! They are places of idol-worship and you are a Christian. All British is Christian. You must not visit them! Better they are knocked down. Do you know Solihull? My cousin has a restaurant there.'

I told him I wanted to cross the river without going back to Nagarjunakonda or down to Vijayawada. He drew a map on the wall with my ballpoint pen.

'The river goes like this . . .' A large loop to the north. 'And there is a place up here at the top where you can take boat.'

'Have you heard of diamond mines there?'

'I have not and I do not want to. Here is Guntur.' The pen had stopped working so he gouged lines in the plaster. 'And Amaravati – not necessary to stop, all idol worshippers, sinful place. From there you take a bus to Sattenapalli and then to the river.'

The following morning I was up early and reached Amaravati as all the water buffaloes were being driven out to the fields. I breakfasted on bananas and tea from a roadside stall, then walked up to the museum. This ancient Buddhist town flourished much earlier than Nagarjunakonda and its greenstone statuary preceded the depiction of Buddha as a man. In these carved reliefs he was shown by five symbols: footprints, wheel of life, stupa, five pillars and the lotus. The seated figure we associate so closely with the religion was a later invention.

From Amaravati I took a second local bus to Sattenapalli and then a third on towards the river. We passed through small country towns where people came to stare at me when we stopped, then rattled off into the heart of the great loop along a narrow single-track road through fields of cotton, tobacco and chillis. The farm tractors were brightly painted with images of Hanuman, the Monkey god. Stands of toddy palms sheltered little settlements of thatched huts, each doorway neatly painted with yellow and on the swept porch of grey slate were mandalas of rice powder – strange swirling figures like plans for magic knots.

The bus stopped everywhere and never turned anyone away. Each man wore a checked lunghi, white shirt and a folded towel over one shoulder; the women's oiled hair was scraped back into a plait and garlanded with white blossom. In profile they reminded me of the delicate sculptures in the Amaravati museum. All of them seemed to be equipped with tiffin-carriers: three aluminium dishes stacked on each other, one for rice and two for curries.

Although the looping river could have been no more than three or four miles away on either side, we saw no sign of it. To the west was a line of low hills which would block any view, but none seemed to match Tavernier's description of 'a high Mountain in the form of a Half-Moon'. The land became scrubby and uncultivated, the settlements scrappy and poorly maintained; most passengers had long since disembarked. I waited, expecting at any moment to see a broad vista of silver water ahead; instead the road turned to rutted mud and we stopped. All I could see were a few shabby concrete shelters, some thorn trees, and a path leading away between two walls.

During the four-hour bone-rattling journey I had attempted to strike up conversation with my fellow travellers, without success. Now they set off up the path and I was left alone. The driver, slouched over the wheel, raised his head for a moment and seeing me, gestured after the other passengers.

I walked slowly as the handle of my bag had broken in getting off the bus at Sattenapalli and was difficult to carry. There was no one around. The path twisted away to the right between thick thorn bushes and left the buildings behind. Quite suddenly, I emerged on the top of a steep bank and there, across a long pale shimmer of sand, was the river.

It was a hundred yards wide, and even at half a mile's distance, I could see that the current was strong. It had a solid muscularity to it, a depth of colour that no idle shallows could produce. On the far side there were steps up a steep bank and a small fortified hill, but I was not convinced that this was Tavernier's crossing.

There was no one to ask: the bus passengers, I now saw, were starting across the sands, heading to the water's edge. One of them waved to me. Two wooden boats, roped together, were being poled across for them. Given the chance that the ferry only crossed when sufficient passengers were available, I realised I had little choice but to follow, foregoing any attempt to explore this southern side.

Halfway across the sands I caught up with my fellow passengers. The youth who had waved smiled.

'You come.'

I pointed back at the bank. 'Diamonds?' I asked. 'Hirak?'

He smiled apologetically. 'You come.'

The boats arrived and the travellers prepared to embark: lunghis and dhotis were tucked up, saris hitched under arms, bags put on heads or shoulders, beedis given a last puff and slotted behind ears; then we waded out, dodging the wallowing buffaloes in the shallows.

When I was seated, I looked upstream to where the river emerged from a narrow passage between hills. A sailing skiff was skipping across the choppy waters. The boatmen began to sing, pushing us free of the sands with long bamboo poles. There was a slither of keel, then the tug of the current and the sudden feeling of instability as the boat began to rock. The passengers had stopped chattering amongst themselves and began to dip their fingers in the river, dabbing it to the holy spot between their eyes and drinking small mouthfuls.

I needed some luck and the river had yet to give it to me. The man next to me waggled his head, beads of water in his hair and specks of green algae on his lips. 'Good!' he said. 'River – you drink.'

I cupped my hand and lifted it to my mouth. The water tasted cool and earthy. I wiped my hand across my brow, felt the dust of the bus journey beneath my fingers, then leaned over the gunwhale and washed my face in the river. Every handful I took from the body of the big brown river came out clear and sparkling. The waves were whipping past, slapping the boat, then tearing downstream. And I wondered if the first man who first found a strange, bright stone in the flood pan, had thanked the river for this gift of heaven by dipping his fingers in the water and touching them to his forehead.

On the far side we jumped down into thick sticky mud, totally unlike the sand of the southern bank. At the top of the steps was a water tank and spout for washing feet. The fort appeared to be occupied and, although it was difficult to estimate its age, the site appeared to be a long-used crossing point. According to Tavernier's map, this was close to where the old Golconda to Masulipatnam trunk road touched the watercourse and where he had crossed to the diamond mines on the south shore. Yet I could see nothing and, though I asked several men, no one could help me. People here did not approach me, preferring to stare from a distance: there was no curiosity, only wariness.

From the vantage point of the high bank it was possible to see how the river had cut away at the earth bank on the north side while depositing sand on the south. There were obviously not going to be any diamond deposits on the outer edge of the curve, but if I could get downstream to the next bend, I would find sand and gravel again – there was also the possibility that the Kimothi's camp might give me an English speaker and, even better, one trained in geology. The difficulty of what I was trying to do was sinking in: without the right person to help, I could never hope to get anywhere.

I sat on the wall above the river, watching the hills upstream turn gold, then fade to dusty violet. I felt sick inside and angry with myself: I should have stayed on the other bank, searched along the shore, slept out under the stars. Crossing the river felt like a retreat; my only hope now was to reach the mining camp and find the right person in residence. But I had convinced myself that even that was hopeless.

After an hour, as darkness fell, a truck appeared and we climbed on the back and paid five rupees to be taken to Jagyapet. It was too late for finding the camp that day, so I decided to head for Vijayawada, a town large enough to boast several hotels. An express bus arrived from Hyderabad and I took the last seat, in the rear corner next to the offside window. Most of the other passengers were asleep and soon after leaving Jagyapet I began to doze.

And then sometimes the mind does something so strange that one can only marvel, as though such things were illusions at a magic show. When I dozed off, I dreamed I was in my bedroom in England and that I was dreaming I was trapped in my own body, unable to communicate, unable to escape. A terrible darkness was forcing me down, stifling the breath from my chest, sapping my will to fight against it, like some thugee with a knotted silk scarf tightening his grip with each exhalation until all the wind is gone and the prey is asphyxiated.

I woke up. I was in my bed in Thirsk. In fact, I was so pleased to have woken, so pleased to have broken the bonds, that I began to lift up, first just floating, gently, then gaining confidence higher and flying over to the door and back, circling up and up. I could go wherever I willed myself and just as I realised that this wonderful sensation was only a dream – that I was not awake at all – I smashed headfirst into the lightbulb hanging from the ceiling. It shattered and I fell, like Icarus, and woke in a bus seat in India and, putting my hand up, found glass in my hair.

I can still feel that sickening moment of incomprehension, of uncertainty. Was I really awake? Was this glass from a lightbulb? Then I felt shards of thick windscreen glass falling down the back of my collar and saw the man beside me shaking glass from his hair. The bus was stationary, skewed across the road, the headlights on the ghostly grey shapes of bare trees standing in stagnant water. I stood up, touching my face to find if blood was there. I could not believe I had escaped the glass uncut.

'It was a lorry,' someone said to me. 'He has gone.'

The man next to me was cut on the arm, glass had sliced through the sleeve of his jacket. I held out my left hand. There was a tingling sensation, as though tiny needles of glass had embedded themselves in my wrist and palm. I struggled out past my neighbour and forwards along the aisle, crunching over glass and baggage.

A crowd of passengers were standing in front of the bus, looking at the damage. The driver was groaning and holding his head over a large puddle of blood. The windscreen was smashed and one corner badly damaged. Somehow a lorry had managed to strike us head-on, then smash down the side. We were surrounded by darkness, apparently miles from the nearest village.

'What will we do?' I asked. 'Will they send another bus?'

'Why should they be doing such a thing?' asked a young man in jeans and tee-shirt.

'Well, look at him.'

The driver was not getting much sympathy, and it crossed my mind that he could be the cause of the crash, rather than the lorry that had conveniently escaped.

'He will drive,' said the young man. 'That is part and parcel of his job.'

And he did. After a fifteen-minute break and a quick cigarette, he bound his head with a towel, took his seat and drove for two hours with one headlight and without a windscreen. We reached Vijayawada at midnight. When I got down with my bags I noticed a peculiar sensation of heat in my elbow, a sensation that was becoming more painful by the minute. I got in the nearest available cycle rickshaw and asked for a good hotel.

'Oh, yes,' said the driver, 'One very good hotel – Hotel Happy.'

I knew, of course, that Hotel Happy was going to be one of the most dreadful experiences that Indian hoteliers could offer, but we were already rolling down darkened side streets where fat black rats swaggered around looking for a fight. There was the rich aroma of fermenting wastes, and buildings that appeared to have narrowly survived a flood.

The Hotel Happy had been somebody's bright idea once upon a time, someone who had seen a real hotel on television and said, 'I can do that.'

I walked up the concrete ramp towards a sign that read, 'Riciption'. Two men in porter's uniforms were loafing behind a counter. Next to them was a fish tank with an internal backdrop of the Swiss alps, dimly seen through a thick pea soup, and one motionless fish with a furry growth on its stomach. Wires hung from the ceiling and the floor was covered in torn and battered carpets, stained with betel juice. Behind the two grinning 'riciptionists' a large telephone exchange box lay on its back with bare wires lolling from its belly. At the far end of the counter, an open door revealed a foul black cavern of a kitchen where a naked man was taking a bath in a sink next to a pile of filthy dishes. He smiled at me too and took the grubby dishcloth off his head to wipe his armpits.

'Twenty-four hours restaurant,' said one of the porters, idly picking at some white goo which had splattered his uniform. 'Veggie, non-veggie and Chinese.'

I only need to sleep here for six hours, then I can leave, I told myself. 'Show me a room.'

He flicked a piece of goo on the floor and turned to stare pensively at the assembled keys. After much consideration, he threw a key to his colleague who also appeared to have been hit by an exploding Camembert cheese. We walked up two flights of steps and came onto a long corridor lit by a few dim bulbs and floored with mauve sacking. He went to the first door and kicked it open.

'Room,' he said and waited for a tip. I gave him one rupee, the smallest coin in my pocket; he handed it back and walked away.

'Used to big tippers are you?' I called after him but he ignored me.

The room was in darkness, and unable to find a light switch, I struck a match. There was the tiny rustle of cockroaches and a glimpse of shiny black bodies sprinting for cover.

I found the switch next to the bed, six inches above floor level. The light bulb was also six inches above floor level and green, but it was bright enough to read the notice on the wall above the bed. '1. Do Not Spit. 2. Intimate departure and cooperate inefficient service. 3. Please turn off water supply before leaving room.'

Fortunately, it was also bright enough to reveal the electric cable that came through the curtains and cut across the room at throat level. I limboed under this and threw back the curtains. There was a flurry of dust and a view of a brick wall. Initially I thought the window itself had been bricked up, but then I saw that a decent three inch space had been left between my window and what was the next building. I closed the curtains.

The bed was covered by filthy sheets; on the pillow lay a single black pubic hair as thick and shiny as a beetle's leg. I threw the pillow under the bed and lay down feeling utterly dispirited, bitterly regretting that I had not stayed on the riverbank.

It was not the fleas that woke me but my elbow. When I looked at my watch, I found I had slept for only five minutes. My arm had swollen from the tip of the elbow to halfway along my forearm and was burning hot. I decided to go down to the twenty-four hour restaurant and get some ice. On leaving the room, I discovered that the lock was broken and I could not close the door.

There was one other person in the dining room, a thin elderly Indian who smiled when I entered. He was toying with a dog-eared menu.

'Have you eaten in this place?' I asked, remembering that I had had nothing since breakfast.

'Frankly, I was just wondering if I had the courage,' he said in perfect English, gently accented with Italian. 'Why don't you join me anyway?'

I discovered he was a designer who lived near Milan. Forty years before he had left India to study in Rome, returning intermittently to explore his homeland. Now he was on his way south and regretting his decision to break the journey in Vijayawada.

[66]

He talked of his childhood in a forest area north of Bombay and of travelling in India after the war. 'I slept in ruined palaces and visited beautiful temples where you could drink from the pool. Now I go back and see rubbish filling the tank, youngsters carrying radios and the priests demanding money. All the beauty that was India is gone.'

He was in a very pessimistic mood and it made me feel better. There is nothing like the long and bitter draught of someone else's misery to rally your own spirits.

'The country is ruined,' he said. 'But the people – some of the people – are still beautiful. In Gujarat there are tribals who claim descent from Krishna and really you can believe it – they are so perfect to look at. I never saw such people.'

We were interrupted by the waiter but neither of us could bear to eat, despite being hungry, and ordered only tea. There was no ice available, the waiter told me, so I gave him ten rupees with instructions to go out and find some.

'Why have you come here?' Mr Shantilal asked. 'Tourists are not often seen in Vijayawada.'

I explained my interest in diamonds.

'Then you should know of the Syamantaka of the Sun god?'

'The legendary gemstone?'

'It is the first diamond in Indian legend, the greatest stone in our history.'

Behind his head, the curtain was moving. A rat appeared on the rail and ran along towards a hole once occupied by an air-conditioning unit. The waiter came with our tea and Mr Shantilal sipped at it before starting his story.

'You know of Krishna – he was a prince who lived in ancient India and an incarnation of Vishnu. The stories about him are in the *Mahabharata* – do you know it? How he helped the Pandava brothers in their struggle with the Kauravas? Later he founded the city of Dwarka which was on the coast of Gujarat before it was lost to the sea – I myself believe this was the origin of the Atlantis myth.' He sipped his tea and grimaced.

'That is horrible. Well, in Dwarka lived a man called Sattrajit who worshipped Surya, the sun, and one day, while he was walking on the shore, Surya appeared before him and rewarded his devotion with a jewel – the Syamantaka. This jewel brought great prosperity to the city and kept away all evil things like famine and wild animals and robbers.'

I remembered Sir John Mandeville and his tales of the properties of diamonds – how a jewel, freely given, protects the virtuous. Mr Shantilal pushed his tea away. 'I would rather not drink that poisonous concoction.'

He resumed the story. 'This man Sattrajit feared Krishna would ask for the diamond, so gave it to his brother Prasena.

'The one property of that jewel was it did good for the good man – but the opposite was true for the bad. Prasena was an evil man: he went out hunting and a lion killed him. In turn the lion was killed by the King of Bears who took the jewel to his cave.

'When the people found Prasena dead there were rumours spreading that Krishna had killed him for the stone. To prove his innocence Krishna had to recover the jewel. He tracked the King of Bears to his lair and fought him for twenty-one days, until the bear gave up the Syamantaka. When Krishna returned with the jewel, the people accepted he was innocent. He then gave it away.'

'This is the story in our Puranas. That was the great diamond which brought prosperity and happiness to the kingdom of Dwarka. They say it came down through history with these Rajputs, then to the Mughals and the British – the Koh-i-Noor. There is no diamond – not any gemstone in the whole world – like it. You should visit these places in Gujarat, walk the forest paths that those heroes walked, then you will feel how it may be true.'

'Where should I go?'

'To the far west: Kathiawar, the Girnar mountains, Junagadh and Dwarka. In those places you will hear more.'

While he was speaking the waiter had appeared with a man dressed only in a grubby lunghi. This man was gasping for breath and shivering. When he stopped, a puddle began to form around his bare feet. On his head was a pad of straw, and on top of that a large column of ice. It was about a yard long and a foot square.

'Ice, sahib?'

The man's knees wobbled. Mr Shantilal looked as surprised as I felt.

'Do you intend to drink this ice?' he asked. 'I would expressly advise against it. They are not using correct sanitation methods in production.'

'I want to put it on my arm,' I explained. 'To reduce the swelling.' The porter's arms, I noted enviously, had begun to shiver uncontrollably; my own left arm was burning hot.

I held my key up for the waiter. 'Please take the ice to my room. Put it in the bathroom.'

His eyes widened. 'The bathroom, sahib?'

'Yes, that's right.'

The two of them headed for the stairs, leaving a trail of icy water.

Mr Shantilal and I went for a stroll outside, but the filthy street only subdued him further. I was feeling quite chirpy by then.

'I am glad to be old,' he said, 'and to have seen India as it was. I think perhaps it was the death of Gandhi-ji that marked the end.'

'Did you meet him?'

Mr Shantilal had something of the look of Gandhi about him: a thin almost wasted frame, round-rimmed spectacles and a gentle manner. 'Yes, I did meet him. We had gone to Poona and he came there to visit a certain doctor. My brothers and I were taking singing lessons at that time and we asked to sing for him. After our performance he came to me and placed his hand here.' He touched his forehead. 'I felt something then, some power. Afterwards I followed his teachings and took the unstitched cloth for seven years. It was the time when the British placed Gandhi-ji under house arrest in Poona. He then refused food. No one knew if he was alive or dead except for a small symbol in the newspaper. It was an open secret: they put a lamp in the corner with the flame burning. Everyone knew that if the flame went out, Gandhi-ji was dead.'

Like Mr Shantilal, Gandhi had come from Gujarat, but further west in the Kathiawar area. There he had been influenced by the Jain religion and its tradition of ahimsa, or non-violence.

'Gandhi-ji's fasting was something incredible,' said Mr Shantilal, 'You saw his real strength, his will. In those days, watching the lamp every day, I saw India as I never saw it since. People were full of excitement and interest. We read everything and discussed so many ideas of how to boot out the British and solve India's problems.' He shook his head. 'Now they discuss nothing and the problems are worse – much worse. Gandhi-ji is forgotten.'

We turned and retraced our steps, weaving through the black puddles.

'In Kathiawar there are so many places we connect with Lord Krishna,' he said. 'And you see his face in the faces of the people and you walk the stories of his life when you walk the forest paths. Next year I will make one more trip to India and visit Kathiawar. After that I will not come back.'

Reaching the hotel entrance, we said goodnight and I went up. The bathroom floor was awash and icy cold, but of the ice itself there was only a small cube remaining. I pressed it to my elbow until it was gone, then wrapped a damp cloth around the swelling and wrote down the names of places that Mr Shantilal had mentioned. Talking to him had calmed my nerves, convinced me that I would carry on, as though a little of the peaceful determination Gandhi had transmitted through his touch had now been passed to me. I took out the map and saw how my journey would sweep westwards, through Bombay, then north and into Gujarat and Kathiawar where the great Syamantaka diamond had first fallen into human hands.

During the night I woke intermittently to curse the fleas which I could feel wriggling under my clothes.

Having no intention of enduring a second night at the Hotel Happy, I left my luggage in the bus station and took the local service back along the Hyderabad road as far as the small town of Nandigama. This was where Mr Kimothi had told me I would find transport down to the river. My arm was less swollen after a breakfast of aspirin, and it was a fine clear day full of promise, I told myself, particularly for finding diamond mines.

Nandigama was quiet. Youths slouched on walls gazing enviously at travellers on the local service to Jagyapet or Vijayawada. Old men picked at their crusty toes and children hung around the speed bumps. I drank some coconut water off a roadside stall and wondered what to do next.

For once I was pleased to see a rusting crate of an autorickshaw come alongside.

'Where to?'

'Chandarlapadu.'

He was initially unwilling to believe me. Chandarlapadu? More than an hour away by the River Krishna?

I had the strong impression that he had never ventured so far afield, an impression confirmed when he went to ask a shopkeeper where it was exactly. Nevertheless, we agreed on a price for the day and set off along a narrow metalled lane through fields of pepper trees, cotton and tobacco. Buffaloes lumbered along the path, silent, heads lower than bottoms, weighed down by vast curling horns.

This looked a prosperous country, blessed with fertile soils and thriving crops, yet the small villages were full of idle men sitting on stones, drinking milky tea with sullen displeasure. We took two of them as passengers and with much gesturing, a few words of Hindi and the driver's halting English I managed to find out that the cause of the farmers' woes was moneylenders. Every year they came and advanced cash to the farmers for pesticides and fertilisers. But this year the cotton had done badly and the farmers had taken extra loans to buy stronger chemicals which had killed some plants. Now desperate farmers had turned the poisons on themselves, committing suicide rather than face financial ruin. This apparently green and pleasant land was choking on the chemicals that had promised prosperity.

My vision had been somewhat selective, I realised, despite Mr Shantilal's warnings of environmental breakdown: next to the buffaloes wallowing peacefully in a muddy pool below the toddy palms was a pile of empty plastic sacks; out in the field of chilli plants a farmer was spraying from a drum on his back, and the ditch beside the road was filled, not with water, but an ugly salty crust.

The autorickshaw driver stopped to let a herd of buffaloes pass and one of the two farmers offered around a pack of beedis. As he held out his hand I noticed with a start that he was wearing a ring. It was the flash of colour that caught my eye: the blue and red, the yellow and green – nine stones in all, three by three – emerald, ruby, pearl, sapphire, topaz, coral, cat's eye, moonstone, and in the centre, diamond. The navaratna, the nine gems, the stones that promise contact with the nine heavenly bodies, the nine gods. After all the disappointments it seemed like a wayside marker, the single footprint in the mud that told me I was still on the right trail.

Chandarlapadu was full of men in white lunghis and jackets, most of them barefoot, all gathered in front of the shacks that sold a few bolts of cloth and essentials like soap. I asked for the National Mineral Development Corporation camp and one of them directed us to a compound on the edge of the village.

We located a rusting gate in a line of eucalyptus trees and a sign almost lost in the undergrowth. Leaving the rickshaw at the gate, I went inside. The squeak of the hinges must have announced my arrival because an old man suddenly appeared outside a tin hut and ran across the track to a larger building next to some abandoned conveyor belts and machinery. The compound had obviously once been carefully laid out with gravel paths and lawns, but the grass had become overgrown, the huts shabby with the passing seasons. An air of lethargy and eternal afternoon hung over the place.

As I rounded the first building, the old man appeared, pressing his palms together and bowing. He led me around the building to a wooden veranda and indicated that I should go up. There was a doorway and peering in I saw a chubby, middle-aged man dressed in neat shirt and trousers. He was sitting at a desk reading a newspaper.

He looked up and removed his glasses. 'Ah, come in,' he said. 'Are you? I mean, you have a card – a business card?'

I confessed I did not.

'But . . . ah . . . proper channels, accreditation for visiting?'

Wondering how many visitors he normally expected, I mentioned Mr Kimothi and my interest in ancient mines. I laid some emphasis on the word ancient. He wobbled his head politely, 'Achcha, achchaaaa,' that lovely Hindi word that sounds like the sigh of a scimitar slicing silk and whose meaning is equally inscrutable.

'We will,' said the man. 'We will, certainly, if Kimothi . . . achcha. I am Muralikrishna – officer-in-charge here.'

He stood up and went into a side room. The shutters were all closed, but chinks in the wooden walls and holes in the roof allowed in sufficient light to see some piles of dusty journals of field geology and a table laid with mineralogical specimens.

'Operationally we are waiting,' he said, moving a few bits of paper around to little effect. 'A move may be imminent. I myself, however, retirement, in one year . . .'

I picked up a specimen and looked at it. He frowned. I replaced the stone where a dark mark showed it had been. In a drawer he found what he was looking for: his own business card and handed it to me.

Putting it in my pocket, I asked. 'Have you found diamonds here?' The direct brutality of the question seemed to startle him. I sensed my own clumsiness.

'Ah, no. Well, yes. But you see not in commercial quantities. We found only tiny traces . . . come, I will . . . we can at least.'

He led me to the veranda and pointed across a patch of grassy scrub to a pile of rusting machinery which looked as though it had been unused for a long time. 'Here the rock is put in to the crusher, then the conveyor to washing and separation, finally we laid out the diamondiferous gravel but so little was . . . actually we . . . well not commercial, not at all, no.'

In fact, they had found about one carat per hundred tons, a very low proportion and totally uneconomic.

'You have taken your snacks?'

We walked across to the other hut, the living quarters and kitchen. A pot of rice and two bowls of curry were already being laid out by a boy. I washed my hands in the tin-walled bathroom with a sliver of soap; the towel was beside Mr Muralikrishna's clothes, all hung over poles in the roof of his bedroom where the ants and lizards were less likely to get at them. Anything in a wooden cupboard would be ruined by mould or moths.

We ate silently and quickly with our fingers. A jungle rat ran across the beam above, chasing a gecko. After we had finished, the rickshaw driver was fed. I was not sure if this was simple camp etiquette – servants eat second – or some delicacy of caste. I suspected both.

Sitting outside, I discovered that Mr Muralikrishna had been here for three years and was hoping to avert any plans to move him for a further year, when he would retire to Guntur. The endless heat, the silence, the simple luxuries like water cooled in a terracotta pot – I felt myself back in the long afternoons of my teaching days in Sudan, snoozing on a rope bed under a grass roof while the tatty heaps of exercise books lay uncorrected on an earthern floor.

The old man was busy pouring petrol from a can into a jeep that sat under a sun shelter. Mr Muralikrishna was still hoping for something official from me, a chit or a letter. The unspoken direct question, 'Who are you?' was behind his elliptical comments, but they were silenced by the engine starting.

'So . . . will we? Go?'

'Where?'

'I can show you – not far – one kilometre.'

I asked the rickshaw man to wait and got in the passenger seat. Mr Muralikrishna drove, the old man climbed in the back.

'Is he a local man?' I asked. Mr Kimothi had said I should rely on local knowledge.

Mr Muralikrishna looked surprised that I should enquire. 'He is a worker.'

We were rattling along a track next to fields of cotton. The land was almost perfectly flat, but away to our right I could see a low ridge. This was the far bank of the river, explained Mr Muralikrishna, the watercourse itself was less than a mile off.

The old man spoke in Telugu and we stopped. Between two cotton fields was an area of scrubby thorn trees about the size of a football pitch. We approached on foot. A dusty path led us to the top of a gravel ridge beyond which was a hollow where some cows were feeding on the bushes.

Mr Muralikrishna translated what the old man was saying. 'This was an ancient mine – he does not know how old – more than three hundred years.'

The old man squatted down and began to sift through the gravel at our feet, chattering all the time.

'He says that the diamonds grow in this soil, so people will come back one day and dig it up again.' Mr Muralikrishna frowned. 'It is their belief – not scientific.'

I bent down and picked up some pieces of crystal. If Sir John Mandeville was a liar then he was a very well-informed one: the belief that diamonds grow is one deep-rooted in Indian culture.

The geologist took the crystals from me and examined them with a professional air. 'Quartz.'

'Did you ever find anything big?' I asked. 'I mean, more than a carat or two?'

'Not even that,' he said. 'We tried gravel from many locations but never got much. There was no purpose to continue.'

We sauntered back to the jeep. I was feeling deflated: duped by boyhood memories of Rider Haggard and Jack London into a hope that I would stumble on something, the dream of every panhandler who came late to the Rush. Now I was here, a couple of centuries after the event, and all I found was some heaps of gravel surrounded by sickly cotton bushes. Nevertheless, I was convinced that this had been part of the Parteal mine – the source of Thomas Pitt's diamond and many others.

We climbed back in the jeep and Mr Muralikrishna drove us down to the river. There were a few dunes, then a mile of burning sand and the glitter of water below the southern bank.

'Do you want to . . . well, walk to that?' He was clearly unenthusiastic.

'Can you ask him – the old man – can you ask him if there's anyone here who knows about diamonds – I mean, the history?'

'There is no one.'

'He might know – being a local.'

'He is not local.'

We got back in the jeep again. The oppressive heat of afternoon was down on us, the sleepiness after food, the overwhelming desire to do nothing much but lie down in the shade and wait for tomorrow. I struggled against it, this was my last chance and I knew it. I turned to the old man.

'*Hirak? Tarikh hirak?*'

He smiled and looked puzzled. Mr Muralikrishna sighed.

I took the phrase book out of my bag and began flicking through, catching desperately at any words that seemed vaguely relevant. '*Ekka da goppavadu tarikh hirak?* Where great man diamond history?'

At this execrable mutilation of the Telugu tongue, Mr Muralikrishna relented and asked for me. The old man immediately broke into a huge grin and began to talk at high speed and at great length, gesticulating violently down the track, tapping me on the shoulder, waggling his head, laughing and finally retying his lunghi with a wild flourish.

Mr Muralikrishna pursed his lips thoughtfully. 'He is trying to say something,' he said, very slowly. 'He is trying to say, "Yes." '

'That's all? Yes?'

The geologist concentrated on getting us through a herd of ambling buffaloes. 'Perhaps we can go.' He thought for a while. 'Yes, we can go. We will. Regular channels would be preferred, but as you are . . . well.'

I kept silent. At least we were going somewhere, not back to the camp and the end of my search. The old man began to shout directions. We came to a small village of mud-walled huts with thatched roofs, each hut with an ox cart parked outside. A small side lane took us down between some coconut palms and hayricks, then into a farmyard. We stopped and got out.

Ahead of us, across a yard strewn with broken water pots, was a single-roomed mud hut with shaggy thatched roof. To the right was a large pile of straw where a few buffaloes were reclining; on the left was a cart with a wheel off, a white bull with enormous pink genitalia, and a rope bed with a sleeping man on it.

He sat up as we approached, and I immediately noticed that he was wearing a long white silk tunic, unlike the other men who began to appear – they were dressed in the simple cotton lunghi. When we shook hands, he did so easily, in the manner of one accustomed to such big city ways. He was small and wiry and his sharp, mischievous eyes darted around, missing nothing, especially not the stencilled sign, 'Government of India', on the side of the jeep.

He shouted to the hut and a woman in a green sari appeared, dragging a second charpoy. We all sat down and large numbers of children appeared, all keen to listen. Conversation began in Telugu, the man nodding and gazing at me all the time.

When Mr Muralikrishna had finished introducing me, the man began to speak, stopping occasionally to allow Mr Muralikrishna to translate.

'The ancient mines were here,' he said, 'where you were taken earlier, and also east of our village. Those north of here, the mines you saw, are called Parteal, those west are Bondulu. Nobody mines at these places now, but sometimes, after the first rains, a farmer may pick up a small diamond.'

Mr Muralikrishna's translation was enfuriatingly brief.

'Are diamonds lucky?' I asked. 'Do they bring good fortune?'

He pressed his hands together. 'The diamond may be lucky. At a birth we cast a horoscope and discover which stone that child must wear. For some it is diamond – but it must not be a stone with a flaw – that is very bad luck.'

'Were large stones found here – famous diamonds?'

As this question was translated the assembled crowd of old men suddenly became animated, waving their sickle handles at me. The man smiled. 'There was one stone – as big as those handles and the same shape – it was found at Bondulu more than 250 years ago.'

'Who took it?'

'Maybe the Nizam or the British – we do not know. Remember that those who find such things cannot hope to keep them, or even to be paid well for finding them.'

I knew what he said was true: if a ruler got to hear of a large gem-stone, the owner was soon prevailed upon to make a gift of it. Shah Jehan, the greediest of all the Mughal emperors, would always force merchants to present him with any large stones that he heard about. The habit of secrecy when it came to large diamonds had been learned the hard way.

As for the diamond as big as a sickle handle it was probably the Nizam, a huge stone that was last heard of in the 1930s when the Nizam of Hyderabad used it as a paperweight.

'And then there was the Koh-i-Noor,' said the man. 'Your Maharani Liz-beth now keeps it.'

'I thought it was mined from Kollur?'

'No, it was here – in fact our village name was that of the diamond, until, in the mouths of Muslims, it became changed to Koh-i-Noor.'

I sat back on the charpoy, smiling widely. The discomforts and difficulties of the previous days suddenly seemed worthwhile.

'When was that?'

'Hundreds of years – nobody can know such things.'

I glanced around me. There was no evidence, of course, there never could be. But why believe what was written in books: if followed back, the story that the Koh-i-Noor was from Kollur probably began with a villager just like this one, telling some traveller what his grandfather had said.

The buffaloes' tails were swishing at flies and sending a golden smoky haze across the farm. It was now late afternoon and I sensed Mr Muralikrishna's impatience. I asked my big question.

'Do they still mine the diamonds? Do you have any?'

The villager's face became closed, his mischievous look turned to a frown, and there was a rapid exchange in Telugu.

'He will not trust a stranger,' said Mr Muralikrishna. 'He wants to know who you are, but what can I say?'

'It's only for information – just information purposes.'

The man became excited when he heard this, whacking the charpoy with his hand.

'Then why did you write his name in your book?'

It was true that I had done this, almost instinctively. Now I tore the page out and screwed it up. 'The name is not important – I have forgotten it.'

The man's face relaxed into a smile again. 'Wait,' he said and getting up, disappeared inside the hut. I could hear a rustling in the thatch, then he came back carrying a small silk purse. 'Hold out your hand,' he commanded.

I did so.

The sun was touching the tops of the coconut palms on the edge of the farmyard and golden sheets of silken light came pouring down. The buffaloes were stirring from their slumbers, raising the dust. When the man took the purse away from over my hand I saw six brilliant shards of light lying there. Six uncut diamonds, ranging from about one carat up to six or seven.

There was a long period of silence, my fingers were trembling. I was right about the mines: they did exist. The oldest diamond mines in the world. I let out a long whistle of excitement and pleasure and everyone, except Mr Muralikrishna, began to laugh. The younger boys jostled for a closer look.

'They are from Kollur,' said the man. 'That is upriver, near where the ferry crosses.'

I told him that I had visited the area and he smiled. 'They will not let you see the mines – but they are there.'

I picked up the largest of them and admired it: the symmetry of the octagonal form, like two four-sided pyramids base to base, eight sides converging on two opposing points. The attraction for ancient philosophers must have been as much for the shape as for the peculiar properties. This raw stone, fresh from the earth after several hundred million years, seemed quite the most beautiful thing I had ever held at that moment.

Mr Muralikrishna had become hunched up on the rope bed, his expression pinched and anxious. He took one of the stones and examined it under an eyeglass. His utter astonishment at seeing the stones was obvious.

'Is it real?' I asked.

'Well, it would seem to be. It must be. This man knows as well as I do.'

'He's a trader – he sells them? Can you ask how much he wants for them?'

But I should have kept clear of any mention of selling. Mr Muralikrishna was clearly unhappy. 'Of course, that is illegal – the selling and the mining – without licence. But how did they find such – we never found like this – I will have to – Kimothi will have to be informed, won't he?'

His look was troubled and I could understand his difficulty: three years searching and here, only months before his retirement, came proof that he had missed the target. All those reports suggesting that the ancient mines were long since worked out were untrue. This was not the quiet, sleepy afternoon the geologist had been expecting. 'Ask the locals,' Mr Kimothi had said.

'Do they take them to Hyderabad?' I asked, but Mr Muralikrishna had stopped translating and the conversation shifted out of my reach into Telugu, a conversation peppered, tantalisingly, with English: 'only information', 'stories', 'generally', 'proper London'. The diamonds were taken from me and returned to their hiding place in the thatched roof. Mr Muralikrishna said we would have to be going and the diamond man gave me a long speech which was translated as: 'He says goodbye.'

The old man started the engine with the crank handle and we reversed down the lane. Just as we reached the main track, a local man nipped out from behind a hayrick and said something to me. I glanced at Mr Muralikrishna who frowned and replied in Telugu. The man turned away.

[79]

'What did he want?'

We had got out on the main track through the village and the geologist put his foot down, sending chickens scattering.

'He asked if you wanted to buy some diamonds and I told him you did not. Never.'

It was almost dark when we reached the compound. Any thoughts I had had of secretly slipping back to the village were gone because I knew I'd never find it in the dark – and anyway Mr Muralikrishna was very particular to see me off on the Nandigama road. His talk had become incomprehensible: like a burbling satellite losing station, he wove crazy circles around me. 'Give my regards to Kimothi – will you see Kimothi? Notice of arrival better – arrangements proper – reports must be – not commercial, not at all . . .'

In a few brief moments we had both found what we were looking for: I had my ancient diamond trade still alive after centuries, and Mr Muralikrishna had his stones. But the discovery had made only one of us happy.

CHAPTER 4

The total amount of diamonds in the world is but one
assload.

Bahr al-Fava'id, *The Sea of Precious Virtues*, a twelfth
century Persian book for princes

T HE night train from Hyderabad to Poona and Bombay was a
shock to someone recently emerged from the simple backwoods
of Andhra Pradesh. Youths in English football shirts paraded
up and down the platform, brandishing mobile phones and Sony
Walkmans. Others, unwilling to risk losing their seat, blew up inflat-
able pillows with flowery cotton cases or took off their leather brogues
and put on slippers, the brogues delicately placed in a carry bag that
zipped shut. You could tell the carry bag was meant for that job and
that job alone because it had 'Shoes – Happy Journey' written on it.

These people were clearly only beginning to get used to having
money; their symbols of wealth were hard-won and they took great
care over them. These were people entering the world of the dispos-
able and dispensable with all the care and circumspection of an earlier
age. But further down the train, the majority of travellers could only
dream of joining them. In third-class the people sat crowded on
wooden benches, cracking sunflower seeds between their teeth and
eating with their fingers from tiffin pots. The men smoked beedis and
talked. In second-class they were reading the newspapers.

Deccan Chronicle Letters page. 'How long will I live this wretched
life?' – 'When will I become a film star?' – 'I suffer from piles and think
that black magic is responsible'. The answers were forthright and

practical: get a doctor for the piles and a psychiatrist for the black magic. A request for an explanation of impotence was, 'Think of a man's penis as a car tyre being inflated by an air compressor.' One can only hope the correspondent's knowledge of English distinguished between analogy and advice.

I had only managed to purchase a second-class ticket, not an actual reserved berth, so I settled warily amongst the triple bunks and watched my fellow passengers chaining their Samsonite suitcases (sheathed in camouflage covers usually) to the bunks. A vast middle-aged lady in an orange silk sari discussed the Northern Railways time-table with a Sikh officer. Two of the flashy Bombay youths chatted politely about how they got their 'positions' – through family connections it appeared. One apologised to me for his English: 'Here, we are only speaking butler English.'

As soon as the train was rolling, the fat lady's eyelids began to droop with sleep. Very gently, hands in her lap, she listed heavily to starboard and with a sigh, suddenly keeled over. The young man leapt out of the way, but his briefcase had become trapped. Outside, it was dark and raining. Occasionally we would see a light in the trees or pass over a marshy area and hear the frogs singing to the night.

I was pleased to be on the move, following the route west and north that all the loot of the centuries had taken: Alauddin's booty, the bejewelled elephants, the war horses, the big diamonds and, most of all, the Koh-i-Noor. Bombay was the world's largest centre for cutting and polishing, but those were diamonds imported from Antwerp and London. I was chasing the Indian diamonds, the big old stones with curses attached, and the smaller, more recent material from excavations of the most ancient mines.

I was nodding off to sleep when the ticket collector came and I discovered there were no more second-class berths: I would have to splash out on first-class.

Two men looked up from their Hindi comic books when I pulled open the sliding door in the next carriage. They wore Levi jeans with white cotton vests. The man on the upper bunk smiled and said, 'Good evening'; the older and thinner man below simply smiled. They had a harder edge to their faces than those in second class and their quality shoes were left on the floor without special slip cases. I had the immediate impression that they had money and were used to spending it.

'I am Rasam,' said the younger man. We did not shake hands – I was getting out of that western habit quickly. 'Are you going to Bombay?'

'Yes – what about you?'

He grinned. 'We are social workers attending a conference in Bombay.' He leaned forward to offer me a cigarette – Marlboro, not the usual beedi or Wills. First-class travel in India is not cheap, I thought, and Indian social workers cannot be that well paid.

I asked a few questions about their work – innocuous enquiries that met with little response. No, they did not work with children, or Dalits, or women, or health. No, they did not live in Hyderabad, nor in Bombay. The subject of the conference was social work, the rest was too difficult to translate.

Rasam got down from his bunk and, with some words in what I took to be Gujarati, went out. His friend lay back and closed his eyes. Rasam returned with some sheets, a blanket and a pillow for me. This time I kept off the subject of social work and we got along better.

They were both from a small town near Surat, 150 miles north of Bombay, but their families were originally from Palanpur, a town in Gujarat close to the Rajasthan border – it was the first of many occasions when I would hear the name. Rasam and I discovered that we shared the same birthday and the same number of children of all the same ages. The friendly atmosphere warmed up even more. His friend bundled himself up in his blanket – the air-conditioner was blasting cold air at us. We were paying for the luxury of being cold, our own hill station on wheels.

'Did you fly from London?'

I nodded and we discussed airlines and routes. They were mystified as to why I had missed the opportunity to fly via Dubai or Abu Dhabi. 'Better shopping. Muscat is no good.'

Rasam asked what I was doing in India and I explained truthfully that I was writing a book about diamonds. The two of them shared a joke in Gujarati.

'What have you found?' asked Rasam.

I told him that Bombay was a big centre – and Surat too. He nodded. 'We have more than 35,000 cutters in Surat and the town is full of workshops. Those people are mostly Kathiawaris.'

[83]

It was a name Mr Shantilal had mentioned and one I had read in history books: the Kathiawaris were a people inhabiting that region of Gujarat which hangs between the Malabar Coast and Kutch, an area once infested by bandits and highwaymen. Their reputation was for quick wits and guile.

'People from Palanpur were the first in this business, but the Kathiawaris are increasing. They are tougher.'

He told me about the cutting trade, how it took six months to learn the basic skills. 'The diamonds are imported in the rough and then exported cut and polished.'

'But not all that comes in goes out?' I said. The man seemed to know what he was talking about and I wanted to hear about the illicit trade.

He laughed and translated my question for his friend. They exchanged words in Gujarati.

'That's true,' he said eventually. 'Not everything is done proper.'

'There's a hidden trade?'

He waggled his head. 'Gold comes from the middle east – there are Indians living there – you can say gangsters. They send gold to India to buy diamonds which are then smuggled back out.'

'Where from?'

'The gold comes in through Daman and the diamonds go out from Bombay and Surat.'

This had the ring of truth. India has long been an insatiable devourer of bullion. The Romans complained that gold was disappearing eastwards at an alarming rate, only to be replaced by useless and frivolous luxuries. When the British came, bearing their heavy woollens, they hoped to trade English produce for Indian. Instead they found the Indian merchants wanted only bullion, while consumers back home snapped up Indian produce. What the Honourable Company had hoped would be trade was actually no more than shopping.

As he was talking, I reached down to my bag and fetched out my notebook – I had some names of diamond merchants in Bombay. I read them out.

'These are all big men,' he said. 'They have no need to use the illegal trade. But that does not mean they are honest.' He repeated one of the names. 'He has been in prison for dealing in fake companies on the stock market.'

The scam appeared to rely, as they often do, on stupid greed. Investors would be lured by the glamour of the diamond business to part with their money, but that money would then be simply siphoned away and, eventually, the company would go bust. Gullible investors would be left with no more than a disconnected mobile phone number.

'You know a lot about the diamond business,' I said with a smile. In my pocket I fingered the cheap navaratna ring.

He yawned and began to prepare his bed. His pillow was the Samsonite case chained to the bunk ladder. 'We social workers learn many things.'

'Don't you ever think about buying a few – doing a little trade?'

His eyes were closed and he was settled for the night. There was a silence and I wondered if he was mulling over whether to reply – or perhaps was already asleep. But then he said, 'Yes, I think about it.'

His friend had already turned his back and was breathing slowly.

I lay down on my back, trying not to bang my elbow which had started aching. Rasam had opened his eyes and was watching me.

'You have hurt yourself?'

I explained about the accident.

'India can be a dangerous country,' he said. 'And what you are doing is different. Do you wish to buy diamonds yourself?'

'No – it's just for interest only.'

His face was impassive but I had the feeling he did not believe this. I didn't believe it myself.

'It is not easy,' he said. 'I was a cutter for ten years before my uncle encouraged me. He lives in the same apartment block as that big dealer I told you about.'

The train was clattering through a small station and I peeped out through the crack beneath the metal grill. Whatever time of day or night every railway station in India has a population of hollow-eyed people, wrapped in shawls, staring into space.

'Your uncle encouraged you to try dealing?'

He sniffed and moved his chin. I was thinking of the young men in the second-class carriage, talking of how family connections got them started. The diamond trade was no different.

'Do you buy in Hyderabad?' I asked. 'Rough Indian diamonds?'

[85]

But his eyes were closed again and this time he made no reply. I lay quietly, lulled by the gentle sway of the carriage, the clack of the wheels and the insistent thought that in his suitcase, where the files of social work notes should have been, was a silk purse of Golconda diamonds.

I woke suddenly, aware that the movement of the train had stopped. There was a man in a red jacket in the doorway saying, 'Mumbai! Mumbai! Coolie, sahib?'

The two bunks opposite me were empty and I felt for my bags. Everything was there. The social working diamond smugglers must have left only seconds before, but by the time I got myself out on the crowded platform they had gone.

Victoria Railway Station Bombay, now renamed Sivaji Rail Terminus, Mumbai, is an impressive brick edifice, not as large, it is true, as some of the post-Independence dams and possibly, as my fellow-travellers on the Nagarjunakonda boat had claimed, dedicated to extracting Indian resources all the quicker from India – but impressive nevertheless. I walked from it in the morning sunshine, pleased to find that the city so often cited as an urban hell had some broad tree-lined streets and less traffic than I had expected. In a street beside the docks I found a hotel and telephoned some of the numbers I had been given for diamond dealers.

Most of Bombay's top dealers have offices in a shabby sixteen-storey tower block called Panchratna – the five jewels. Its rubble-strewn corridors are like some seedy oriental souk: dark and narrow, busy with merchants and muttered conversations. Everyone who works there knows everyone else because they are either related to each other or will be one day. The only outsiders are the buyers who trek up and down the bare, betel-stained stairway, comparing deals and dealers, occasionally whispering into a mobile phone. Once past the security men, the offices are like the tightly folded scrips that the diamonds are kept in: narrow rooms filled with hunched figures peering down over low lamps.

[86]

The top-floor offices are more spacious: doors swish back and liv-eried staff ply you with soft drinks, snacks and company reports. In the white marbled office of Mr Harshad Mehta, one of the big players, I was invited to take lunch – alone.

'We Jains are not in the habit of lunching,' Mr Mehta told me, which was how I discovered that all these interlinked families of dealers were of the Jain religion, a faith which practises vegetarianism as well as non-violence and is similar in many respects to Buddhism.

There was something rather other-wordly about it all: the smooth uncluttered curves of the rooms, the preference for white, the ascetic denial of food, the low voices; but on leaving the building I noticed a very different scene. In the grubby side streets around Panchratna was a crowd of several hundred young men in white shirts and black trousers all milling around.

'Who are they?' I asked the man who Harshad Mehta had sent with me. We were in a car, emerging from the underground car park on our way to see the rest of the family empire.

He looked surprised I should ask. 'Dealers.'

'They buy and sell on the street?'

He gave the driver some directions. 'They are small. It is nothing.'

'Selling illegally? Illicit stones?'

He seemed not to hear me. 'If you like, we can stop here at this shop. It is a part of the company's expansion into costume jewellery – we can see the range if you like. Harshad's daughter is running the bou-tique.'

Next day I was back at Mr Mehta's tower block, but this time I wan-dered around the streets below, amongst all the hundreds of young men in black trousers and white shirts. The lanes were choked with parked motorcycles and scooters and it was on and around these that the men were lazing, chatting to friends and smoking. Many of them carried mobile phones and were busy talking to business contacts. I stood outside a paan kiosk and bought a wad, watching the men in the street while the youth pasted the lime on the leaf and sprinkled the areca and spices over it. In front of me were two motor scooters sur-rounded by a group of five men. The paan-seller tapped me on the shoulder and I turned. At precisely that moment, something changed hands between the five men. I just saw a hand come to meet another over the scooter seat and the brief flash of something white. When I turned back with my paan, all neatly folded up into a triangle, the men were chatting again.

I waited, enjoying the sweetness of the paan and its gentle stimulation. When one of the men caught my eye, I nodded. He came over.

'Yes, mister – you American?'

'English.'

'You buy?'

'What do you have?'

He slipped a hand in his trouser back pocket and brought out a leather wallet. Keeping his hands close into his stomach so no one could see, he flipped out a white sachet and opened it enough to catch a glimpse of a black diamond.

'You want ringstones?'

The black diamond was gone and his fingers slipped out a second sachet. I could see that there were upwards of thirty such packets in his wallet. This one held a small cut diamond of no more than half a carat.

'You buyer?'

'No,' I said, meaning to put him at ease. 'I'm just a tourist, but I like diamonds.'

It was as though I had switched a light off. He slapped the sachet back inside the wallet and returned it quickly to his back pocket. Without a further word he turned away. Until that moment I had been aware of others watching us, but now, picking up on the man's body language, I was ignored. My mistake had cost me dearly: in the same moment that I had discovered the Bombay street market for diamonds, I had lost the chance to penetrate it. Here you were either in the game or not – nothing in between. I resolved that, should the chance come again, I would not make the same mistake twice.

I carried on watching for a while, working out how things operated. Panchratna, the dilapidated building that towered over us, was for the big boys, the Mehtas who could afford offices and to entertain foreign clients flown in from Japan or America. Down here was the chasing pack, the lads with quick wits, a dash of cunning and enough up front to keep at least a couple of poor quality stones in their back pockets. This was where my social worker friends would come to sell their Golconda stones.

Some of the dealers looked only fifteen or sixteen years old with thin, feral faces that spoke of hard years spent working up to owning a neat shirt and trousers and sufficient capital to enter the market. The paan-seller saw me watching them.

'Kathiawaris,' he said. 'Too bad boys. You no buy. Maybe bad stone.'

Stalled by my failure at the street market, I decided to pursue a different line of enquiry. There was plenty in the history books about the old trade in large diamonds, but I wondered if it still went on. A series of contacts led me to an astrogemologist who, after a brief initiation into the arcane art of manipulating fate with gemstones, wrote down the telephone number of someone who would help. The following afternoon I rang the man and introduced myself.

'Yes, I will see you,' said a voice. 'We are in K____ Villas in a street full of human beings.'

I put my arm in a sling – it was still painful some days – and set off. After an hour of wandering through streets full of human beings, I had still yet to find the place. Then I came to a quieter neighbourhood, with large old apartment blocks and some big mango trees. Outside one block was a sign for 'The Society for Universal Naturopathy' and a man called to me from an open downstairs window. 'From where are you coming friend?'

I went up the short drive and stood next to the barred window. He was sitting at a desk, neatly dressed in high-collared grey shirt and dhoti, his Hindi newspaper lying before him, at the rear of the room were some glass-fronted bookshelves with Hindu stone gods on them. For a full five minutes he questioned me in order to reveal how I had arrived at his gate, or as he put it, 'This remote place in the world.'

He shook his head in amazement. 'So you are spending your father's money wandering the globe? No? Well, your mother's money – that is Sanskrit by the way. Mother, brother, father – have you really never enquired as to why all your family relationship names are coming from

[89]

our Sanskrit?' He stood and walked around the room, tutting to himself, hands massaging his lower back.

'What you are doing is surprising, not to say . . .' he paused and appeared to pluck something from the air, 'Not to say, rather dashing.'

He came up to the bars. 'Are you veggie?'

'I have been since I arrived in India – only by chance, really.'

He nodded sagely. 'Tigers and those are non-veggie, but humanity is naturally veggie. My brother is interested in veggie. Did you want to see him?'

'Actually, I just wanted to . . .'

He interrupted. 'But he is free now. You go up the side passage and knock there – where it says Professor of Mathematics – he will see you.'

I thanked him and followed his directions. His brother's wife let me in and sat me down in a waiting room. There was a large painted statue of the Elephant god, Ganesh, a television and two chairs. After a few minutes his brother appeared and, seeing my arm in a sling, assumed that I had come for a consultation.

'You must imbibe the four elements: earth, water, sunlight and oxygen,' he advised. 'I personally go to the hill every morning to imbibe the sunlight – that is our suryanamaskar programme – and on my return I drink one toothglass of my own urine.'

He must have noticed something doubtful in my expression because he began to expound on the benefits of urine.

'Your body is a filter, isn't it? And so urine is pure water of life, the water of the blood. Look at me, not one day sick in twenty years of urine-drinking. All my family too – they have all taken up this practice. Also I recommend that you rub your urine into the affected area every night and morning. Then you should soak a bandage in urine and tie it – yes.'

I didn't fancy walking around smelling like a public toilet. 'Isn't there a cure involving gemstones?'

His face dropped. 'We are dealing only in Ayurvedic. I make my own medicines with various tree seeds and ginger and, of course, the water of life.'

'But the gemstones?'

'Actually some are putting that navaratna – you know? – in water for twenty-four hours then drinking it with some benefits they say, but I myself only deal with Ayurvedic.'

'Has anyone tried jewels in urine?' Seldom does the opportunity for such questions arise.

He frowned. 'No – no. You can boil it and leave for four days then wash in it – that is possible. Very good for the toning of skin.'

I thanked him for his help and promised to bandage myself that evening.

'Did someone send you?' he asked at the door. 'Two years ago some English people came in and asked questions like yourself. Did they send you?'

'I'm afraid not. By chance I was passing on my way to K____ Villas. Do you know it?'

He was looking crestfallen. 'So nobody sent you? A pity.' He stood up and led me to the door. 'Well, goodbye then.'

I returned to the front of the house where his brother was ready to invite me into his study. He had obviously been waiting.

'How did you find him? What was he telling you?'

I mentioned the urine.

'Ah! That is correct.'

'Do you take it?'

'Ah, no. He tells us to but we ignore his requests. Urine is waste, isn't it?'

'But the body is a filter – doesn't it purify the blood and make urine?'

He smiled sadly. 'No, no. The body is a machine, it creates waste by-products, for example, urine – a dirty, smelly liquid better you get rid of it – OUT!'

He flung his arm violently and his hand struck the bookshelf. 'Ouch.'

'What about washing with it – toning the skin?'

'Mumbo-jumbo, or is it Mumbai-jumbo? Poppycock. Piffle. Brother, do you want to walk around the streets smelling like a public place?'

'Not really.'

'So do not drink or wash in this smelly substance. You will take tea?'

'No thank you.'

He toyed with a small figurine paperweight on his desk. 'My

brother is reading books, you see, and believing them. But I am reading books and not believing them.'

We sat in silence, mulling over this. It was as if a wall had been drawn between the two halves of mankind, as neatly as the wall between his brother's apartment and his own. Truth had no relevance in such matters, the distinction was in personal temperament: some can believe, others cannot.

'Did you want to ask some particular questions?' he asked. 'Of my brother?'

'I'm interested in gemstones,' I said. 'There is a place called K____ Villas, do you know it?'

'Yes. It is a short way. Just carry on this road and you will see it on the right.'

He accompanied me to the gate, past the weather-beaten sign.

'Has the Society for Universal Naturopathy been popular?' I asked. 'Do people join?'

He looked solemn. 'Actually it is simply a sign,' he said. 'My brother put it there some years ago – when he first drank urine – but apart from an English couple who came some years ago . . .' I stepped through the gate and he remained inside looking up at the trees. 'Did they send you? The English couple?'

'No.'

'He might have liked that. Do you have mangoes in England? No! But how to manage – it is the King of Fruits. Good bye then.'

I had walked a few yards when he called to me. 'Really? No mango trees in England.'

'None at all.'

He made a face and turned away, returning to the house with his hands massaging his lower back.

I soon located K____ Villas, just as they had said, in a street full of human beings. There were beggars, housewives, taxi drivers, porters, ox cart drovers and tiffin-wallahs, their turbanned heads bearing a plank on which stood a dozen or more tiffin-containers. An archway led through to a central atrium decorated with potted plants and hung with washing. Old ladies lay on charpoys. In the ancient creaking lift a notice declared, 'Servants are not allowed to use the lift unless accompanied by children.'

The dealer was a neat middle-aged figure dressed in Nehru-style summer suit. We chatted about his family background and how his ancestors had got into the business. The telephone rang continuously – an old-fashioned dial model, not like the plush telecommunications in Panchratna. He spoke quickly, never for more than half a minute. I had noticed how brusque they were: no apparent greetings or fare-wells, they were the conversations of a close-knit group where every voice is known.

'After 1947,' he said, 'the pearl business died and the maharajas lost their status. Some began to sell off diamonds.'

'Did your father get involved?'

He smiled at the bluntness of my question. 'He travelled a lot.'

'In India?'

'Oh, I don't mean overseas. It was in Saurashtra – we had some family connections there – in Junagadh, for example.' I recognised the name as the town Mr Shantilal had recommended me to visit. 'Those were topsy-turvy times, you understand, people went to see that family members were all right. It was not all business, but those big diamonds certainly helped start the Bombay market – like pump-priming.'

'Did you handle large stones?' I had asked this question of every-one, but all had either dodged it or said no. This man sipped his tea before answering.

'Of course, it was a hush-hush business,' he said carefully. 'Sometimes you would not know who was selling or who was buying, only intermediaries came.'

'I realise you cannot tell me those details,' I said. 'I just wondered how big the stones can be?'

I sounded like a small boy asking, 'What was the biggest fish you ever caught, Grandad?' But I was the fisherman.

'There were large stones,' he said. 'I remember a 132 carat stone inscribed with the name of Shah Jehan. In fact, I had two inscribed stones come through – very rare.'

I felt a jolt of adrenaline. That was a big stone, one that ought to be recorded or mentioned somewhere.

'Does that business still go on?'

'No, it began to dry up in the 'seventies. The maharajas lost their status as princes in 1971, you see, so that flushed the last of the jewels out. It's quite rare now to see a good piece. Those that had need of money sold their possessions at that time; the richer ones, or those clever in business, they have survived. Now they will not sell.'

'But they have large diamonds?'

'Oh, yes. All of them. I was taken once to the house of a raja living here in Bombay. He showed me an underground garage – a secret place – where he kept his Rolls Royce. Behind a wall in his dining room there were many treasures: statues, vases, jewelled weapons, big diamonds – many things. You see they keep it hidden, undeclared. They fear that if it is known they have these things, then someone will make a law to take them away. And diamonds are a good thing to hide – very easy.'

'Are there more big diamonds than anyone realises then?'

He smiled. 'It is not in my interest, or theirs, to say yes to that – rarity is all – but I think you can make up your own mind.'

'What was the attraction of diamonds? Just money?'

He pressed his fingertips together. 'And competition. I was in the middle east once and these sheikhs were quarrelling: 'My diamond is bigger than yours.' Such-like – very childish. One produced a 60 carat stone, a second produced a 70, then finally the third pulled out an 80 carat diamond. Later on, each of them came to me independently and asked me to get them a 100 carat stone.'

'But did the maharajas have any beliefs about diamonds – a spiritual need for them?'

He laughed. 'Possibly they did. The maharajas would give their children the nine jewels to play with – as though they were playing with the universe! Then there were some stones, like Koh-i-Noor, it was a symbol of greatness. Look at the men who owned this stone before you – it must be true that you are their equal – and the first of them was a god, Krishna!'

A telephone rang and he lifted the receiver and began to talk. While doing so, he opened a drawer and took something out. He examined it for a moment, out of my sight, then leaning forward passed it to me. It was a pearl the size of a bantam's egg.

He put his hand over the receiver. 'That is a Basra pearl – a *real* pearl!'

I examined the piece closely: physically this was the same thing as those tiny milky chips sold in Hyderabad market, but in reality there was no comparison. On this specimen the colours mixed and swirled, subtle shades of pink and grey like a sunrise in the rainy season.

He put down the telephone. 'Have you seen the cultured pearl?'

I nodded.

'Now you see this – a true pearl. The difference is very enormous, is it not? Well, there is the same difference between a small diamond and a big one, between the ringstones they sell in the street and the ringstones a maharaja might wear. You have seen the stones they sell outside Panchratna?'

I nodded, then remembered to change it into the Indian affirmative waggle. 'Is that market legal?'

He smiled. 'Some of it. These Kathiawaris ... You see, traditionally the dealers were of the Jain religion and that gave them a peaceful philosophy. But now the Kathiawaris are starting in business and they do not follow this way.'

'Do they smuggle?'

'We are not involved in anything like that.'

'No, I realise that – I mean the Kathiawaris.'

'Nobody asks such questions.'

I had overstepped the mark. 'Are there other similar markets?'

'Yes, at Surat and Bhavanagar in Gujarat.'

I knew then that I would get a second chance to see a diamond market. The telephone rang again.

'Is there anything more?' he asked, holding his hand out for the pearl.

I returned it and stood up. 'No, thank you. It was good of you to see me.'

He gave a nod of acknowledgement and turned to the insistent telephone.

I left his office and walked down the stairs. On a landing stained with the blood-red paan juice where an old lady lay asleep on a charpoy, I stopped. In my bag I carried a list of the known large diamonds of the world.

I put the bag down; the old lady did not stir. The list did not claim to be exhaustive, but on one point it was definite: inscribed diamonds were extremely rare. There was the Shah which bears the mark of Fath

Ali Shah, a Persian ruler of the early nineteenth century, who used it as a gift to placate Tsar Nicholas I, hence its current home in the Kremlin. The second stone was the Akbar Shah, inscribed with the names of Jehangir and his son Shah Jehan. This stone was said to have been set in the eye of the Peacock Throne but was almost certainly looted by Nadir Shah in 1739, along with the Shah. It later turned up in London where it was recut, obliterating the inscription, and was sold back to India to the Gaekwar of Baroda, Mulhar Rao. Finally came the Jehangir, a pierced stone bearing the names of Jehangir and his son. This stone had been sold at a London auction in 1954 by the Maharaja of Burdwan. In doing so he had violated India's antiquities export law and was duly fined, along with his Calcutta jeweller.

What excited me about this was that none of the inscribed stones exceeded 116 carats. If the man was correct, then this 132 carat specimen was an example of a large diamond unknown to all but those who had owned or handled it.

Back at my hotel, I pored over my maps and books. The Kathiawar area of Gujarat was looking more and more interesting: not only for its legendary associations with Krishna and the Pandava brothers, but there appeared to be a strong connection with the modern diamond trade. And if that trade had been stimulated by royal jewels in the 'sixties and 'seventies, then it was significant that western Gujarat had once been home to more royalty than anywhere else in India – 282 princely states in an area no bigger than Ireland. Junagadh had been one of the largest and richest, but most had been tiny, often less than ten square miles in area. The smallest was Vejanoness where the Thakur managed an income of 450 rupees from two hundred subjects and twenty-two acres. Monarchs such as these, I reasoned with cavalier enthusiasm, would not have had the resources to buy a second life in Delhi or Bombay – as the richer princes had done after Independence – but rather would have sunk back into genteel decay and obscurity. It was these people who would have time to talk. If the reasoning seemed impeccable at the time, it was not entirely wrong.

CHAPTER 5

Suratt is reckon'd the most fam'd Emporium of the
Indian Empire, where all Commodities are vendible.

Rev. F. Ovington,
A Voyage to Suratt in the Year 1689

Wee preferr your imploiements in dyamonds before all
other interests.

East India Company president in Batavia
to factors on the Coromandel Coast, 15th June, 1624

Bombay Central Station was littered with sleeping people, each
wrapped from head to toe in a bedsheet. I found the correct carriage and my seat by the barred window on the Surat train.
There was a large family opposite, surrounded by the vast quantities
of luggage and snackables: plastic water tubs, tiffin-carriers, bags of
fruit, drink containers, soggy newspaper-wrapped delicacies tied up
with white cotton, and still they bought something from every hawker
who chanced his luck at the window: small bitter oranges, bananas,
slabs of sesame biscuit, warm peanuts in a cone of newspaper, a bottle
of mineral water, a packet of beedis for Dad, and a lurid masala movie
magazine for Mum.

The man in the next seat was grinning at me: forty-ish, moustache,
hair flecked with grey and a cheeky almost lecherous face. He caught
my eye and pursed his lips; one eyebrow arched slightly. I looked out
of the window. A porter was staggering along under a vast white
package, a human snail leaving a trail of sweat. I could sense my

neighbour's eyes on me and turned back. He was slightly hunched forward, eyes sparkling with secret thoughts. I noticed the expensive pair of loafers and the gold watch. Two more porters staggered past, burdened by vast white shapeless packages. The man pressed his palms together between his legs. I looked at the family. They were totally absorbed in themselves, wiping babies, counting heads. The man leaned over, his eyebrow twitched, his breath touched the hairs behind my ear and, when it came, his voice was low and conspiratorial, the voice in the bazaar with the once-in-a-lifetime deal, the voice of the Great Game and the secret society.

'Both of my boobs are yours.'

There was a long silence when he seemed to be coiled up ready to spring. At such moments, even the hardiest traveller is exposed as a defenceless alien. At such moments, he falls back winded and is suddenly conscious of being alone amongst strangers, a little pink prawn in the fishing net of life, waving his pathetic feelers in the air and watching the hungry fisherman of fate reach for the mayonnaise.

I heard myself apologise. 'Sorry – no thank you.'

I stared straight ahead, trying, telepathically, to attract the attention of the family man opposite. If I stared hard enough he would see my cry for help. I could sense how awkward my posture had become: my neck seemed long and foolish, my back too straight, my smile fixed.

My neighbour's shoulders shook a little, then he was leaning in for another go. His lips came close to my ear. 'Lights out! Knickers down! Open knees!'

The family man was staring back now and I was forcing out the silent message, 'For God's sake – go and get a policeman!' He didn't move.

The sexual monster was coming back for more. 'I love acronymns.'

He was laughing now. The full implication of what he had said was sinking in. There was a sudden moment of realisation and I started laughing, too.

'Your spelling is terrible!'

He was crying with laughter. 'Your face! Both Of My Boobs Are Yours! BOMBAY. It's good, isn't it? And I mean knickers and knees with an 'n'.'

He tapped me on the thigh. 'I knew you were English because of that notebook in your top pocket. You can't buy them here, but I used to sell them. I had a newsagents in Twickenham – I mean in "Lights Out, kNickers Down, Open kNees." Oh, your face!'

He was whacking his knees in pleasure at the memory of my discomfort. 'You see the newspaper today. They are calling the millennium 'Y2K' – it's good isn't it?'

He opened his case and took out a pack of cards. The children opposite left off snacking and showed interest. Four of the cards were offered to a child who selected one, put it back and found that card had disappeared from the four.

'It's easy,' he said, grinning at me. 'What's your name? I'm Sanjay – I used to live in Twickenham but I live in Bombay now.'

He made two coins disappear, found one of them in someone's hair and it had become an English ten pence. A crowd gathered and we set off, hardly noticing the journey as Sanjay kept up a continuous patter with his audience. A torn envelope put in someone's pocket reappeared whole with the ten pence coin sealed inside.

'I was making good money in Twickenham,' said Sanjay. 'And spending it, too. I had good customers and everything but I wanted my kids to grow up in India.'

His case was even more strange for the fact that he himself had not grown up in India: his family had been in Canada until he was a teenager. 'We had a newsagents in Vancouver.'

A handkerchief now seemed to be emerging from the base of his thumb to gasps of astonishment from the children. He dropped the false thumb back in his case while they were trying to do it themselves with the 'magic handkerchief'.

'My brother's eldest daughter is a teenager and she started going out all night and seeing boys. Then there is problems with drugs. I thought I don't want any of that, I'll move back home.'

He was not alone. Daily reports in newspapers described how expatriate Indians were returning – responding to the economic liberalisation set up by the former prime minister, Narasimha Rao. Sanjay had been in Bombay for two years but had yet to realise his dream of a knitwear factory.

The man opposite had been following our conversation and now chimed in. He was an expatriate returnee too, from East Africa. Then two Sikh youths asked Sanjay if he was going to make 'suitings and pant' in his factory and another man turned out to be the nephew of a clothes shop owner. Within an hour he had half a dozen useful contacts, business cards exchanged, while we swayed gently through the flat featureless countryside.

'That's what I like about it here,' he said. 'It's easy to meet people. The only thing is – you need them. You can't do anything without contacts.'

He missed football and the British sense of humour, but otherwise was happy. 'It was strange,' he said. 'We spoke Gujarati in the house all my life – but never outside. Then I arrive here and everyone speaks it. It was like coming home – really.'

'Do people know you are an expatriate Indian?'

'Sure they do.'

'How?' And as I asked, I realised. It wasn't his English, which was better than most, but his nods and shakes – he had learned to move like an Englishman.

'It's true,' he agreed when I suggested it. 'My Hindi is fluent but my body language is not. Mind you, in the north it's different.'

Somewhere along the way we were crossing a border: the line that marked the extent of long-term Mughal influence. With the Muslims had come handshakes and headshakes, pushing the wagglers and palm-pressers back into the Deccan.

At Daman station we stopped for some time and I walked up the platform, remembering the diamond smugglers on the Bombay train who had told me about gold bullion coming in through the old Portuguese port. Sanjay joined me. I sensed that he missed English friends, despite the firmly optimistic face he put on life.

He began to tell me about London, recalling customers. 'There was a woman who came in the shop. Very beautiful Italian woman. She drove a Mercedes coupé and lived in Belgravia. She kept saying I should go to her house for the evening. For a year or more she said this and eventually I couldn't resist any longer. I went there and spent the night. It was the first and only time I did such a thing.'

He had begun the story with the gleeful twinkle of a naughty child but had ended uncharacteristically glum. I wondered if it was this incident, or the guilt of it, which had precipitated the move 'home', fear of the erosion of his own morals, more than his children's.

Our approach to Surat was as darkness fell. From the train I watched as we passed the dead rivers, the culverts choked with rubbish, the smokestacks belching yellowish fumes and finally pulled up in the blackened suppurating cess pit that passed for a city centre. 'This hideous city', as *The Times* described it, had suffered an epidemic of the Black Death in 1994, losing half its population as refugees. As I stepped down from the train, with a handshake goodbye from Sanjay, there to greet me was a deformed beggar on a wooden trolley. 'Welcome to Surat,' he said. 'One rupee.' I decided there and then to like Surat, if only because no one else did.

The city's reputation has long been one of a useful money-making spot with few pleasant attractions to distract from the enterprise. It is said to have been founded by a Hindu merchant who fancied the location on the broad but shallow River Tapti. By 1516 it was successful enough to be noted by the Portuguese, but they preferred to control shipping trade through forts at Diu and Daman. In 1573 the town fell to Akbar who built a fort and established a Mughal governor.

The English East India Company arrived in 1608 and by 1620 had a factory established, plus that very necessary facility of the time, a graveyard. This graveyard, I understood, was still in existence, although the factory was said to have long since disappeared.

I walked into the town, through the choking fumes of vehicles run on agricultural fuel, pining for the fresh air of Bombay. The scabbed and patched concrete buildings were trapped in a filthy web of cables and pipes. Air-conditioners drooled green fluid down the walls. I found a hotel and once in my room, lay down on the bed stunned. The sulphuric sting of the street was still in my nostrils, the black and white television was hissing venomously, and through the smog of static I was startled to hear the familiar gay warble of a 'seventies sitcom voice, 'Captain Peacock! I'm free!'

In the morning, Surat did not appear quite so terrible. I hailed a cycle rickshaw and we rattled through the old streets between the station and the river. Having read nothing but complaints of the place, I was surprised to see beautiful old town houses with elegantly carved facades, upper casement windows and balconies supported by sinuously curving corbels shaped as elephant trunks. Glimpsed up side alleys were paved courtyards where women sat on steps gossiping and the slatted shutters were painted blue and yellow. Some of the doors were magnificent ancient timbers, the jambs and lintels festooned with dusty arabesques. Not all was so beautiful, of course: concrete pillboxes had been dotted amongst the older dwellings, original doors had been replaced with scraps of plywood and tin, breeze blocks used to divide rooms and close antique windows, and all was tied together with cables, drooping and tangled over the narrow streets with dozens of toy kites trapped like dead flies.

I had asked for the river but now I spotted what I was looking for: a sandy, black-streaked dome appearing over the ragged shops. Paying off the driver, I found my way up some back alleys and emerged through a gap in the wall into a graveyard.

A white dog growled and slunk away with her pups. There were a number of grand mausoleums with pediments, pilasters and domes; the place had clearly been tidied up recently and lime put down. An inscription revealed that this was the Dutch graveyard and beside it were the Armenians who played an important role in the economic life of the city. Like Mr Gregory in Madras, most had come from Shiraz or else New Julfa.

The English graveyard was only a short walk from the others and it too had been cleaned and limed. It was here that the plague had begun after the river flooded in 1994.

I walked around the humbler graves first: less fortunate folk who had died by the dozen before their hopes of fortune were ever given a chance. A seventeen-year-old sailor buried by 'his grieving shipmates', children of all ages dead of cholera, and 'Mary Price, wife of Will'm And'w Price Esq chief for affairs of the British Nation & Gov'm of the Mogul's Castle & Fleet of Surat Who thro the Spotted Veil of the Small Pox rendered a Pure & Unspotted Soul to God – April 13th, 1761'.

The largest monument was actually two tombs, one built over the other. A narrow passageway inside the wall led up to a turret where I sat looking out at the gentle golden light of the early morning. Small squirrels chased each other through the fallen dessicated yellow flowers of the trees. A few pariah dogs that I had disturbed crept away to sleep in a patch of sunlight, nothing else moved.

The tomb in which I was sitting was that of George Oxinden and his brother, a solid and impressive testament to the opportunities for personal gain in the seventeenth century – if you could survive long enough. The reputation of East Indiamen for ostentatious displays of wealth was already apparent by the time the Reverend Ovington described the graveyard in about 1690: 'they endeavour to outvie each other in magnificent Structures and stately Monuments, whose large Extent, beautiful Architecture, and aspiring Heads, make them visible at a remote distance, lovely Objects of the sight, and give them the Title of the Principal Ornaments and Magnificencies about the City.' It was the seventeenth century equivalent of buying a snot-green Porsche and parking it on the double yellow lines outside your City of London office. But those 'celebrated Fabricks set off with stately Towers and Minorets', as Ovington puts it, had lasted four centuries.

For the men who took part in this competitive tomb-building, the diamond trade was an undoubtedly important means to an end: a single stone acquired from Golconda and sold on to some European monarch could make a man's fortune in a single trick. Thomas Pitt realised a profit of about 600 per cent on his celebrated diamond – and was bitterly disappointed. Less remarkable stones passed unnoticed making a precise assessment of the trade difficult, but significantly the notorious pirate John Plantain who preyed upon the Indiamen around the coasts of Arabia and Madagascar had sufficient to deck out an entire harem with diamond necklaces.

George Oxinden had come to Surat as president in 1662, his mission, as it was to be for so many new bosses, was to clean the place up. Andrews, his predecessor, was still there, and by way of a welcoming gift handed Oxinden a large diamond. It was a significant choice: the diamond trade was growing fast and completely beyond the Company's control. Everyone seemed absorbed by it: Armenian go-betweens criss-crossed the city and double-crossed each other; arrivals at the port were minutely searched by the governor's men, eager to misappropriate gems, even the good Reverend Ovington secretively acquired two fine specimens. Likewise, the new broom,

Oxinden, seems to have been a man of his times. there is no record of him dutifully handing the diamond back.

It is interesting to speculate on the role gemstones might have played in the motives and sympathies of the men sent to carve out an eastern trading empire for His Majesty. Spices were a profitable commodity but too bulky for the side-deals that would enrich individuals. For this, precious stones were a far better proposition and they were found in India, Ceylon and Burma, not the Spice Islands. With the Dutch putting up stiff resistance to English advances further east, it would have made good sense from any individual's point of view, if not the Company's, to settle for the Coromandel or Malabar Coasts.

Soon after Oxinden's arrival in Surat, the Company saw the folly of outlawing this vast hidden business and announced an amnesty: 'If any with you . . . shall consigne any dyamonds or jewels unto us and desire their transmitting to any other place, wee doe hereby promise really to comply with their directions' – for a small percentage, of course. The glittering trail from east to west was well and truly opened and would not shut until Victoria had her Koh-i-Noor.

Oxinden proved to be a very successful president, keeping both London and locals happy. His clean-up campaign could be deemed a great success by all concerned, especially those accused of foul play. The factor, William Bell, was found guilty of 'scurrilous and saucy language', while Oxinden's predecessor, Andrews, was forced back to England where he was knighted, became an MP and died on his private estate at the age of eighty-two. Sometimes it seemed that all one required for success in the east was to remain alive.

Oxinden was certainly a survivor. In 1664, the Maratha warlord Sivaji invaded the town, looting and despoiling. The factory and the Mughal fort held out, while the rest of the city was looted and razed. Oxinden was rewarded with a robe of honour from Aurangzeb, plus a £200 bonus and a gold medal from the Company. It was one of those moments which, repeated two centuries later, became the stuff of imperial legend – Rorke's Drift, Mafeking and Khartoum – but in 1664, when an exchange of letters could take two years, the reaction was more muted. It was the scene of this stout defence I wished to find, but all I had to go on was that it had been fortified, was close to the river and had stood next to the house of a merchant named Zahid Beg whose balcony window had doubled as a gun emplacement. I was not hopeful.

The way to the river skirted the edge of the old town, passing through what the rickshaw-puller referred to as 'the girlie market'. This was a busy street where each doorway was amply filled by a lady in her nightdress. Behind was a tiny cell containing a bed. School-children in neatly pressed school uniforms were strolling past.

'You wanting girlie?' asked the driver.

'No, I want the English castle – the old one – the fort – factory – godown.'

He looked confused. 'English girlie?'

'Factory.'

'Yes, facking, what you like?'

'It doesn't matter.'

We rode into a small square busy with traffic. On one side was an old mission school with boys waving at me from the barred windows. Paying off the rickshaw man I began walking, exploring the alleyways and lanes around the square. I asked a few people for directions, but no one spoke English. Then I heard a voice behind me: '*Isa?*'

I turned to find a middle-aged man in white shirt and trousers.

'*Isa?*' he repeated. '*Isa bin Miriam? Nabi al-masaheen?*'

I suddenly realised he was speaking Arabic. '*Aiwa*,' I said. 'Jesus son of Mary – prophet of the Nazarenes.'

He looked pleased. 'You speak Arabic?'

It transpired he had worked in Saudi Arabia for two years.

'I'm looking for the old fort of the Europeans,' I said. 'The English.'

'There is an old building,' he said. 'Come.'

We walked across the busy square opposite the school and up a narrow lane into a second open space with a flagpole in the centre. On the far side was a long two-storey building with yellow, paint-peeling walls and two large carved doors, one open. It had the right look about it: obviously old and built to be defensible, the shuttered and barred windows on the upper floor. A stone ramp led up through the door to the foot of a wooden staircase. We went slowly, calling greetings.

Over the dusty banister, a face under a Parsi hat appeared for a moment, then disappeared. At the top of the stairs we found ourselves in a cool spacious room with a wooden floor polished by years of bare feet. I took off my shoes. On one side was a table under an old portrait of a severe-looking Parsi. Beneath it, three elderly white-haired people were eating soup. They did not look up. A fourth man, dressed in a long robe and wearing a Parsi hat, came in and smiled. My Arabic-speaking friend, Jalal, chatted to him in Gujarati, then turned to me.

'He will show you around. It has been a Parsi lodging house for one hundred years, but before that he does not know.'

We went out onto a rear veranda, a pleasant shady place under the broad eaves, then into a large room at the front of the building. There was nothing much to see except some fine old teak beds, all with a carved central pillar at each end for draping a mosquito net. This, I decided, could have been a meeting room for convivial factory dinners or a useful vantage point for shooting locals.

We walked into a smaller room where an elderly man in his vest and trousers was washing at a tin bowl on a washstand. An open suitcase was on the floor. I realised we had just barged into his room, but this seemed to be quite alright.

He straightened, patting his face dry.

'Good morning, young sir,' he said. 'Please feel welcome to look around.' His voice was that of a 1930s radio newsreader on the BBC. 'Are you of an historical frame of mind?' He put the towel on a wooden rack. 'The building is 350 years old and was the headquarters of the Portuguese trading company for a while. Before that it belonged to a great merchant named Zahid Beg.'

I looked out the door back to the balcony, realising that this spot was where the English had set up their guns and held off Sivaji's attack. Oxinden wrote that the English had broken through a wall into Zahid Beg's godown and 'kept a garrison in a belcony [sic] that cleared all the street'. There was little doubt that this was the spot: the commanding view over the square was unchanged. Not that it prevented Sivaji looting the city: 'Hee hath carried away in gold, pearle, pretious stones and other rich goods to the valew of many hundred thousand pounds . . . The towne is utterly ruin'd.'

The Parsi went to his suitcase and removed a white shirt that had been carefully starched. Next to it were a pair of striped pyjamas and a dozen ladies' brassieres. He turned, buttoning his collar.

'I travel in ladies' hosiery and undergarments,' he explained solemnly. 'Are you from London? I used to be a salesman for Monson's in Albemarle Street.' He pulled the cotton shirt straight with a crack. 'I first stayed here in 1958 when you could still see the river. Look at this construction – built to last, I should say.'

'Was the English factory next door then?'

'In the very early days, yes, but there is nothing left of it. After Sivaji's attack they moved to a bigger better place. That is the one you should search for.'

He took a comb from his pocket and put a precise parting in the wisps of grey hair.

'Do you know where it was?'

'Can't help you. Like Monson's – long gone. But the Irish Mission school and the Anglican church are just over there. Go and scout round – why not?'

I left him to finish dressing. On the landing, the three old people were still eating soup.

Jalal took me across to an alley on the left of the mission school. Behind the tatty houses we found an elegant church with columned portico and the dimensions of a London Hawksmoor. The caretaker came across to us and took us to see a grave at the back. A stone recorded the death in 1840 of missionary Reverend Alexander Fyvie who had designed the church, helped build it and finally fell from it, landing on the spot where he was buried.

Taking a second alley, we found ourselves on the river bank, or rather the edge of a long green flat that led to a distant shimmer of water.

'Boats used to come here,' said Jalal, pointing along the bank. 'But now the mud has moved in.'

Half a mile downstream, I could see the white walls and towers of the small Mughal fort, almost hidden behind the trees and the iron foot bridge the British had constructed. Deducing the position of any other old buildings was difficult in the scabby and untidy development that had pressed right up to the edge of the flood bank.

'It is gone,' said Jalal. 'Like you British. All gone. Only the old men remember the British times and most are dead now – you will find nothing.'

He left me to continue searching alone, but after a fruitless hour spent wandering the lanes, I had to admit he was probably right. I went up to the Mughal fort, now government offices, and read the sign left by the British to record their capture of the place in 1759 – two years after Plassey. The Mughal was still on the throne of Delhi, but his kingdom was shrinking and the British were rushing into the vacuum. Soon the emperor's empire was no more than the area bounded by the walls of the Red Fort in the capital. Surat in the meantime had been eclipsed by its southern neighbour Bombay, the Company having bought it for £10 from Charles II.

After a lunch of masala dosai, I went and found a quiet spot on the grassy riverbank with a teach-yourself book of Gujarati for company. 'It is likely that there are banana-skins, rubbish, pot-holes, etc on the roads,' I read. 'And there is traffic too; therefore, walk with care', 'Don't lean to look into wells', 'Keep your bowels clear', 'Don't scratch', 'There is no limit to the nuisance committed on our railway platforms.' But in the proverbs section I found what I was looking for: 'Diamond cuts diamond.'

As the sun dropped, armed with the word for diamond in Gujarati, I set off back into the old town, hoping to track down the market and some of the small workshops I had heard about.

I was soon pointed down a narrow side street and found myself surrounded by beautiful old houses with lovely carved facades – lotus blossoms scattered along lintels under a ragged fringe of pan-tiles. In the shade of one veranda an old man was getting a cut-throat shave, while a white sheep lay stretched out fast asleep on a charpoy.

All the streets were lined with motor scooters and bikes, but now I noticed that the quantity was greater. The street became narrower. Up ahead I saw a crowd of men milling around, all dressed in smart shirts and trousers. I stopped then and stood back under a balcony, pretending to admire the wood carving. My heart was pounding. A woman in an upstairs window was watching me. I bent down and tied my bootlaces tighter. This time I knew I would have to go in under the guise of a buyer. But was my knowledge up to it? The few bits of jargon and the odd trick were all I had picked up. I tightened the straps on my camera bag and wished I hadn't brought it. Cedric, the African diamond smuggler, had warned me: 'Never go to buy diamonds with your money. These are dangerous characters.'

Nothing could have prepared me for the rumpus my arrival would cause. As soon as I was spotted, I was surrounded by excited laughing youths. 'Come, brother! Buy diamond?' The mob propelled me along the street, shouting to their friends. There would be no quiet infiltration here.

On the verandas, older men sat at small tables while customers examined stones. White packets slipped from hand to hand in front of the carved doors and balconies. These were a rougher crowd than Bombay, wild-eyed, uncombed hair, the clean shirt being the entry ticket. No mobile phones, no need: the diamonds were all here on the street, glittering from a man's palm as he leaned over a scooter seat, gripped between grubby thumb and forefinger as they raised it to the light, tumbling across the blue velvet of the dealers' tables. In the centre of a mass of youths, I was propelled forward to the main sellers. There were characters here to be wary of, sharp shifty eyes darting away from mine or thuggish strength shouldering past. I remembered what I had been told in Bombay: 'Those Kathiawaris use strong-arm tactics – they are not too fussy, you know.'

'You a diamond buyer?'

'Yes.' There were shouts of pleasure at the news. 'Don't you get foreign buyers?'

But this touched their sense of cosmopolitan pride. 'Yes! Many – from all the world. Africa, Taiwan, Pakistan.'

I looked at some stones, all inferior quality and colour. I had been learning to distinguish good from bad during those visits to Bombay dealers: the 4 Cs – clarity, colour, carat and cut. Most of the stones I saw failed on at least two of these criteria.

'I want to see good stones,' I said, and immediately every other dealer had just the right thing.

'Come in here.'

I was led across the flag-stoned pavement into a narrow room filled with machinery for the rough shaping, or bruting, and polishing. There was no room to sit, so the cutters stood and worked at chest height, their heads brushing the ceiling. With the diamond gripped in a wax mount on the end of a short stick, it was slowly ground into shape, a pan collecting the dust that would be used to grind others. These were tiny stones, almost invisible in the wax mount. I thought of Flann O'Brien's surreal desk sergeant in *The Third Policeman*, delicately producing tiny boxes that no one could see, let alone put anything in – apart from an even smaller box. Under a lens, however, the stones sprang into reality as perfect geometric shapes, though the colour was often poor.

One particular man had been following me since I had arrived. When I left the workshop, he pressed forward. 'Come with me,' he said. 'I have better quality – you cannot find what you are looking for here. I mean good stones.'

We went up the street a short way. He was about twenty years old and well-dressed with a stylish suede jacket that distinguished him from the others. He also had a new foreign motor scooter. We sped away through the narrow streets, dodging cows and people and the occasional belching lorry, those vast black asthmatic monsters that wheeze and fart across India.

'My job,' said the wide boy, 'is girlfriends. My hobby is diamonds.' He pulled up at a shop and bought us both a quid of betel. 'Here look.'

He took out his wallet and showed me all the white packets inside. 'These are rubbish,' he said. 'But come in here.'

I noticed two men watching us in the street. They were also on a scooter and I'd seen them in the market: one clean-shaven and young, the other middle-aged with fine grey moustaches curling up at the ends like tusks.

'Do you know them?' I asked.

He shrugged. 'Sellers. Market is down – like cloud-mood. They need buyer.'

We went into the house, not one of the elegant older buildings but an untidy, dusty block with barred windows and padlocked doors. I was on my guard now, wondering if I had been stupid to leave the safety of the street. He sat me down on a nice old sofa with a cool tiled back and went away. Two minutes later he returned with some packets: slightly larger diamonds, some of one carat, but his prices were inflated.

'Have you got Indian diamonds?' I asked.

He made a face. 'They are diamonds.' He selected one envelope. 'This one is Indian.'

'From Golconda?'

But he gave no sign of having understood. It was a good stone: a subtle blue light playing inside the brilliance of its facets, and there were no poor cuts along some of the edges as I had seen in the street market. He named a price which seemed far too high. I remembered Pitt, haggling over the great diamond in the Fort at Madras, forcing the price down over days of discussion. My offer was less than a quarter of what he had asked. He began to pack the envelopes away.

'In the market they are multiple talking,' he said. 'But here I am doing my level-best – not such multiple talking.'

I thought that this was a prelude to a round of bargaining, but his manner suggested he was serious: the diamonds were taken away and locked up, then he reappeared. 'Maybe you prefer to buy womans?'

'No, thanks.'

We went back down on to the street. The two men were there and they followed us. I was crouched slightly on the scooter seat, waiting for something to happen. We were zig-zagging between rickshaws. I had a tight grip on my bag.

'Which hotel?' my dealer friend asked. But I didn't want to tell him, and I didn't want to be dropped in front of it.

'Just leave me at the station,' I said. 'I can find it from there – I've forgotten the name.'

'You think about that diamond – it is good price. Come tomorrow.'

It was a price beyond my means, unfortunately. We said goodbye, and I took the opportunity to go in and buy a ticket to Ahmedabad for the following evening. On my way back to my hotel I kept glancing behind, but there was no sign of the two men. I assumed I had lost them in the crowd at the station. I was wrong. Later that evening, sitting in a crowded teashop, I spotted them. The older man grinned and beckoned me over.

'You are an Englishman and must take tea.'

I was not sure I wanted to meet him and his friend. 'I was just leaving.'

'Hurry, worry, curry, my friend. Slow down. Tea drinking is your custom – and ours.' He called for three fresh cups, and as he turned, I saw he was wearing an ear-ring: a clutch of eight tiny rubies around a single diamond on a golden flower.

[111]

'Nine stones for luck,' he said when I asked about it. 'And for me, ruby is the best one. No bad things have come my way since wearing these jewels.'

His friend began to laugh. 'But before that – plenty!'

'Really?'

He waggled his chin but did not say any more. We talked about Hyderabad, their home town, and they told rude stories about the Nizams – stories too difficult to follow as they repeatedly digressed into Urdu at the critical moment. Then Malik, the older man, would roar with laughter and twirl his splendid moustaches.

'What is your salary?'

No one bats an eyelid at such a question in India, and no one really expects the truth. I made a rapid calculation of what a realistically 'comfortable' salary might be in India.

'Oh, about ten thousand rupees a month.' That was roughly £300.

Malik sucked air noisily. 'Ten thousand! You make whoopee with your rupee!'

'Yes, but in England that is not a lot. I'm not a rich man – nowhere near.'

'Do you have a car?'

'Well, yes. But most people have one.'

He looked sceptical. 'And you say you are not rich? Electric rice cooker?'

'Yes.'

'Touching telephone?'

'What?'

He jabbed at the air with a finger – a touch pad, not dial.

'Yes, touching telephone. All telephones in Britain are touching now.'

The list went on: television, computer, camera, house ... all of them I had to admit to owning. Eventually I could take no more. 'Okay, so I'm rich,' I snapped, a little petulant at being uncovered as fat cat in an impoverished Indian teashop.

Malik smiled. 'Ten thousand rupees is nothing in England. I was there six months ago. That amount of money would last a week – if you are lucky. Your salary is higher, isn't it?'

I gulped. 'Yes.'

They began to laugh, having tricked me into thinking they were ignorant country boys.

'But everyone needs more money, hey?' said Malik. 'No money, no honey. You buy something from your friend today?'

It was just a simple question, slipped into the banter, nothing to take much notice of, or to worry about. Stupidly, all that entered my head as I answered was that I didn't want them to think me a tourist. I had to keep up the pretence of being in the diamond business and the obvious way to do that was to say yes.

'Oh, a few souvenirs.'

They both laughed.

'A few souvenirs! I think more than "a few" – isn't it?'

Immediately I saw my mistake, but the damage was done. They thought I was carrying diamonds – lots of them.

'Really, the market prices were too high, I only bought samples.'

'Market is down,' said the younger man who was called Raghu. There was a silence.

'When will you return to England?' asked Malik.

'Another month or two.'

He glanced at his companion. 'Too long.'

'For what?'

Raghu changed the subject. 'Where will you go in India?'

'Through Gujarat, Rajasthan, then Delhi and the Punjab.'

'You are like me,' said Malik. 'Always on the move – a rolling stone gathers no boss.'

'You travel for your work?'

Raghu laughed. 'He has no choice in the matter.'

'Why is that?'

Malik waggled his chin, eyes twinkling. 'More tea? In Hyderabad they say you must take a cup and a half.'

'Come on, I was honest about my salary,' I said, dishonestly. 'Now it's your turn. Why do you travel?'

Raghu nudged him, laughing. 'Go on. Tell him.'

Malik twirled his moustache thoughtfully for a moment, then said, 'All right. I jumped parole.'

'In India?'

His arm reached around me and lay on the back of the bench seat we were sharing. 'No, it was in Hong Kong. I was caught at the airport carrying currency.'

I had heard of such operations: illegal importation of hard currency into India.

'How much did you have on you?'

He chuckled. 'It was 16.8 million US dollars.'

'What! But you couldn't possibly carry that much – physically.'

'Only a million was in cash notes – the rest in other ways. They found it and took me to prison. That was horrible. A cell six feet by three and rats everywhere. After two weeks my godfather put up some cash and I was out on bail. Then he got me a passport and I left.'

'So you are a wanted man?'

'Yes. They had some other men from the gang and they were sentenced. As for me, they decided in my absence that I should get 314 years.'

His hand slapped my shoulder and they both roared with laughter. I was aware that in hitting my shoulder he had hit the strap of my money holster that sat under my arm.

'What do you do now?'

'I am . . .' He thought about it. 'I am freelance.'

He handed me a business card: 'Malik', I read, 'Freelance.' There were phone and fax numbers. They were talking in Urdu. I felt Malik's fingers on my shoulder, very gently resting on the strap.

'You should come to my place for a drink – you like whisky? There are some moneymaking ideas we can talk about.'

There was a story I had heard in England: a friend of a friend who had accepted just such an invitation while in Goa and was later found with his throat cut.

'Business?'

'You say you will go back in two months?'

'Oh, maybe a month – maybe less.' I was intrigued to hear what possible scheme he might have in mind, but I preferred the teashop as the place to hear it.

'A month is okay.'

They muttered together in Urdu. Malik had left his hand on my shoulder, just an absent-minded friendly gesture, but I could feel his finger-tips very gently feeling the width of the strap.

'I want you to take something,' he said. 'To London.'

'What is it?'

'A package – it's a compact disc – but all sealed up in a box. You just take it by hand and the man there will pay you.'

But Raghu was looking doubtful and spoke quickly in Urdu. I made out the phrase 'one month' a few times and guessed he was persuading Malik that this was no good for their purposes. It looked as though my chance to be a diamond smuggler – which is what I imagined – was slipping away. When they finished their discussion, they were both cheerful and relaxed, suggesting that we meet in the same spot next morning. I agreed. Walking back to my hotel, I wondered what Malik's game might be: I had completely forgotten that I was, in their view, carrying a large quantity of diamonds.

The following morning at nine, I sat in the teashop waiting. The mysterious money-making plan had intrigued me, but I also wanted to see if they would mention my diamond-buying: overnight I had decided to take the first opportunity to correct their false impression. Two cups of milky sweet tea later, I conceded that the chance was not going to come; neither of them had appeared. After half an hour, I gave up and set out on a final search for the old East India Company factory. As I planned to leave Surat that evening, I had no reason to think I would see either Raghu or Malik ever again.

I first took a rickshaw back to the Irish Mission school, then began to explore all the alleys and streets in the area. There was one particular lane down to the river that I walked along several times. The walls on both sides were whitewashed plaster on stone and at the far end was an arch leading out onto the river bank. Halfway down this alley, where it curved first right then left, was a large gateway with two spiked gates. Above was a tumbling roof of pan-tiles and some closely shuttered windows. The previous day the gates had been shut, now they were open and tyre marks had been made in the mud.

I went through, following the track around to the left. There was a compound, partially in ruins. On the right was a small empty bungalow where plants grew from the roof and gutters; a sign read, 'Cooper Villa', and the English name alerted me. Further along were more houses, two-storey whitewashed buildings with shutters open and curtains closed to keep the hot, dead air of mid-morning out.

In a patch of sunlight, some puppies were playing, watched by an elderly couple. He was tall and noble-featured with white hair, she was wearing a headscarf and cardigan. They were watching me, obviously puzzled to see a stranger, but friendly when I spoke.

'Yes, this was the English Company's compound,' the man confirmed. 'They came here for safety after Sivaji's attack, but there is nothing left of it – even the river's gone.'

He took me up to the edge where the buildings were ruined. 'They could load and unload here, you see, but the flood in the 1960s moved the river.'

He had a sad face, much lined with the years, and was wearing a jumper despite the heat.

'I went to school at the Irish Mission over there and now we live there.' He nodded at one of the neat two-storey houses that backed onto the alleyway. 'My wife's parents had it before us and she's lived there almost all her life.'

'Was Cooper an Englishman?' I asked.

'No. He was a Parsi. We are all Parsis here – Aryans. We had a good relationship with the British, you see.' I thought of the Armenians of Madras, another of the British allies. 'Cooper left in 1965 and no one has lived there since.'

We strolled back to the bungalow and he pointed to the derelict land behind. 'That was the main British building there, but the last owner gambled it away.'

He made it sound like it had happened brick by brick – chips of history in a poker game. 'Before Independence we had governors and all sorts come to look at it.'

We stood silently. His wife had gone into the house. I asked him about the Parsis.

'We are fire-worshippers,' he said. 'Refugees from Persia when the Muslims came. Our ancestors brought the sacred flame to a place near Daman. We worship the elements: sun, moon, earth, water and fire – so the fire must never go out.'

Their language, he explained, was Parsi, but over the years it had been corrupted with Gujarati and they could no longer understand the sacred prayers that they recited every evening at sunset. 'Some Parsis went back to Persia recently and found our religion had changed too,' he said with a sigh. 'Even our religion is not pukka.'

I nodded. 'Last year, I came across an abandoned Parsi temple,' I said. 'It was on a hill above the town with three circular walls around a central well with a pillar in the centre.'

'That's right. They put the bodies out for the elements to take, you see. We believe burial is not correct. Where was that – the place you saw?'

'In Aden – it's a town in Yemen – have you heard it?'

But he did not answer immediately. He was staring at me. 'Aden, you say?'

'Yes.'

He sat down on the stone bench beside the bungalow. The puppies began playing around his feet. 'I left Aden in 1968,' he said. 'We had a business – my uncle and myself. Our people were laid to rest in that place.'

One of the puppies got hold of his trouser leg, growling, but he didn't push it away. He was thinking, remembering. I sat down next to him, glad that I had not mentioned the skeletons lying in a careless heap inside the temple, thrown there by treasure-seekers and pariah dogs. A gang of urchins had appeared and begun pulling sun-bleached bones from the pile. 'We're going to sleep up here one night,' they boasted. 'And if a jinnee appears, we'll pull his beard.'

When I asked, they had no idea who had put the place there.

'It's two thousand years old,' said one.

'Three thousand!' said another. In fact it had been used until the 1960s.

The old man was lost in thought for some time, then he roused himself and said, 'You had better come in – take some tea or coffee.'

We went up the steps and into the cool darkened room. It was like stepping back into the 'fifties: leatherette sofas with home-crocheted cushion covers, souvenir ornaments like the Black-and-White Whisky Scottie dog, a vase of plastic flowers, the television under a lacy doily, and the kitchen hidden behind a cotton curtain. In one corner was a convenient plug-in sacred flame, flickering gently.

'Our friend has been in Aden,' he said to his wife. 'You had better make him some coffee.' She went out through the curtain and we sat down.

'I went in 1949,' he said. 'After Independence here, things were not good. Many of us Parsis were in the liquor trade and our stock was smashed, so I left. My uncle was in Aden and it was really booming. We had a cold storage business in Tawahi – you know the place?'

I got him to describe the exact spot and told him the building was empty except for a grocery shop on one corner. All that he remembered was still the same: the Rock Hotel, the signs for Elizabeth Arden cosmetics and BSA motorcycles, the Crescent Hotel with its surreal cocktail-bar mural of a harlot's leg emerging from a banana.

'We supplied frozen food for the ships, you see. Smedleys canned food, fruit cordials and squashes, Players cigarettes . . . Is the P&O building still there?'

Together we rummaged through our memories. His wife brought the coffee and went quietly into the other room. He was back in the 1950s boom town, the Aden of Gilbey's gin, the RAF and Humber motor cars, the Aden where the hot breeze blew endlessly and the Arab dhows were beginning to be outnumbered by the steamers, a place that was constantly in motion, making money from the sailors or the passenger liners.

'It was a good time,' he said, reeling off the names of all the Parsi merchant families.

'What happened?' I asked, half-knowing the answer already.

'The last years were very bad,' he said. 'The British said they would stay and then they simply packed up and left. The Parsis and Indians were defenceless then. Once the British had gone the fighting continued, but between the NLF and FLOSY. Those NLF were the hardliners – Marxists – and when they took power there was no hope for us. They had a way of telling you to go: a bullet would be sent to your home – just a single bullet. If you did not go within twenty-four hours, you were dead. Friends of ours lost their lives that way.

'One morning I went down to the door and there was an envelope on the step. Inside was one bullet. We each packed one suitcase – just necessary things – cash, small valuables – and then we left.'

'The business?'

He waved a hand. 'All gone! We left everything. One moment we had a house, a business, customers, stock, friends, a life – next moment we were gone to Bombay with one suitcase.' He looked at me. 'Very strange you should have been there. I haven't spoken to anyone who has seen Aden since the day I left.'

I sipped my coffee; he hadn't touched his. 'What became of the other Parsis?'

'They dispersed. Some went to America – my own children are there – others to Europe or India. Most married outside our Zoroastrian faith. My children are married to Americans and no longer follow our religion.'

I asked him about his childhood in Surat.

'In those days Surat had a population of 200,000 – the same as in Mughal times – now it is 2.5 million. Then the streets were paved with stone and every house had beautiful carved doors and windows. Now you see they have put concrete buildings up in between the houses; there are wires and cars everywhere. In those days, after 6 p.m. the streets were quiet and there was no pollution at all.'

I was looking to my left, examining the structure of the house as he talked. There was a barred window on the back wall, high up and deep-set, so deep-set, in fact, that it was almost hidden from me; the wall had to be four feet thick.

'Your house is strongly built,' I said.

'Yes, that part is old,' he agreed. 'Actually, it is the only piece of the old English fort that survives – a few yards of the outside defensive wall. When they built the house, maybe ninety years ago, they used the old wall.'

Having lost his livelihood twice to political decisions taken in Whitehall, the elderly Parsi was living out his days in the shelter of the last fragment of the Honourable Company's base in Surat. I had, at last, found a physical reminder of all the fortunes made and lost, the place where many an Englishman had quietly hoarded his gemstones, waiting for his time to finish and the long voyage home. Those that succeeded bought themselves country seats and county status; those that succumbed were in the majority, and as often lost to good living as to disease.

My thoughts were interrupted by the elderly wife. 'Would you like more coffee.'

'No, thank you.' I finished my cup. 'I'd better be going.'

The old man had obviously been tired by our conversation and I thought it best to leave. He came to the door to say goodbye. 'Do you know Middex?' he asked. 'It's a place in England.'

'I think you mean Middlesex.'

'Yes, I have a nephew there – but we haven't heard for some time.' He smiled sadly. 'We Parsis are an easy-going people: we lost our language, we lost our religion, and now we are losing our families.' He held out his hand. 'Well, goodbye then. Take care.' Then he stepped back into the unlit room.

CHAPTER 6

In Every Handful of Earth, Souls are Imprisoned.

A.L. Basham on Jainism

THE rail journey to the Ahmedabad was slow and uneventful. Non-Muslim travellers hung shopping bags on the hooks by the windows and ate apples and cucumbers with salt and masala relish. Ramadhan had come. We passed through banana plantations and vineyards, then stopped briefly at the ancient port of Broach; there were no boats to be seen.

The staunchly Muslim town of Ahmedabad was lively by night with lantern-lit barrows selling dates. I stayed only one night and caught a bus west, heading into Saurashtra – Kathiawar country – a flat, dusty land punctuated by white temple buildings. At Bhavanagar I stayed in a former ruler's palace, converted to a hotel of modest proportions. The town had some lovely old buildings with scalloped archways and wooden columns entwined with carved ivy, but I had arrived too late to search out the diamond market. It was Saturday evening and the market would not open until late on Monday, so I decided to continue my journey into the heart of Gujarat, moving on to Palitana, a pilgrimage town for the Jain religion. In my mind I had switched from the small-time smugglers of diminutive diamonds, the Maliks and the Raghus, to the bigger stones and the old princely states. I wanted a raja and I wanted him broke and bitter. I wanted him to sit on his crumbling veranda, stirring crushed diamonds into his afternoon tea and telling me who had taken the big rocks.

*

Even by the standards of India, public transport in Gujarat is particularly crowded. When I reached the bus station next morning, it was packed with travellers and every bus that came growling to a halt was besieged. Chaos and dust. I was in a throng of people jammed together so tightly that struggling towards the bus door seemed pointless. A green sari wrapped over a silky cheek next to mine slipped and a golden flower on an ear caught the sunlight; there was the delicate jangle of glass bangles on a wrist as a silk-skinned elbow jabbed me in the solar plexus; a youth waved a cricket bat, shouting at me, 'Back to the pavilion!'; the women's embroidered bibs were like armoured breastplates, adorned with tiny mirrors, sparkling as they cut through the crowd; I saw a throat tattooed with the holy chakra wheel and a nutmeg of gold and ruby jauntily bouncing on the hairline. I moved gently backwards in the stream of humanity and, when I finally struggled aboard, all the seats had long gone, leaving just enough space to plant my feet.

The youth next to me introduced himself and his friend. Perhaps the display of feminine beauty and supple strength had excited them because their first question as we bounced gently out onto the Palitana road was, 'In proper England, is there love marriage?'

My answer rushed through the promiscuously packed travellers like an orgasm.

'Most marriages in England are for love.'

I suppose I had simultaneously confirmed all their best and worst expectations.

'I have been in true love only once,' declared the younger of the two. 'But she disdained me.'

He was a student of English literature and liked nothing better than sitting on a hilltop reading his favourites: Milton, Dryden and the Romantics. The effect on his spoken English had been remarkable. 'My ambition is to love and be loved,' he whispered so his friend would not hear, adding more loudly, 'I am a shepherd by caste and he is a Patel – a farmer.'

Young Patel, bridled slightly at this. 'I am no longer a farmer,' he said. 'I am a diamond merchant.'

'In truth, I say to you, we both are school students,' said his friend.

With one on each side, I now began to carry on two simultaneous conversations.

'I am absorption with *A Passage to India* – do you know this volume?'

'My uncle was a farmer who became a cutter and saved enough money to travel to Antwerp. He had one phone number in his pocket and he could not read or write. Now he is a millionaire.'

'I read it a few years ago. Have you seen the film? Are there diamond factories in Palitana?'

'No, but I am much entertained by Arnold Commando – he is an esti-mable movie star.'

'Plenty, I will show you.'

'What he is doing is unliggleliggle.'

When I worked out what this meant, I asked the literature student. 'Illegal? Your friend's business is illegal?'

'Yes. He is smuggling.'

The friend treated this as a joke. 'It is business,' he said. 'But my uncle is doing things proper. It is true many are going to Surat to buy and then smuggle, but my uncle goes to Antwerp twice a month and buys diamonds. He is a pukka diamond man.'

As we talked, two other men in front were drawn into the conversation, also small-time diamond dealers. The whole country had gone diamond-crazy, Patel told me. It was the only way to get rich and everyone wanted to do it. As if to prove it, he showed me what was inside the plastic tube he was carrying: a set of plans for a thirty-six-unit apartment block. 'My uncle will build it in Palitana.'

The other men were impressed by the rags-to-riches story, not least because neither of them could read and write. In modern India, with its increasing demand for qualified workers, it was becoming more and more difficult for the quick-witted but illiterate boy to succeed. Diamonds gave them a chance. Under democracy, the stone of kings had become the stone of everyman.

Palitana's connection with gemstones was an early one. In 1656, Prince Murad (two years away from death at the hands of his brother Aurangzeb) granted the village to a leading Jain jeweller of Ahmedabad in return for a generous loan. Temples and stupas soon began to be built on the mountain behind the village, which prospered as a result.

At certain times of the year, Palitana is inundated with pilgrims, many of whom walk right across India to pray there. Even at other times it is busy with Jain mendicants.

The religion was founded in the same period as Buddhism and in similar circumstances. Mahavira was the son of a clan chief living in the area to the north of the Ganges. Like the Buddha, he threw off his privileged lifestyle in order to seek enlightenment and release from the endless cycle of death and rebirth. He abandoned all clothing and took a path of extreme asceticism for twelve years until he achieved full enlightenment and became *jina*, 'conqueror', from which his followers took their name. In about 468 BC, at the age of seventy-two, he died by the traditional Jain method of voluntary self-starvation.

As a religion, Jainism is inspired by a great animistic belief that all things connected to nature are inhabited by souls, including plants, rivers, flames, even raindrops. Extreme reverence for life characterises the faith, to the point where lighting and extinguishing a flame is frowned upon and the path ahead of the traveller is lightly brushed lest a tiny creature be crushed.

Perhaps surprisingly, this austere faith became popular with mercantile classes in Gujarat who adopted its philosophy of non-violence and vegetarianism. With this small but influential group behind it, Jainism has had a greater effect on Indian culture than might be expected – notably, in recent times, through Mahatma Gandhi who came into contact with Jain sadhus during his youth.

Of all the Jain temples in India, those on the hill of Satrunjaya that rises 2,000 feet above Palitana are the most important. The hotel manager advised me to rise early and, 'like the real pilgrims', climb to the top in time for sunrise.

He gave me a brief summary of the religion too, dismissing my undiplomatic claim that Jainism was a minor faith. 'You cannot say it is a small religion,' he declared. 'There are 25,000 Jains in Leicester.'

At 5 a.m. I woke and dressed. It was bitterly cold and in the street I found a horse and trap with the driver fast asleep, completely enveloped in blankets. I woke him and we trotted through the streets, passing more and more people as we neared the base of the hill.

Here the shops were open, preparing vegetarian breakfasts of nuts and cups of tea. Men were renting out walking sticks, while others offered to take the unfit or sick to the top on a palki – a palanquin (our word comes via Portuguese from the Hindi). This extremely uncomfortable form of ascent is on a small wooden palette slung by four ropes from a beam which two men shoulder. The palette gives just sufficient space to sit cross-legged.

I could hear the temple bell and the drums. Groups of pilgrims dressed in white unstitched cloth came hurrying by, feet bandaged after the miles of walking and faces filled with ecstatic determination. In the temple there was a frantic scene of men and women praying, drawing swastikas in rice grains on little benches, or simply rocking themselves, palms pressed together. The drummers had hit a loping loopy beat above which wailed a reedy pipe.

I started up the steps towards the darkness at a brisk pace, but soon old ladies in white were trotting past me. The sky was paling in the east and I was caught by their urgency to be at the top before the sunrise. I began to move like they did, trotting up the shallow steps. There were water pots at stopping places but no one halted. It was cold and a strong wind was whipping across the hillside.

The noise of the temple faded and I glanced down to see Palitana glittering below. I passed a palki bearing an old man who was reading a holy book, except it was still too dark to see and the words must have been words known by heart. Others fingered prayer beads, one for each step, their bare feet beating the rhythm on the stone. Some young women were leaving trails of milk poured from brass ewers, as though unwinding a string of gleaming white to retrace later their steps from the heavens.

I moved at their pace, zig-zagging across the steps, feeling that this was the sun we were honouring. Why else climb to the mountaintop at dawn? For the first light of the day from the sun god. Once I had been in a remote African village during a solar eclipse and the people had run into their huts, crying with fear, then begun bashing cooking pots together. This, one of them told me afterwards, had brought the light back.

The path flattened out and I looked back to see the Gulf of Cambay gleaming like burnished steel. After more steps I reached a crenellated wall and a gateway. The path curled to the left, then the entire hilltop appeared, covered in temples: each a pale stone lotus bud, elegantly fluted and tapering; at the top, twenty or thirty feet up, was a flagpole and a ribbon of wind-blown cloth. Beneath each of these squarish buds, inside a darkened hall would be the image of the Jain saint, one of the twenty-four *tirthankars*, the men made god, the jewels in the lotus.

I left my shoes at the gate with the rest – there were very few as most had come barefoot – then continued up, following the mass of people. Some stopped to join a long queue but most pressed on. The white stone under foot was like ice. I was propelled up the steps and over the lintel into the dark interior of the largest temple. Women were kneeling and rocking on the floor and I stumbled into them in the gloom. Each had a small bowl of cardamom paste into which the priest would dip his thumb and mark their forehead. Most wore a silk scarf over the mouth.

A temple attendant pulled me up and held an incensor in front of me, miming that I should waft the smoke across my face three times. Then a lamp was passed to me and I swung it three times before moving across in front of a latticework screen, and behind that, behind the flickering lamps and the candles, loomed a massive seated figure.

The first thing I noticed were the eyes. Mirrored and protruding slightly, as if pressed by some force within, their cool gaze appeared to follow me as I shuffled sideways. The figure was solid, heavily built, almost crude: look at me, it said, an ordinary mortal become god, yet not so high or mighty that I will not look back. There was a garland of jewels, a silver crown, and in the centre of the brow, enclosed by a downward V, was a sparkling cluster of large diamonds. In a religion where stones have souls, the diamond is the perfect mineral embodiment, the perfect gift from the rich man to his god.

A priest, his body bronzed by the candlelight, was brushing the pediment with the feathers of the sacred peacock. Across his mouth was a mask to prevent him exhaling on the god or inhaling any wind-born creatures. There was no time to linger; I pressed my hands together respectfully and stepped back through the crowd. The temple bell was rung. By some trick of the lattice and the candles, the image was visible only close to the front, as though that strange and unsettling gaze could be endured for no more than a few seconds and never without a charm of smoke in the throat and three creaks of a lantern chain.

In the courtyard I wandered around the outer colonnade, my feet numb with cold and scarcely feeling the prick of the rice grains on the marble. The sun, now risen, was gilding the temple tops and slowly its warming gaze spread down the courtyards. I sat on a bench, enjoying the warmth and sketching some of the carvings: Krishna playing his flute, lions on the cornices, and the floral designs of the carved doors.

Some of the pilgrims came and spoke to me. Dressed in thin cotton they were shivering with the cold but not at all unhappy. Having walked to Palitana from Calcutta, they would spend two months performing the pooja, the prayers, walking up and down the hill twice a day until 108 visits had been made.

'Why 108?' I asked, the ek-su-aat, as they called it.

'These gods know all about the past, the present and the future,' said one elderly man who looked like he might be a bank manager in normal daily life. 'They have no attachment to the good or to the bad. They predicted all that science has discovered long ago. And they decided that it should be 108 times. We do not question that. But 1 plus 8 is 9 and nine is the number of chakras which we touch with the slurry of cardamom.'

He gestured to the spots on his body: hips, belly, forearms, shoulders, chest and brow. I thought, nine is the number of heavenly bodies, and something prompted me to glance up at what I had been sketching – the decoration of a door – and I saw that the ancient carpenter had used a schematic representation of a lotus flower to adorn the corners. It was this beautiful carving that had caught my eye as the early sunlight raked across it and I had copied faithfully the eight petals around the central crown.

The ancient oriental love of the lotus always seemed totally appropriate to me, simply for the flower's stunning beauty. There is the warm yellow centre surrounded by creamy white and the fact that it emerges from water and opens when the sun touches it. Examined closely, there is a symmetry and perfection in its construction that is almost like the mechanical beauty of a well-built timepiece. Yet now I saw something else in the fascination: the one in the centre with the eight satellites in a ring – the 1-0-8 – was the mirror of the heavens with the central sun and eight heavenly bodies surrounding, the mirror also of a man with his eight cardinal pleasures and the eight chakras that complement the central third eye, the door to the soul. Redrawn as a square this archetypal pattern would form the navaratna, and the diamond, with its eight-sided crystal, would echo the pattern. It was a symbol seized on by early men: eager for symmetry and order in their universe, they sensed the fingerprints of the gods in the patterns and numerological coincidences of their world.

Like the stem of the flower itself, spiralling down into the murky waters, it was the lotus that connected the temples of Palitana through the millennia to the earliest beliefs of man rooted in the mud of the Nile. In ancient Egypt the god Ra was born in the lotus whose eight petals symbolised the eight gods.

The group of men now moved away: an office had opened and they were collecting small tokens in order to complete the pooja. They had stopped shivering as the sun's warmth had taken the chill from the marble stones at last.

'It is an honour for us all to be here,' said the elderly bank manager. 'We will be returning at sunset time.'

The pilgrimage was a time for living in harmony with the earth: to mark sunrises and sunsets, to start with the new lunar phase and end at the death of another; each number and each action was symbolic, an affirmation of man's connection with the cosmos. Modern science holds back the chaos of the universe with General Theories and Unified Theories: arrangements of numbers based on huge particle accelerators and nuclear explosions; these pilgrims used numbers too, based on a flower.

I sat until I had warmed up, then finished exploring the whole temple complex – the most exquisitely beautiful place I had seen in India, certainly more beautiful than the one lotus pond I had come across at Sri Rangam, all choked with weeds and rubbish.

Reclaiming my shoes, I set off down the hill past the crowds of people, pilgrims and visitors, many bearing little trays of flowers. The palki-bearers were doing good business: passing one particularly large lady and two gasping bearers, I wondered if they charged per pound.

At the foot of the hill I had my breakfast of *bale*, a vegetarian concoction of seeds, beans and spices, then took a pony and trap to the bus station. The more serious pilgrims were walking back to their lodgings, stick in hand, waiting for the shadows to shorten, then lengthen, and it would be time to do it all again.

My route now was further west, but first I had to go south to the sea, passing through Alaung where I stopped to see the bizarre sight of three hundred vast ships drawn up on the beach as though they were rowing boats rather that 50,000 tonne tankers. This was the biggest shipbreaking 'yard' in the world, a strip of oil-soaked sand between sea and high water where tens of thousands of unskilled labourers tear, ant-like, at the leviathans. The gate guard wanted to refuse me entry, as though he knew there was something shameful within, but I insisted and a worker I had met on the bus promised to watch over me.

After the pale serenity of Palitana hill, Alaung came like a blast of hell. Blackened men carrying slabs of steel, women in saris wading out through the motionless grey water to a gash in the belly of a Russian freighter. Some vessels were whole, others almost gone, eaten away to the waterline, their engines torn from them and ripped up the beach by hawsers.

The worker who had befriended me was under instructions from his boss to find a certain type of electrical generator that a client had requested in Bombay. Armed with a few tools and a torch, he was planning to disappear into one of the behemoths. We stepped across the tangle of cables and mud, then up a notched pole onto the lower deck. This Panamanian bulk carrier had been cut down to the waterline for half its length, leaving a vast cliff of rusting steel ahead of us. We picked our way towards a hatch. In one place a hole barely one foot in diameter had been cut into the deck and when I glanced down I saw a man crouched in the darkness, lit only by his cutting torch.

'You go Palitana?' asked the worker, stopping by the bulkhead.

'Yes.' Jagged edges of steel plate jutted out as though the front of the ship had been wrenched away by some incredible power.

'I go there. Every month, go to temple.'

'Your family?'

'No. Family in Calcutta – one time a year I go – Diwali.'

His entire life then, was divided between this infernal place and the elevated peace of Palitana, except for one religious festival in Calcutta. For four years he had done this.

'Bad place,' he said. 'Last year big explosion on ship. We find no bodies only pieces – some feets and hands. You want to come inside? But it is not good for you, I think.'

I looked inside the hatch, into total darkness. Far away I could hear a man singing.

'Maybe a quick look?'

'Okay.'

But as he clambered through, I heard shouting and glanced back. A man in shirt and trousers, a foreman, was waving angrily from the top of the beach.

'You go back,' said the worker. 'Better for you.'

The last thing I saw were his grinning white teeth as he stepped away into the hole.

I walked back, placating the angry foreman by insisting I was not planning to go in the ship, only look.

In the hinterland were mile upon mile of scrapyards where you could buy yourself a Panamanian lifeboat, a Russian mug or half a million chipped ashtrays. It made me glad not to be a sailor.

From Alaung I headed further west on a bus whose conductor played the flute, one leg crossed over the knee of the other, just as in the statues of Krishna. I spent two nights at Diu, an island now linked by bridges to the mainland, and a Portuguese outpost until 1961. The fort at the eastern tip of the island was begun in 1535, one of a Portuguese armed necklace hung around the Indian Ocean from Mozambique to Malacca. In the golden grass lay piles of rusting cannonballs and abandoned World War One howitzers with which the Portuguese had made their last defence of an empire that had outlasted the British, though to little effect for the final three hundred years.

The old town had cool empty streets with Portuguese colonial architecture and faded colours of pink, blue and gold. An old man in a black beret sat on a stone balcony and bemoaned to me the ending of the dhow trade. The bughlas from the Persian Gulf had brought dates with which the locals made a powerful spirit, he told me. All he had now was coconut fenny from Goa, so we drank a tot for breakfast and then I went to catch the bus to Junagadh. It was Christmas Eve.

CHAPTER 7

Aureng-zebe:
I'm tired with waiting for the Chymic Gold,
Which fools us young, and beggars us when old.

Nourmahal:
'Tis not for nothing that we life pursue;
It pays our hopes with something still that's new:
Each day's a Mistris, unenjoy'd before;
Like Travellers, we're pleas'd with seeing more.
Did you but know what joys your way attend,
You would not hurry to your journey's end.

> Dryden, *The Tragedy of Aureng-zebe*,
> first performed, 1675

The Nawab of Junagadh had perverse habits and a sad-
istic nature – although he never ruled, really; it was the
Dewan.

> A Kathiawari prince quoted in
> *Lives of the Indian Princes* by Charles Allen

ARRIVING at Junagadh after dark, I walked through the gaggle of
rickshaw men and a rank of taxis – all either Ambassadors,
which is the Indian-made old Morris Oxford, or enormous
black Ford 8s from 1948 with running boards and acres of chrome.
Opposite the concrete shell of every Indian bus station is the inevitable
row of concrete lock-ups, selling piles of snackfood, cigarettes, soft
drinks and sachets of betel. It was above such a row that I found a hotel.

I almost left immediately: the carpets were speckled with the stains of squashed cockroaches and when I sat down on the bed, a brazen specimen strolled nonchalantly out from under the grubby pillow. But I stayed, too lazy to move, and the owners were friendly. I asked for a wake-up call at 5 a.m. as I planned to climb Girnar Mountain on Christmas Day. The 3,666 foot hill is part of a range of wooded crags and peaks that overshadow Junagadh, and on top of the highest are a number of Jain temples, said to be inhabited by some of India's wilder sadhus or holy men.

But if I had imagined a re-run of my Palitana experience, I was to be disappointed. As I approached the base of the hill in the chilly night air, I could hear the clamour of amplified voices and music. Thousands of youths in their best natty clothes had turned out to climb the hill while listening to ball-by-ball cricket commentary on a one-day international. In their fake crocodile-skin shoes and imitation silk shirts they paraded their consumer durables for the passing delectation of each other – the demurely beautiful girls took no notice. Binoculars, sunglasses, personal stereos, and ghettoblasters by the score, these were the petty princelings of democracy parading their treasures. Waistcoats draped over their shoulders, emboldened by each other, they nagged at me like crows over an injured animal: 'Hey, you! Come on! Come here! You donkey!'

It required the patience of a saint to reach the upper reaches where they were momentarily diverted into stoning some monkeys. From the top, there were marvellous views over the Girnar but all too little opportunity to dwell on them. A few sadhus living in cracks in the rock impassively ignored the mob. One doled out water and blessings, his forehead daubed with ashes, his eyes as yellow as a lion's.

'I have lived here for thirty-nine years,' he said. 'At night I hear the trees talk and watch the water bags fly across the sky. What is this material world? Nothing!'

He let out a sudden screech of delight and jabbed me in the chest. 'Illusion!'

'Actually, I did feel that.'

'All illusion. All of it.' He jabbed me again and caught me on the left nipple – through my shirt, of course, it was him who was bare-chested. It hurt.

'This world is only pain and misery,' he said.

I leaned back a little, hands protecting my nipples. 'I see what you mean.'

His possessions were limited: a saffron robe, a necklace of seeds, a few pots and a 300 watt public address system – most of our conversation was broadcast to the passing rabble and he seemed to be taking the chance to deliver a small sermon. 'Up here we are close to the next world. Only saints live here. Merry Christmas!'

The sadhu leaned closer, away from the microphone, his wispy grey beard tickling my cheek. 'Do you know Rosie? From Leamington Spa?' He winked at me. 'She stayed here for five nights with me. Doing yoga. Very strong girl – very athletic. If you see her, tell her to come and visit me again.'

At that moment the crowds parted and a naked man emerged: no croc-skin shoes or double-breasted brown pin-stripe suit or cowboy hat, just a naked man carrying a fan of peacock feathers. His face was radiant, his gaze set faraway, there were no marks or dirt on him, his hair was short and neat, his teeth perfect. He walked easily, without effort on the steep steps, and on his face was a gentle smile.

'Digambara Jain,' said the sadhu, with a hint of professional jealousy. 'Believe in absolute non-violence; sweep the floor in front of their path in case a small insect is there; very powerful in fasting.' It was like an excerpt from I-Spy Holy Men. 'No clothes,' he added unnecessarily.

Jainism is divided into two sects both of whom agree that wearing clothes is wrong for monks. However, the Svetambaras, 'white-clads', hold that nudity is not possible in this imperfect world, while the Digambaras, 'sky-clads', maintain that it is. In almost 2,500 years this is the only major schism that has emerged in Jainism – something, perhaps, for the Pope and Archbishop of Canterbury to consider.

This sky-clad ascetic had obviously sensibly decided that no living thing could have survived on the steps because he was not using the fan. He passed by without a look at us nor anyone else, apparently oblivious to his surroundings. Like a creature who discovers his ancient migration path overrun by humans, he would carry on regardless to his final destination.

There is a Jain parable which tells how a man was travelling through a wild forest when he was charged by a mad elephant. Turning to run, he found his path blocked by a terrible demoness. The tree next to him was too smooth to climb so he leapt into a well. Halfway down he managed to catch hold of some reeds and hang there. At the bottom he saw no water, only poisonous snakes waiting for him. Then two mice appeared on the reeds, one black and one white; they began gnawing through the stalks and the mad elephant, enraged by the loss of its victim, charged the tree and dislodged a bees' nest which fell on the man. As he hung there, stung by bees and waiting to fall, a single drop of honey fell on his lips, and suddenly all he could think of was how to get another drop of that delicious nectar.

I set off back to the base of the hill, trying, less successfully than the naked ascetic, to retain my composure. Wild peacocks screamed in the teak forest and packs of langur monkeys waited to beg for food. Once out of the mêlée, the route back to Junagadh passed the Upparkot, a vast crenellated fort which was abandoned to the jungle around the seventh century AD. The town lies below the silent walls and I walked down from the impressive gate into the narrow streets.

Almost immediately Junagadh began to interest me. Behind a narrow high street of silversmiths and other shops I found a small courtyard that led into an old graveyard. Here were strange mausoleums laden with gothic domes, all knobbled and spined like fossilised sea creatures, the stone streaked and stained by centuries of rain. It was the graveyard of the nawabs of Junagadh, but it was like no other Muslim cemetery I had seen. This was architecture maddened by isolation and the dark legends of Girnar's stunted forests.

Intrigued, I retraced my steps to the hotel and asked if they knew of any local historians, experts on local legends and the nawabs. After some discussion in Gujarati, they agreed that Shantilal Bhatt was the man I required: a very old man now, they warned me, but one who had been personal photographer to the last nawab. I was given directions – of the vaguest kind, as always – to his studio.

Walking through the town, I was struck by how dirty and shabby it was: buildings had been torn down and patched up, rubbish was piled high and covered in flies and scavenging pigs. The people, too, looked thin and dirty, but some of the buildings suggested that things had

[135]

once been very different. There was a clocktower gateway leading into a semicircle of once elegant shops, the lemon yellow paint still apparent. Opposite were the former palaces and administration buildings of the nawabs, beautifully adorned with traces of coloured glass, balcony windows, traceries and towers. One had been taken over by a bank which had thrown in some concrete pillars and made a mezzanine floor; others appeared empty, the glass and shutters smashed. Everywhere things were broken, decrepit, unpainted, patched and peeling. The crescent of buildings now looked out on a concrete podium where crippled dogs fought over scraps, and rickshaw men over passengers. This, I decided, was definitely a town of ghosts, but it was also a town that had once seen great wealth. If I could get close to the former royal family, perhaps I could discover more about the trade in big diamonds.

Bhatt Studio was not quite what I had expected: a small shopfront with empty window and inside the walls lined with artistic portraits of sadhus and beautiful girls. A thin-faced man sat at the desk reading a magazine and when I asked for Shantilal Bhatt he simply ignored me. I thought perhaps he was deaf and shouted the name, at which he glared and pointed outside.

I went along the street a short way and asked in a pharmacist's shop. Like all the shops, it did not appear to be thriving: a few bars of soap, some toothpaste and ointments on the shelves.

'Shantilal was the best photographer,' the old owner said when I asked. 'But he died three days ago. Did you know him?'

I explained why I had wanted to meet him.

'Yes, he would have told you many things. He was present at so many historic moments with his camera.'

I made some comment about the state of Junagadh, the filth in the streets.

'People do not appreciate these old buildings,' he said. 'And then many came from outside when the Nawab ran away.'

'When was that?'

'He declared for Pakistan in 1947, he and Shah Nawaz Bhutto who was his diwan.'

The diwan was a chief minister, the man who ran the kingdom. The old man noticed my reaction to the name. 'Yes, that Bhutto – the same family – Bhutto was Benazir's grandfather. When they declared for Pakistan there was fighting in the streets between Hindu and Muslim. The rich Muslims left for Karachi, leaving only poor people behind – so you see what we are like.'

'Did the Nawab take all his possessions?'

'No. He went by Dakota plane which is a very small plane and he expected to return. All his things were confiscated and are kept here in the Durbar Hall Museum. Now the man to speak to would be Shambhubhai Desai – he, I believe, is still alive. I see his son walk past here sometimes. He is a lawyer but Shambhubhai was District Collector here – a famous man, I tell you – and also present at those events.'

He scribbled down an address and telephone number. That evening the hotel manager rang for me and made an appointment to see Mr Shambhubhai Desai at his house.

It was a smart villa set behind a high wall near the town hall. I pushed open the metal gate and found myself in a pleasant yard lined with palms and dotted with plants in terracotta pots. Calling out, I heard a hoarse, elderly voice answer, 'Yes, come in, come in.'

I went up a few steps and, leaving my shoes behind, stepped inside a large cool room. On the right was a set of rattan furniture and on the left a traditional Gujarati swinging sofa, hung on chains from the ceiling. An elderly man with a noble face was sitting there wrapped in shawls, looking rather frail.

'You are an English character,' he said. 'Punctual.' He struggled to his feet in order to shake hands, using a chair on wheels as a walking frame. On it was a commodious wooden box containing medicines of all descriptions. 'My knees are bad and my throat,' he said. 'We will talk but I will soon get tired.'

We sat down. 'What is the long and the short of your visit?' he asked.

'I'm writing a book about the diamond trade,' I said.

'Of that I know nothing – I cannot help you.'

'But – I've become interested in the Nawab and Junagadh – what went on here in 1947.'

He sighed. 'Ah! yes. There I can be of service. Many have written on that subject but few are left who remember as I do – I was there. You will take coffee – I like it black myself.'

He clapped his hands and a serving girl appeared. He spoke to her in Gujarati.

'You knew the Nawab?'

'I met him many times, of course, and because he lost they say he was a bad man. But I swear at sunrise on an empty stomach to a stranger that the Nawab was a gentleman – no angel, certainly, he had nine wives and liked the company of boys – there was a lot of silly talk about that – but in administration he was a gentleman, and very fair, whatever religion.'

He began to root around in the large pile of envelopes, papers and books that stood next to him on the sofa. 'This is the fellow.' He passed me a black and white photograph of a stout young man with rather saturnine features and a brooch on his frock coat in the shape of a sun – the symbol of Junagadh.

'I remember one occasion when a well had been restored. The idol was to be placed in the mouth of the well, as is our Hindu custom, and the Nawab was invited. His ADCs all told him not to go but he insisted, and when he did, the priest came forward to place the mark,' he gestured to his forehead, 'and the Nawab accepted it. On another occasion he paid for the restoration of a temple – something forbidden to him as a Mussulman. I tell you, both his eyes were open.'

The girl returned with the coffee – 'black' turned out to mean 'less milk'. Having no milk was unthinkable.

We talked a little of his life, one recorded in breathless style in a short biography where the young Shambhubhai 'girdles up his loins' and struggles with demons of 'red tapism', imperialism and banditry. As a young journalist he had been commended by Gandhi and became a lifelong follower of the man. In 1947 he had been working in the upper echelons of the Junagadh civil service when the dewan, or chief minister to the Nawab, had had a heart attack and left for treatment in the USA.

'They replaced him with Shah Nawaz Bhutto from the Sindh – a dangerous man.'

Throughout that summer, negotiations were under way to partition India, with the rulers given the choice of Pakistan or India. In some areas of the country there were Muslim rulers governing a largely Hindu population. Junagadh was one of them.

Most of these potentially divisive situations were easily defused by the ruler acceding to the democratic inevitability of the majority, usually expressed in the shape of heavyweight politicians such as Sardar Patel and V.P. Menon. Of those that did not, Hyderabad is well-known, but Junagadh, that remote and unsung kingdom, was also to lurch into the limelight.

Before August 1947 the Nawab had given people to understand he would be for India, but under the influence of Bhutto, he changed his mind, or at least was too weak to disagree. In August, Bhutto announced the decision, triggering a mass exodus of Hindus who feared similar massacres to those taking place in the Sind. Though this never happened, most were robbed of all their possessions as they departed. Shambhubhai was summoned to see Bhutto and asked to use his influence on people to accept the declaration and stay. He refused.

'V.P Menom himself came,' said Shambhubhai, 'And Bhutto told him "Nawab is ill". Nobody could get past Bhutto to see the Nawab. Menom said, "As a courtesy then, let me see the Nawab's son". But Bhutto said, "Oh, he is busy with a cricket match." After that, Bhutto sent the Nawab to Karachi to meet Jinna.'

'Did the Nawab know he was leaving for ever?'

'He may have guessed. We cannot know, but I think not.'

'So he took very little – I mean his jewels and diamonds and so on?'

'He had his personal kit, of course, and he took his favourite dogs – he was a great lover of dogs.'

'Then most of his possessions were left behind. What happened to them?'

'The jewels are in the Old Palace, I believe.' He could not, or would not, say more.

On 9th November, Bhutto realised the position of Junagadh was hopeless and fled.

'My sister was a minister with the Arzi Hakumat and they came in.' I asked who they were.

'The refugees formed a government of Junagadh in exile and they marched back in.'

But his own eyewitness status stumbled here: three days before the 9th November he had escaped to Ahmedabad and returned to Junagadh only two days after Bhutto fled, missing the critical moments.

Our conversation moved away from those events: his son, Harish, had arrived home for lunch and I was invited to stay. We went through into the dining room where the table was laden with various dishes prepared by Shambhubhai's wife and daughter.

'In Hindu scripture,' said the son, Harish, 'it is not a rule that you must be vegetarian, but here our social custom is for it – that is the Jain influence.'

The women filled up the little aluminium pots with vegetable curries, soups, salads, chutneys and puris. There was a glass of buttermilk. 'If we do not drink two or three glasses of buttermilk, we feel we have not eaten.'

The menfolk tucked in, using their right hand to mix up a wonderful mess of rice and curries, tipping gollops of curd in to cool the spices.

In western cuisine, it has been said, there is a kind of symbolic evolutionary progression to the meal: soup, the primordial ocean, is followed by fish which crawls onto land to be meat and then takes to the air for the fowl, then man uses his intelligence to create the sweets and the cheeses. Sweet and savoury are as distinct as night and day; the vegetables are cooked separately.

In the east, the meal is not a recapitulation of the creation myth, all the sweet and savoury are eaten together, the vegetables mixed up, chutneys created; there are no courses or stages. It is the people, the diners themselves, who are separated.

'If I drank alcohol, my father would throw me out of the house,' said Harish, a grandfather himself. 'If I ate an egg, he would leave the table in disgust. Many younger people have picked up this habit of the west to eat eggs, but the older folk cannot abide by it.' Brother against brother over an omlette.

I was trying to tear a puri in half and brought up my left hand to hold it steady.

'Here we are using only right hands,' his wife reminded me sharply. I apologised.

They began to tell me of the calorific content of each dish, the seasonal nature of ingredients, the health-enhancing attributes of certain preparations. 'If you are eating two of these urudia for breakfast, you will pull on all day!'

Then they gave me a solemn warning of the horrors of meat-eating. 'Some restaurants just grab a street chicken or use diseased animals.'

The Brahmin priest at Sri Rangam had said to me, 'A man believes with his belly.' Now I began to understand what he meant.

After finishing, we went back into the front room. Shambhubhai fell asleep on his sofa, while Harish chatted.

'In some states – like Bihar and Andhra Pradesh – they still make a big thing about eating with your caste,' he went on. 'They have not accepted this equality principle of democracy.'

The British, like previous invaders, had presented a problem to the caste society that they appropriated. Where and how to fit them in, especially at the dinner table? Obviously they could not be high caste – that was for priests – nor could they be shudras or low caste – that was not suitable for rulers. Many British incomers were treated, as I had been in Bombay, to a meal without a participating host. One memsahib, Marguerite Bunyard was invited to supper by a raja who made a brief appearance before dinner, then left her to enjoy (in order of serving) sardines with egg and potato, tinned soup, tinned salmon, mutton cutlets with vegetables, a joint of beef, strawberry pudding, roast snipe with chips, jelly, savoury eggs, then to finish, candied fruits, chocolate, coconut ice, pistachios and coffee.

Decried by most British as unjust, the caste system was not unequal to subtle revenge on its masters. During the last years of the British Raj, the last Viceroy, Lord Mountbatten, was holding a formal reception at Viceroy's House in New Delhi when his wife's lap dog had an 'accident' on the carpet. Mountbatten's daughter Pamela recalls, 'It took such a long time to find the right grade of servant to clear up the mess that my mother, in formal long white dress, diamond tiara and elbow length gloves, got down on her hands and knees and cleared it up herself.'

Perhaps there was a subtle kind of vengeance too when, at the

Nawab of Oudh's palace in Lucknow, the khansamah, or chief waiter, thought to delight his British guests by serving the food in a particularly attractive set of large bowls that he had found in the European shop in Lucknow. *Memoirs of a Cadet* (1839) records: 'In due time, when the ladies and gentlemen were ushered into the supper room, the most conspicuous objects were these very vessels plentifully bestowed about the table, laden with jelly, blancmange etc etc.' Unfortunately, they were chamberpots.

Harish had the language of equality and democracy, the liberal socialism of Nehru and Gandhi, but when it came to the crunch he was a traditionalist. 'We believe in marriage within our community,' he said. 'You can come in my house and we can be friends, but this is not my language we are speaking, our thoughts are different, our food is different, our culture, our houses, our skin and our religion – all different. You can never be part of this.'

The message was delivered with surprising force, a message of uncompromising pessimism for a country containing so much cultural diversity. Forbidden to eat together and so unable to understand each other.

After saying goodbye to my lunch hosts, I walked across the river, a foul grey slime where some women were attempting to wash clothes, and into the town again. Once again I was struck by all the grand abandoned buildings: there had been a civic pride in the place and Shambhubhai's claim that the Nawab had been an able administrator rang true. In one corner I found the public library, a fine octagonal building lined with glass-fronted bookcases, all padlocked. Here were forgotten favourites such as, *Electrical Amusements* by C.R Gibson, the three volume set of Gladstone's Scottish speeches, *My School and Scoolmasters* by Hugh Miller, plus many works on Indian history and culture. They were not to be read, however. Pigeons swooped around the clerestory and sent delicate white feathers down onto the octagonal reading table. No one had the keys and the library assistant looked at me curiously. It was a considerable time since anyone had asked to see the books. Were they of any value?

I went up the street and emerged opposite the palaces in Circle Chowk. Around the back of the buildings was the door to the Durbar Hall Museum where I paid my one rupee and climbed a flight of steps into a large open hall. Although I had no means of knowing for sure, it did not strike me as a grand durbar hall, the durbar being the court. There were a large number of kitsch glass chandeliers, some paintings and a raised dais with two silver chairs upon it. I wandered through and found two more smaller rooms containing a few weapons and costumes. There was nothing more, so I went back to the entrance and found one of the museum-keepers.

'Can I see the other rooms of the palace?' I asked.

He smiled. 'That is not possible.'

'But isn't there any more of the Nawab's treasure – furniture, jewels, gold and silver?'

'This is all that was left,' he confirmed.

'But the Nawab had seven palaces. All that is here barely fills one room! Where is the rest?'

He paused before answering. 'There are ten boxes of jewels in the State Treasury.'

'Can I see them?'

'It is not possible.'

'Have you seen them?'

He signalled that I should follow and we went through into a side room where there was a large grey metal cabinet. Unlocking the cabinet he rummaged about inside, casting glances at the door to make sure no one was watching us. When he had found what he was looking for, he beckoned me towards him and used the cabinet door to shield us from view.

'Here. These are the jewels.'

There was a small colour photograph showing a basement room and a table with an open wooden box. Inside was a jumble of golden ornaments. I could make out some chunky bracelets studded with 10 carat diamonds, a few necklaces and pendants. He flipped the photo book shut and quickly replaced it in the cupboard.

'There are nine more boxes?'

'Yes. We hope to display the contents, perhaps in five years time. There are security problems.'

I reminded myself that more than fifty years had now passed since the treasure had fallen into Indian government hands. 'Is there a catalogue?'

'No.'

He relocked the cabinet and led me out to the lobby.

'Have any pieces gone missing?' I asked ingenuously.

He thought long and hard. 'There was a belt, studded with jewels. It disappeared and was never seen again.'

I thanked him and walked out into the bright sunlight of the street. It was clear to me now that some time after the Nawab's departure an enormous theft had taken place: seven palaces of treasure emptied. Quite possibly courtiers had helped themselves to the odd piece – understandable in the perilous circumstances of the times. The Nawab would have taken any prime pieces, but what remained in the ten boxes was clearly the dregs, the bits that got left behind when everyone's hands were full.

I walked back around the building to Circle Chowk. The once grand entrance to the palace complex was now choked with sari shops, tin shacks open on one side where the dealers sat cross-legged, surrounded by bolts of brilliantly colourful cloth. Beyond these I found a doorway leading through a hall of scalloped arches, then a flight of steps up to the second floor. There was no one around. I went up and pushed the ancient studded door open. Inside was a large room full of shelves on which lay bundles of papers stitched into white cloth. There were huge old doors, little latticework alcoves for water pots to cool in the breeze and thick stone walls. After the heat and bustle of the street, it was peaceful and quiet. Passing through one doorway, I found myself in a long room lit by dusty shafts of light breaking through closed shutters and bits of coloured glass. At the far end three men were working at their desks. I coughed.

'Welcome,' said one. 'You will take tea?'

I was ushered down to their end of the room and a muddy brew was fetched for me in a cup and saucer. I had stumbled on the Public Records Office, housed, so they told me, in part of the Nawab's former private chambers. One of them took me through to a second room: it occupied a fine corner position with beautifully carved wooden cupboards and an archway leading out onto a covered balcony – a jarokha – with fluted columns and scalloped arches.

'The Nawab stood here and watched parades,' he said. 'Elephants

[144]

would come along, or he would watch performances by dancing girls in Circle Chowk.'

He took me upstairs, around the empty derelict palace rooms where pigeons fluttered and the walls were stained with rain damage. Roofs and ceilings had fallen in and there was a musty carpet of bird droppings and feathers. The man showed me the roof pavilion where the Begum had slept on warm nights, the hooks still in the rafters where the wooden cot had been tied. Across the roof was a pavilion for the Nawab, smelling of bats, the glass all broken.

'India government not taking care for it,' he said. 'Old building all ruin.' He grinned and sent a spurt of blood-red paan juice slashing down the wall.

In the office they discovered an old picture book for me to look at, and I found a photograph from 1907 of the Circle: the road freshly swept, all the men in turbans, and only one stray goat. 'The windows of some of the apartments,' went the text, 'look down on the main thoroughfare. And after sunset, when the bazaar is ablaze with flaring lamps, and the shopkeepers are busy, and sturdy Mussalmans, gorgeous in bright silks and fine linen, fill the streets; when the Palace gleams with light, and the wild retainers, armed with quaint guns and half a dozen knives, go swaggering by, and mounted sowars come clattering through the crowd; when the moonlight transfigures the picturesque houses, and casts bold shadows, and every dim recess seems a haunt of mystery, Junagadh becomes the typical Indian city of the imagination, unchanged and unchanging.'

There was a map too, showing Junagadh state as an odd collection of land areas, bits missing, pockmarked with tiny enclaves. 'What are these?' I asked, pointing out one of the tiny blank spaces close to Junagadh town.

'That one is Bilkha,' said one of the clerks, squinting at the lettering. 'It was a very small state inside Junagadh.'

'With a ruler?'

'Oh yes. It had a raja even though it was only seven miles wide and ten long.'

'Is he still there?' I hardly dared ask. It seemed too easy, to stumble on exactly the sort of place I needed.

'That I do not know. The palace is there. You can go and see. Take the bus and when you reach, say to someone in the market: "Take me to your former ruler." That will do.'

Later that evening, I returned to Circle Chowk and sat on the steps under the clocktower. It was almost nine o'clock and the town was quiet; the dusty scent of paan and spices came welling up with the night air; the dim lights of the watchman's room were caught behind fragments of red glass and behind me was the creak of a sofa, swinging gently as someone lay awake in the gloom. For the English writer in 1907, Junagadh had been a place to appreciate the unchanging nature of India, the India that his predecessors had found. Now I was trying to catch faint traces of that world and beginning to appreciate that India had changed all the time, Junagadh, too; only what we outsiders wanted it to be had remained the same.

The bus out to Bilkha was a real country vehicle: battered and bent, laden to the gills with dusty-footed people smiling at me with sun-dried faces. The road skirted Girnar mountain, passing through small villages and over clear streams. There were more trees around and a feeling of solid rural life, not exactly wealthy but certainly not poor. It was late afternoon and a golden glow lay across the hills and the stone-built houses with their tousled fringes of coconut palms.

Bilkha proved to be a small place, built on both sides of a small river just two or three miles from the foot of the craggy mountain range. In the town there was one cool narrow street of shops, empty of traffic except for buffaloes and with some pleasant old carved windows and balconies. At one end was a small square fort, but I was directed out of town to a second building, a high wall with twenty-foot gates spiked with iron to stop elephants pushing at them. There were two small cannons painted black and a side-gate on a chain. I knocked, but there was no answer, so I lifted the ring off the hook and let myself in.

If I had expected something palatial, one of those vast dwellings that maharajas put up for themselves, full of soaring towers of clapboard, and ridges wriggling with Victorian wrought ironwork, then I was wrong. There was a dusty yard where a large hunting dog lay asleep, undisturbed by my arrival; beyond was an unkempt garden filled with pepper trees, and to the right stood a small square villa with porticoed entrance. Under the shade of this was a World War Two American jeep with a pair of stout muscular legs emerging from underneath it.

I walked over and called a greeting.

'Ah! Where are you from?' A big, booming voice. There was the clash of a spanner flying off a nut and a grunt of pain.

'I'm English. I heard about Bilkha in Junagadh and came to see you.'

'Correct. I am just attending to this jeep. Go inside and sit on the terrace. The boy will show you. Ra-joo! Ra-jooo!'

A barefoot lad of about fifteen with a big, white-toothed smile came padding around the corner and beckoned me to follow up the steps.

At the top I went through a fly door into a darkened vestibule. On the left was a huge copper-bound chest as tall as myself with an old palanquin on top. I followed the boy through some heavy curtains and into an unlit room. Large paintings were laid against the walls, there was a collection of darkwood furniture, a glass-fronted cabinet containing several hundred glass bangles on rods and a heavily-laden washing line – men's jeans and shirts only.

'Sahib?' The boy was out on the terrace, showing me a wooden sofa to sit on. The house was built around a central courtyard with a veranda running around it on three sides. There were numerous pairs of dusty antique wooden doors leading off this, but clearly the occupier spent most of his time on the chair opposite me. Next to it on the desk was a pair of spectacles and some unopened letters. Further down the hall was a table bearing a pair of porcelain elephants and two toy cannons identical to those outside. Beside the table was an easel holding an oil painting of a young boy dressed as a raja in plumed turban and pearl-strings. The courtyard was empty and a battered old screen hid the kitchen door.

The boy reappeared carrying a metal cup full of tea, a wad of paan and a cigarette, all of which he placed on the desk with gestures that I should help myself. After a few more minutes my host came through, a middle-aged man, big in the belly with a large friendly face and impressive grey moustaches.

'It is a Ford jeep – 1942 – but the starter motor has gone and I can only get spares from US. Drink your tea and have a puff. I will take bath.'

He went through one of the doors and I caught a glimpse of a vestibule piled high with old volumes and documents. Sounds of happy splashing drifted through, then a silence after which he re-emerged, neatly dressed in Levi jeans and shirt, moustaches combed and eyes twinkling.

'So! It is fortunate that you found me here. I came this morning from the Gir – the forest, you know. We are making a study of the lions there.'

The Gir is a national park where the last Asiatic lions live, or are meant to live. As Bilkha (the man and town being synonymous) explained, the lions had always lived near man, so when the people were cleared from the park, the lions simply followed them.

'We have some here,' he said, pouring a glass of black tea from a flask. 'On the slopes of Girnar.'

This was unexpected – the lions are thought to be restricted to one last location. 'They move singly, not as prides, and they can be difficult to see but there are about eighteen or nineteen of them. I will show you. Where are you staying?'

I told him and he shrugged. 'You can move your things here. Why not? I am alone. My family are in Poona. Bring your things and we will go and look for the lions. Correct? In fact, you open that door.' The boy who was listening carefully began to grin when he saw his master point to the door. I got up and, pulling back the bolt, pushed the double doors open. As the light fell into the room, I gave an involuntary start. Standing directly in front of me was a large lioness, amber-eyed and jaws forever open in a ferocious snarl.

'My grandfather shot that lion not seven kilometres from here. Of course, we are conservation-minded nowadays, but in the past we were sporting types.'

He showed me around the room which was hung with trophies. 'This portrait is my grandfather spearing a leopard. He used to go with the Maharaja of Bhavanagar hunting black buck with trained cheetahs. When I was younger we had a Humber Super Snipe specially converted for shooting parties – searchlights for the guns and walnut picnic tables for each seat. Sherry in the jungle! There was a thunder

[148]

box, too, and a guy who would come to know you were there and take it out and clean it.'

Unlike the shooting, cars remained a passion – and horses. 'We did not always live here. Our place was the fort, but the government took it from us. Did you see it? Underneath are stables with secret passages so you could gallop out. There was a special breed of Kathiawar horse – gone now, in the pure form anyway.'

The cars had gone too: Rolls-Royce 1939 Phantoms, Chevrolets, Packards, Hispano-Souzas, Bentleys – all sold off. One neighbouring raja had even had a Rolls-Royce built in the shape of a swan, complete with a tiny copy to be its cygnet.

'It's in our blood,' he said. 'Horses, hunting, cars – we are Huns! What about you? What is your family history?'

'Do you know England?'

'I do.'

I explained that we were from Lincolnshire originally, though there was no connection now. 'I was driving through recently,' I said, 'and stopped at a churchyard – just by chance. The graveyard was full of Rushbys and, when I checked, one turned out to be my great grandfather.'

It sounded rather careless – to lose a great grandfather and stumble on him by chance. 'We're not an old family,' I said, making light of it. 'As far as I'm concerned, we go back to the 1960s. What about you?'

Bilkha laughed. 'Our ancestor was the Sun. The court poet used to sing the genealogy back through Rama's son to the Sun god. I forget how many hundred generations.'

He led me out of the room back onto the veranda. Raju locked up after us. 'I've never met anyone descended from the sun before.'

He grinned. 'It was the moon on my mother's side. Come, I will show you.'

We went out into the yard and across to some rooms that were part of the surrounding wall.

'Raj-ooo! My key!' Raju came galloping past and unlocked the door. He and Bilkha kept up a constant banter in Gujarati, a relationship more like father and dutiful son, an impression bolstered by Raju calling Bilkha, 'Bapu', or father. It was, I would discover, what everyone in town called him.

[149]

Inside the room was a small shrine with a garlanded picture of the Sun god riding a lion. Around the walls were portraits of various ancestors and a war banner embroidered in gold and silver with a blazing sun.

'My grandfather and father would get up every morning at sunrise to worship the sun, but nowadays – who gets up that early? No one! Correct!'

We stood outside in the yard. The sun was setting and Raju had disappeared into the garden. 'They have a temple there to the snake. They say there is a snake living in there – cobra.'

'Isn't it dangerous?'

He laughed. 'No! These things are not dangerous. Like the lions. If he runs at you, just stand still. They won't attack. When Raju comes back – Raj-ooo! – he will take you to the bus stop. You come tomorrow for lunch and bring your baggages.'

Raju returned and led me out onto the street. Once on the bus, I remembered that I had forgotten to tell him why I had come in the first place. As for Bilkha, he had yet to ask.

The following day I found Bilkha sitting on his verandah talking to two youths who were cross-legged on the floor at his feet.

'Come!' he called, when I appeared. 'Sit here, where you sat yesterday.'

Raju took my bags away and came back with tea. Bilkha was listening to the youths who were excitedly telling him something in Gujarati. Eventually, their tale finished, they politely took their leave, palms pressed together and bowing.

'That boy has seen a panther,' Bilkha reported. 'A black one – it's very unusual.'

'Are there many leopards?'

'Yes, many of them, but never black ones – the boy's father watches my buffaloes for me up on the Girnar. We used to have cattle, too, but every one was taken. The buffalo survive by forming a circle, you see, to protect each other, but the cattle do not – so they die. You should walk over the mountain to Junagadh one morning. Maybe you can see a lion.' He noticed Raju standing near the kitchen. 'Come. Let us take lunch.'

We went through into his dining room, paint peeling from the walls and Victorian pictures of dancing nymphs damaged by the monsoon humidity. There was a fine old sideboard from which Raju fetched various pots of curry and chappatis.

'Where have you been eating?' he asked. I told him the name of a restaurant.

'But this is proper Gujarati food. In town they put sugar in everything.'

I tried to mix things up properly. Raju was watching me, grinning, making comments to Bilkha.

'He won't eat with me,' said Bilkha with a chuckle. 'Our family never followed these restrictions but our servants still do. The man who comes to sweep the courtyard needs his own water cup – like that. Even now the village headman – you will meet him later – he now eats with me but before he would make an excuse: 'Oh, I already ate' – something like that. Very polite.'

'But your family were the rulers. Wouldn't it be an honour to eat with you?'

'Not at all. We were warriors and outsiders and so respected. But not all rulers were necessarily high caste. Take the Scindias of Gwalior, they were shoe-keepers.' He began to laugh, belly shaking. 'Shoe-keepers, I tell you, they looked after the rulers' shoes. Then they had their chance and became rulers. Well, why not? The Gaekwars of Baroda were shepherds. But these servants here: some, like the lady who cooks, her family have been with us for six generations but they will not eat with us. Why? Because they are Kolis and that caste were once, long ago, rulers themselves in Gogha.'

At this point Raju produced some more chappatis, wrapped in a linen cloth. He slipped a question in for me, through Bapu.

'He wants to know if you have a Walkman.'

'I'm afraid I don't.'

'It's his ambition, you see, to own one, and a television, although his house doesn't have electricity.'

Raju looked abashed, such ambitions, run-of-the-mill as they would appear in Bombay or Ahmedabad, seemed the wildest daydreamings here. He put his hands behind his back and leaned on the sideboard, smiling at the floor.

[151]

Bilkha and I finished eating and went out onto the veranda. 'Take a puff if you like,' he said, gesturing smoking. 'There are some books you can look at here and your room is over there. I will take some rest now.'

He disappeared through the curtain, past the bookshelves into his room. I picked out a few volumes and went back around the terrace into my room.

It was a lovely cool dark space with an antique hardwood bed in the middle, all carefully made with sheets and blankets. On the walls were various portraits from the 'twenties and 'thirties. The bathroom was through a pair of creaking teak doors and had obviously been installed during the same period. There was a small wooden stool to sit on while washing – something done with liberal sploshings of bucket-water.

I pulled the heavy curtains across the doorway and lay on the bed, examining the books. One was a detailed exposition on the ruling families of Saurashtra in which I discovered that Bilkha as a state had come into being in the 1920s when the Privy Council (presumably in London) had recognised Bilkha's grandfather, Rawat Wala, as ruler. According to legend the Walas had been mentioned in Assyrian inscriptions, fought against Alexander and finally moved into Saurashtra in the sixteenth century. The fort in the centre of Bilkha might easily have dated from that time, but this house had obviously been built when the recognition as a state came through.

The rulers had all built impressive genealogies for themselves, tracing their lineages back to the heavens. And, like the American tourists gawping at London's Tower, the British lapped it up – the new masters in awe of their predecessors (the imperialistic arrogance would come later). Some wrote scholarly works that have remained classics of Indian history. In the mid 1820s, a young British colonel, James Tod, sat down in the library of Udaipur and began his *Annals and Antiquities of Rajas'than*, a massive work detailing the origins of the ruling peoples, including that of Bilkha's ancestors: 'his religion, his manners and his looks, all are decidedly Scythic . . . [He] still adores the sun, scorns the peaceful arts, and is much less contented with the tranquil subsistence of industry than the precarious earnings of his former predatory pursuits.'

The second book I had borrowed from Bilkha's shelves offered practical advice and was entitled *Etiquette for Ladies and Gentlemen*. I wondered if the grandfather had bought this to emulate his British mentors, or to understand them, or perhaps both.

On the Art of Chewing, it recommended a closed mouth: 'It is often neglected with the most unpleasant results.' The Art of Walking was clearly a trick only achieved after some practice: 'the upper part of the body should be held erect, and balanced alternately on each hip without perceptible swaying or rolling.' Naturally, there was an extended disquisition on the Art of Being a Passenger on a Ship: dinner – 'just a dinner jacket rather than a swallow-tailed coat, with a silk shirt, and a freshened leisurely air are all that is necessary.' Air travel was in its infancy, so much so that passengers were reminded to pack pyjamas and clean linen, close all bottles of hair oil firmly, and never, never, to tip the stewardess.

I lay down on the bed. A cold wind was whistling in the shutters, setting up all sorts of bangings and creakings. Heavy snow had fallen in Kashmir and this north wind was coming straight down to us from there.

When I woke, the light outside the door had become golden and I could hear the whistling of a steam train – Bilkha is still served by a coal-fired locomotive. Raju had put a bucket of hot water in the bathroom for me and was busy making tea. Far across the fields between the house and village I could distantly hear the sound of drumming as local musicians prepared for the wedding season. Bapu was sitting in his chair, with yesterday's newspaper on his knee. Two village men were sitting on the wooden sofa smoking beedis. They were barefoot, dressed in the simple white cloth of the farmer.

'Are you refreshed?' Bilkha asked me. 'Good, good.' After a polite pause he returned to business with the two men, speaking slowly and gently. When he finished, they grunted in assent and got up to leave. I had the vague impression that Bilkha had delivered a judgement of some kind, but their careful, guarded faces gave no hint as to whether they approved or not. Raju came through with the inevitable tea and saw them out.

'Did your father and grandfather hold court here?' I asked. 'I mean sessions where the people could come with complaints or whatever.'

He smiled. 'Yes, and they still come occasionally: these men wanted advice from me, although I am 'uraju' – heir apparent – my father is still alive in Poona. You see to go through the courts might take years and ruin them financially. So it is easier to make a friendly agreement – where there is no crime involved, of course. We don't have those powers any longer.' He picked up the newspaper and finished reading it while I drank my tea. Then he tucked his spectacle case in his shirt pocket. 'Shall we go?'

We found Raju was outside, cranking the jeep up.

'There are some people to see,' said Bilkha, climbing into the driver's seat. 'Then we will do a tour up along the bottom of the mountain. We may be lucky and see a lion.'

We made stately progress around the village, stopping to talk to several men, then rumbled out along the dirt tracks into the surrounding fertile lands. Bilkha talked about his plans for businesses in the area and I realised that my initial impression of a former ruler down on his luck was well wide of the mark. The family had built a new life in Poona, but now he, as the eldest son, had come to reactivate the family interest in Bilkha – one that had lain dormant for some time.

We watched a herd of black buck grazing in a field, then set off towards the mountain. Families of mongeese sprinted across the track, huge bushy tails held horizontally behind them. Bilkha asked about my visit to India and I told him about the diamonds – how I had found the mines and now wanted to discover more about the rulers and their stones, how this had led me to Junagadh and the questions over the Nawab's wealth.

'What have they told you already?'

I outlined what I had heard: Bhutto's role, the Arzi Hakumat invasion and the Indian Army's capture of the treasure, now in the State Treasury.

He chuckled, changing gear as we bounced across the railway lines. 'Most of that is complete eyewash,' he said. 'Do you want to know what really happened? I'll tell you. The Nawab declared for Pakistan and the Indian Army invaded. It was led by Brigadier Gurdial Singh and his men were Punjabis, all fired up by the massacres in their homelands. This Arzi Hakumat was got up later to make it look better in the history books.'

'And the treasure?'

'You have seen the Durbar Hall? How much is left? Nothing. And let me tell you most of that was brought in from Mangrol, another state, to hide the fact that there was so little left in Junagadh. People became rich overnight. There were twenty tons of silver in the treasury, porcelain, jade, a crystal bed – a whole room of crystal, in fact. The Nawab had many many things. Even in the 'fifties I can remember seeing his Chippendale chairs in the flea markets of Junagadh. He had horses, too, and they pulled carts around the town – racehorses became rickshaw pullers!'

We had moved beyond the fields now, working our way through the dry teak forest, the broad fallen leaves crunching under the tyres like popadoms. Peacocks screamed and ran for cover. The sun had gone down and a half moon was rising over Girnar hill, the sky behind it an exquisitely soft blue.

'And did he have diamonds?'

'All the big rajas and nawabs had diamonds. In 1917 when there was the Russian Revolution, many jewels came into view and were bought up by Indian princes. Then Cartier reworked them. It was a competition for them. Jamnagar had emerald drops and a pink diamond, the Nizam had the Jacob diamond – which he kept in a shoe for years. The Gaekwars had good diamonds – I saw them in the 'seventies – Eugenie, Akbar Shah, Shepherd's, the Star of the South . . .'

The Baroda collection had been built up by Mulhar Rao in the 1870s, until his penchant for poisoning caught him out. The state's Prime Minister had died mysteriously, but it was only when the British Resident discovered a strange powder in his morning glass of sherbet that the plot was uncovered. The powder was found to be a mixture of copper, arsenic and crushed diamonds.

'There was a string of twelve pearls all as big as pigeon's eggs.' Bilkha continued, 'Now the two brothers are in dispute over the jewels so no one can see them.'

'But the Nawab?'

'The Nawab was not mixing up much with people and no one knows exactly what he had.'

'Did he love jewels?'

'He loved dogs. My grandfather attended a wedding ceremony back in the 'twenties – for the Nawab's favourite bitch. It was all done exactly as a proper royal wedding.'

He explained how, on the morning of the wedding, the Nawab had gone to the railway station on a bejewelled elephant with 250 dogs also riding elephants. There a red carpet was laid out for the arriving bridegroom – a golden retriever from Mangalore named Bobby. After inspecting the guard of honour, Bobby and the wedding party moved to the palace for a sumptuous breakfast, the Nawab flanked by the happy couple and faced by 700 guests from all the royal families of India. Only the Viceroy, Lord Irwin, declined to attend, on the grounds that such a union was 'unprecedented'. Poor Irwin, his mark on history is as a party-pooper at a dog's wedding.

'The bride and groom wore silk gowns,' said Bilkha, 'They had gold chains on their paws and necklaces of jewels – it was very colourful. Dancing girls were brought from Bombay and all the guests brought jewellery as gifts. They say it cost the Nawab over £20,000.'

Bobby's moment of glory was fleeting, however. His wedding night bliss was interrupted by the Nawab, who had him thrown in the common kennels so his darling bitch Roshanara could resume her place on His Highness' bed.

We had swung around and climbed out of the teak forest into an area of long grass, white in the moonlight and gently sighing as the breeze stepped through it. The lunar crescent was climbing towards Venus. In Bilkha a few lights had come on, but most of the land was in darkness now, a subtle shaded carpet of smoky greys and blue.

'Do you see that rounded hill?' he asked, stopping the jeep and pointing up the slopes to where the peaks were silhouetted. 'This place was a place of kings from long back, from the times of the *Mahabharata*, the times when the Pandava brothers came to hide in their twelve years of exile. The god Krishna walked these paths. That hill was where the demon wife of Bhim did her cooking, and those two mountains are where she put her hammock.'

Not only had I found my ex-royal, but I had also stumbled upon the landscape that Mr Shantilal had told me about all those weeks before in a grubby Vijayawada hotel restaurant. This was the region where the legends of the great Syamantaka jewel had begun.

We moved on again. Something dark flipped up from the track and over our heads. A nightjar, the goat-sucker bird of folklore. We were on a slight ridge with scrubby thorn below on either side. 'One night we met a lioness walking along here,' he said. 'And she would not give way. After some time I pulled close to this edge and she walked past. Here, as close as you could touch.'

'Would she attack?'

'No, no.'

'Have there been attacks?'

'There was a lioness came to the railway lines near the houses. Some youths were there and one of them stoned her. So, naturally, she became angry and chased him. He fell down and lay flat, then she sat on him.'

'And killed him?'

'No, she bit his bums off!'

'Bottom-pinchers of Girnar' did not have the same thrilling ring as 'Man-eaters of Tsavo', but I asked if there had been any cases. It clearly pained him to say anything bad about a wild animal. 'Not really. Occasionally. A panther killed and ate three people about a year ago.'

'Was it caught?'

'It must have moved away because nothing else has happened.'

Above the hills, the moon and Venus had missed a conjunction by a few degrees. Other stars had appeared now and there were more night-jars lying in the dust until the wheels were almost upon them. Then they would come flying across the bonnet and up over our heads – all in silence, no cry of fear or warning. We left the track once more and passed through grassland.

At a T-junction in the track, Bilkha waved his hand up to the right. 'This way leads into the mountains. You will take it when you walk to Junagadh. I have arranged for someone to go with you.'

Our safari for that evening was over and we drove back to the house. At the sound of the motor, Raju came leaping from the shadows to open the elephant gates ('Yes, we used to have one,' said Bilkha, 'but when he died, we did not get another.')

In the dining room, supper was waiting: napkins neatly laid beside the aluminium trays and dishes. Raju got the kedgeree from the side-board and a mint chutney. There were three curries and a pot of warm chappatis. The buttermilk, a thin watery yoghurt, had begun to thicken but was still welcome.

After eating, Bilkha went and put his pyjamas on, then reappeared to take his betel. Raju was squatting at my feet, intently watching me read. Bilkha had a battered old volume in his hand, the cover dangling off. 'This will be of interest. It has the family tree of the Nawab.' He found the relevant page and handed the book to me. 'There, you see, they were governors for the Mughals, then they declared themselves nawabs in 1748.'

It was a similar story to that of Hyderabad where the nizams had assumed power in the vacuum left by Nadir Shah's despoilation of Mughal Delhi in 1739. Mahabat Khan III had been the ninth in the Junagadh dynasty, brought to the throne in 1911 by the premature deaths of his two elder brothers. According to the chronicler, 'enormous booty' had been acquired by the Junagadh nawabs during successful military campaigns in the eighteenth century. 'Valuable presents' had also come from neighbouring lesser states like those adjacent to the Portuguese island of Diu: Una, Delwada and Porbander.

The previous, legendary, history of the area was of the Yadav king, Sri Krishna, settling in Dwarka on the coast and the Pandava brothers roaming its forests. Krishna was said to have had a son, Samba, who married Rama, the daughter of the King of Egypt, and their descendants had moved into the Sind from where internecine warfare had since scattered them.

Bilkha's book ended its record with the birth of the heir apparent to the throne of Junagadh, Muhammad Dilaverkhanji, in 1922.

'Is he still alive?'

Bilkha thought, arms crossed over his stomach. 'I do not know. I think he became a lawyer or diplomat in Pakistan.'

'Did they all leave? Are there any relatives of the Nawab left in Junagadh?'

He laughed. 'Oh yes. They are here.'

'Can I meet them?'

'I will take you there.'

'Are they rich? Do they claim the throne?'

His eyes twinkled. 'You will see for yourself and you will ask for yourself.'

We talked for a little longer, then I retired to my room. The teak doors needed a good lift and pull to close. A shutter was banging in the wind and I secured it. The bed had been turned down for the night and I lay awake watching tiny flakes of yellowing plaster spiral gently down from the ceiling. It was the coldest night of the year and the wind had a bitter edge to it.

CHAPTER 8

The last Begum of Avad, who once ruled one of India's most powerful kingdoms, squatted in Delhi railway station for 10 years before going out in style drinking a phial of poison laced with crushed diamonds.

Daily Telegraph, 23rd March, 1997

I slept a lot and read Bilkha's books over the days that followed; in the cold mornings, I would be up on the roof to catch the first warming rays of sunlight, then, in the hot midday, I would withdraw to the veranda behind the cotton curtains. Twice daily, a young Brahmin would come to perform the necessary rituals at the family temple. When that was finished he would bring the smoking incensor to the house and give a taste of holy air to each room. During the day Bilkha would be meeting local people or out visiting, but at sunset we went lion-hunting, bouncing along all the dirt tracks on the skirts of Girnar. He would point out features of the landscape that legend associated with the heroes of the *Mahabharata* and his own ancestors. Then I began to see the landscape as a record of all that had happened, a way of casting the stories in stone, even when men had forgotten them. Their own court poet and storyteller, he said, had died five years previously, taking to the funeral pyre his epic ballads that wove the thread of Bilkha's rulers right back through the offspring of Lord Rama to the sun. It was to walk through these legendary mountains that I now waited.

On the last day of the year, I woke shivering at dawn. The cold weather had taken a grip: bitterly cold night winds rushing straight down from the Himalayas and swirling around the Girnar. The youth who was to guide me through the hills to Junagadh was waiting at the gate, leaping on the back of the jeep as we set off for Ramnat Temple, the start of the footpath.

'Do you think I'll see a lion?' I asked Bilkha.

'A pair were seen on the track two days ago,' he said. 'So it is a good chance I think. This boy Raghu knows how to look for them.'

'And they definitely do not attack?'

He chuckled. 'When they are in heat the females can be aggressive. If one charges at you – remember – just stand still.'

I could not imagine anything I was less likely to do, but I kept quiet.

Ramnat Temple stood on a wooded knoll at the mouth of a narrow valley that emerged from the hills. After Bilkha had driven away, we climbed up the steps to pay our respects to the god. The Brahmins were all wrapped up against the cold and greeted us with cries of 'Jaya Ramnat!' We were served tea in saucers which we lapped at like cats, then went to ring the temple bell. The god was a red stone idol who gazed out over the scrubby forest and the fields beyond. Somewhere beneath him, in a sealed room, were the bones of a Jain sadhu who had voluntarily starved himself to death. In a society where food and eating marked the position of the man, the final release from earthly restraints came with total abstinence.

We walked down to the river and crossed by jumping from stone to stone. The water was cold and clear; there were no plastic bags caught in it, no foul foaming pools, not even a broken flip-flop. In the bushes peacocks ran from us and mongeese chattered. I tried to walk quietly, but it was an impossibility with the dry teak leaves scrunching under foot. When the wind rattled through the trees it sounded like water dashing over rocks.

We moved quickly, following an earthern path upwards. Occasionally there was a view across to the far side of the valley where the trees were becoming greener and taller. In the dry season, when the plain had dessicated and yellowed under the breath of the cold wind, the mountain retained its water and animals retreated to its slopes.

After an hour we began to descend towards the river once more, and eventually, after passing through stands of bamboo, emerged beside a deep dark pool surrounded by cliffs. The youth whispered something in Gujarati and we crept across a rocky ledge to an overhang in the rock. Glass bangles had been hung in the small trees that clung to the stone and there were red tridents painted on the cliff-face – the mark of Shiva. The idol was red, too, and shawled in silk; the ledge in front of him was carpeted with broken coconut shells. The youth prayed to the stone god for a long time and I waited, gazing out at the beauty of the forest and rocks. When he had finished, he led me around the edge of the water, gesticulating that there was something in the pool, some creature, and we should take care.

On the far side we scrambled up the smooth sides of huge boulders and then claimed a lookout point from a family of monkeys. Behind us was a cave where, according to local legend, the Pandava brothers had hidden. Red leaves were scattered on the ground below like spent firecrackers. An eagle glided over and butterflies settled in the warm fingers of sunlight that broke through the trees. It was that fleeting moment of balanced perfection when the coiled chills of the night are undone, and rise, twisting in the sun. My guide had gone up into the trees, collecting fallen fruits to gnaw on; I could hear him singing to himself, and then he had moved so far that there was only silence. On the far side of the pool, I saw a slow movement. A large crocodile, perhaps eight feet in length, slid gently from his rocky ledge into the water. There was scarcely a ripple, his eyes remained above the surface for a moment, then with a swirl he had gone. I climbed down to the water's edge, to see if I could catch a second glimpse, and found myself on a small muddy beach. In the soft ground close to the water was a single paw mark.

I stood very still. The animal, a lion or leopard, had been here recently, probably climbing by the same route from the smooth boulder above. There had been various droppings up there, some no doubt from the monkeys, but the big cat might enjoy the warmth of the rock beneath his belly in the late afternoon. This was an undisturbed place where such pleasures could be taken. The animal would look out over the water and the shrine where men came to make their offerings. This was the India whose existence I had thought was confined to books, long since banished by the rising tide of humanity and economic development; the India of sparkling rivers, mysterious jungle and memories of legendary heroes, an India where lions moved out of National Parks to be near the villages and where the advice 'Just stand still' seemed to be purest wisdom distilled from centuries of tranquillity.

There was a thud behind me. I yelped in surprise and leapt around to find Raghu grinning from ear to ear and pointing excitedly at the water.

'Magar! Magar!'

I turned again, in time to see the swirl of water as the crocodile disappeared once more.

We left him in peace and continued upwards, stopping every few hundred yards at a shrine. Then Raghu would slip off his shoes, kneel before the idol and press his hands together in prayer. Each place marked some event recorded in the *Mahabharata*: where the Pandavas slept, or lit a fire, or faced some terrible foe. At the top of the pass was the Bor Devi Temple where we rang the bell and some boys ran out from a hut to greet us. In this simple temple, a few years ago, a silver box was found inside a copper box inside an earthern pot on which a seal of King Rudradama was made in the second century AD. An inscription discovered nearby records the monarch's achievements in the use of sword and shield, management of elephants and banishing snakes. His treasury, it reads, 'overflows with the accumulation of gold, silver, diamonds, beryl stones and other precious things'.

All around were soaring mountain peaks and a valley led through them towards Girnar Mountain itself, the temples on the summit gleaming in the sunshine. It was hot now and the dust was rising. Under the trees were the blackened ashes of hundreds of fires lit by pilgrims who come once a year to walk the stories of the paths. The landscape had threaded the great narrative into itself, each page become a stopping place, the word become stone, water and wood. Here the pilgrim could move in the footsteps of the great heroes: Arjuna, Bhim, Yudhishthir and Krishna. The man-god with blue skin had struggled with demons here, perhaps had tracked the cave bear on his way east, then fought for twenty-one days before the Syamantaka jewel was given back. Krishna had then returned to Dwarka and restored the diamond to Sattrajit. But jealousies had been ignited and Sattrajit was murdered by another who escaped with the jewel. Although Krishna chased and killed the murderer, the diamond had disappeared, falling into the hands of a good citizen, Akrura. For many years, the town prospered due to the hidden presence of the jewel. 'Through the virtue of that gem,' say the Puranas, 'there was no dearth or pestilence in the whole country.' At the end of this period, however, Akrura was forced to move away and various calamities immediately befell the city, so much so that the coincidence was noticed and Akrura encouraged to return. When he did, the disasters stopped. Krishna then knew who possessed the jewel and invited Akrura to confirm the fact before the tribal assembly.

'Akrura drew forth, from his garments, a small gold box, and took from it the jewel . . . the whole chamber where they sat was illuminated by its radiance.'

Krishna was now called on to adjudicate as to the rightful ownership: 'This jewel . . . should be taken charge of by a person who leads a life of perpetual continence. If worn by an impure individual, it will be the cause of his death.' So saying, Krishna returned the diamond to Akrura, the only one present worthy of the jewel – Krishna ruled himself out on account of his 16,000 wives. 'And Akrura moved about like the sun, wearing a garland of light.'

There is little doubt that many of such tales recorded by the Puranas and *Mahabharata* are based on actual events that occurred between 700 BC and 1000 BC. Archaeological evidence suggests the great war between the Pandavas and Kauravas took place around 900 BC and actual sites for the cities mentioned have been proposed. However, the stories were constantly added to and altered, making them unreliable sources on life in ancient India. The legend of a great jewel, capable of working wonders, also appears in Muslim stories of Noah, who is said to have given a magical inscribed jewel to his son, Japhet. Perhaps this was the source of Sir John Mandeville's pronouncements on the attributes of the diamond – 'it protects him from quarrels, fights, debauchery, and from evil dreams and fantasies.' Whatever the origin, the great liar who is supposed never to have left fourteenth-century St Albans certainly managed to capture the essence of the Syamantaka stone with astounding accuracy.

As for the treasures of King Rudradama, they may lie buried somewhere in the mountains or, more probably, they moved on, until the memory of their origin was also lost.

A few miles beyond Bor Devi we passed a lone sadhu, his hair matted and caked with mud, smoking cannabis in a clay pipe and muttering to himself. The end of the track was the gateway at the foot of Girnar Mountain, the place I had passed through on Christmas Day. Raghu took me down the road a short distance and showed me the Damodar Kund, a pool whose waters are said to dissolve the bones of the dead. Behind it was a temple where we squeezed through a tiny door and crawled into a cupboard-size cave. According to one legend, Krishna slew a demoness on the same spot.

Once we reached Junagadh town, Bilkha met us in the jeep and we drove around visiting the Nawab's other palaces and guesthouses: vast overgrown gardens where Bilkha pointed out tumbledown roofs – 'That was the squash courts and over there a swimming pool. This was the cinema hall he built for his wives and mother.'

The ornate pavilion architecture was long-neglected, streaked with rust and algae, broken and forlorn. Where once the hothouse had stood was now jungle. Panthers had been seen. The water filtration plant was broken: in the Nawab's time the town had drunk clean water. The lake where lotus flowers had blossomed was choked with thick green slime, parts of it filled with rubbish on which shanty slums had sprung up. In many of the old palace grounds, new concrete blocks had been brutally forced in front – the new masters stamping their identity on the old. When Independence came, Bilkha told me, there had been extensive forests in the area which the people had then gone out and chopped down. The carcasses of wild animals were dumped on his family's doorstep, as if to say: 'You can't stop us now!' It was an understandable reaction but disastrous for the environment. Now he saw signs of hope: the teak forests were returning, the lions and deer, too.

For the architectural heritage, however, it was probably too late. Shambhubhai's son, Harish, had told me how he had rescued a small piece of carved panelling, part of an entire traditional Gujarati facade thrown on a builder's rubbish heap. In other parts of India, traditional doors and windows were being torn out for sale to tourists, but here even that limited salvation was yet to appear. After some supper with an architect friend of his, Bilkha asked if I was ready to meet the Nawab's last Indian relatives. I nodded.

We drove up through the modern part of town, across the railway and into the older part, parking in a square near the strange old graveyard that I had discovered on my first day in Junagadh. The streets were jammed with rickshaws, people and pigs. The mosque on the street corner, like most city mosques in India, seemed to be floating on a raft of small, brightly-lit shops, all selling cheap watches and clothes. Children played cricket amongst the traffic with a stone for a ball. There were very few cafés or tea shops, so people tended to walk, meeting friends on the street. Over the whitewashed wall, gloomily unlit, the nawabs' graveyard sat at the centre of it all, its gothic domes covered in boils and crazed arabesques, trees sprouting from its cornices, the black stains of its stonework ready to grow into hideous faces for any child who dared look.

A few steps from the main thoroughfare, the noise died and the lights faded. Behind the graveyard there was a large old house with a high arched gateway. We passed inside and stepped through a door to our right. Ahead was a darkened courtyard filled with fallen masonry and broken fragments of elegant stucco. Against the night sky I could see the jagged edges where parts of a first floor arcade had been ruined. Some of the lower arches had been filled with cheap mud bricks or breeze blocks.

'These rooms are rented out or sold off,' said Bilkha. 'The family will be upstairs.'

We took a stone flight of steps up and at the top came to a huge antique wooden door. Bilkha called out and someone answered. The door swung open to reveal a scruffy roof terrace with a sitting area. A face peered around at us, a thin bird-like man with straight lank hair and intelligent eyes, dressed in shirt and trousers. The noise of families squabbling and shouting in the lower rooms came up to us. We stepped inside.

'Welcome, welcome,' said the bird-like man. 'Please – my brother.'

The last Indian heir to the throne of Junagadh was lying on an iron bedstead smoking a cigarette. There was a thin dirty curtain over a doorway beyond and on the walls two old photographs showing young men with dead leopards, the only reminder of former glories. He struggled up and greeted us, then sank into an armchair with a sigh. His speech was slurred and his memory vague.

'Are you . . . hum . . . so you came, Bilkha . . . and a friend.'

The younger brother brought chairs and we sat while he fussed around. 'You know, my brother is the rightful heir to the Nawabs of Junagadh. We have some disputes – land here in town. I'm currently trying to . . . but the legal process is very slow.'

'We were at Raj Kumar together,' said the Last Heir, rousing himself to offer me a beedi and light one himself. 'Bilkha and I.'

He meant the Princes' College in Rajkot, one of a small number of premier schools set up by the British in order to produce brown-skinned Old Etonians: men capable of playing bridge, running small principalities and discriminating between jelly bowls and chamber pots. The Last Heir became quite distant and misty-eyed as he recalled the good old days. 'Do you remember Rogerson? He wrote to our father, "Your son is a stylish stroke player."'

'Very good opening batsman, my brother,' said the younger man, his head pecking forwards, like a sycophantic aide-de-camp, eager to flatter. 'Fine stroke player.'

The Last Heir was murmuring about an innings against Mayo College. It was a shock to realise that these two men had been con-temporaries of Bilkha; he sat beside them, smiling and pleasant, in good health with a sharp mind and neatly attired in new Levis, loafers and polo shirt. He was every inch the modern successful Indian, while they were scraping a living in the ruins of the past.

'Our ancestor was the Nawab's brother,' explained Last Heir But One. 'When they passed him over, he disputed it. The case went all the way to your Privy Council. Our ancestor is buried here in the maqbara.' He meant the graveyard we had passed on our way in.

I pointed at the photographs. 'And this is a relative of yours?'

The Last Heir snorted. 'It is me!'

Last Heir But One smiled. 'Yes, look, come look.'

I got up to be given a tour of the picture collection.

'This is myself with a leopard. It was at Kalwar Chowk, very close to town. Of course, hunting was very popular with us ruling families.' There was a young handsome man crouched with a rifle beside the corpse of a big cat. We moved on to the second, and last photograph. Like a bankrupt millionaire rattling the small change in his pockets, he took pleasure in the remnants of the royal life. 'And here is my brother – rightful claimant, as I said previously.'

'Did you know the Nawab very well?' I asked.

The Last Heir moved uneasily and his brother answered. 'We were not keeping on good terms with His Highness.'

'He visited us once at this house,' said the Last Heir, 'when our father died. Otherwise there were some problems because of our claim.' Naturally, the Nawab would hardly have smiled upon those who disputed his position.

'Can you remember his visit?' I asked. 'What was the Nawab like?'

But the Last Heir became vague. He could not recall anything about the visit or the Nawab.

We were interrupted by the clatter of feet on the steps outside and the door being thrown back. A youth came bursting in and came directly over to me, staring. I sensed the disapproval of the Last Heir But One.

'Say "How do you do?"' he commanded, rolling his eyes in exasperation for my benefit.

'What is your country?' was all the youth managed, after some thought. He could have been any streetcorner layabout.

The Last Heir But One let out a gasp of irritation. 'Hah! Look – no education. What are they doing but playing cricket all day long! You should pay attention to your masters like your father did at Raj Kumar.'

As all the father could recall of school was cricket, this seemed a little harsh, and the son had obviously long ago stopped hearing the favourite homilies of his uncle. He slouched away to be with his friends on the street, leaving an awkward silence behind him. Perhaps we were all reflecting on the flimsy and insubstantial veneer that separates the prince from the people, a veneer buttressed with vast genealogies, legend and wealth, yet one that could be torn down in one generation.

'It is not easy,' said the Last Heir But One, 'to be Royal and adjust to this democratic way of life.' I reminded myself that 1948 was fifty years away.

He picked up a parcel of papers and documents that had been lying on the bed. 'If you will excuse me, I have to go, but if you would like to return later – shall we say 9 for 9.30? Then we can talk more. It would be interesting for you – I think you would like to know more history – I can show you some documents.'

He left us to chat with his brother, a task that soon dispirited even Bilkha's capacity for good humour. Eventually we took our leave of the Last Heir and went down the steps. When we were out on the street, Bilkha explained how, after their father's death, the sons had frittered away their inheritance, selling off lands and houses and failing to adapt to a new role as businessmen or government officers in the new India.

We wandered on through the streets, rejoining the main thoroughfare.

'You mentioned Bhatt Studio,' said Bilkha. 'Do you wish to see it? The true one?'

'You mean there is more than one?'

'Correct.'

We strolled along in the road: the pavement was impassable with deep potholes, broken drains and tangles of motor scooters and bicycles. The second Bhatt Studio proved to be close to the first but far older: I saw instantly that this was the place I had been searching for at the very beginning of my time in Junagadh. Bilkha left me at the door, having arranged to meet later.

Inside, the walls were plastered with dozens of black-and-white photographs showing scenes from the Nawab's life and the arrival of Indian troops. It was all there: the Nawab, sleek and plump, with his dogs and at his own wedding (no canine wedding albums, unfortunately); various British viceroys in pith helmets standing over dead lions; Bhutto looking Machiavellian and austere; Brigadier Gurdial Singh, who led the invasion, with a panther he had shot near Ramnat Temple. The old photographer had indeed died, but his brother was keeping the place open as a sort of museum. Dusty negatives hung from wires above our heads and bits of antique photographic equipment stood in the corners. Mr Bhatt showed me the letter of appointment, making his brother official court photographer, then box after box of prints. At the bottom of one was a newspaper cutting of an old Dakota plane landing.

'That was the Nawab's aircraft,' he confirmed. 'The one he left for Pakistan in.'

And with it, I reflected, had gone the secret of the Junagadh treasure.

[169]

By the time I came to return through the old town towards the ruined house, shops were closing up for the night and there were fewer people around. I passed through the archway and up the steps to the door. There was no answer to my knock. I went back down into the ruined courtyard, a dog slunk away from me. Last Heir But One was coming in. 'Do they not answer?' he said. 'Please, come on up.'

We went up the steps and across the terrace to the ragged curtain. Behind it was a door which led into a dark kitchen. I could make out a clutter of pots and pans, then a table with a stout man in a night shirt stretched out fast asleep on it. The newspaper over his face was rising and falling with his snores. We squeezed past a wardrobe and some broken chairs, through a door and along a grubby narrow corridor. There was no lamp, only the reflections of moonlight to find the way. 'Here,' said Last Heir But One, 'but take care some steps are missing – why can't they repair – ah! It's very difficult.'

He had started up a ramshackle stairway that clung to the crumbling wall. Far below I could see a courtyard filled with rubbish; the stars wheeled above me; the handrail moved when I touched it. There were battered doors with panels missing that led to empty space. I kept as close to the wall as possible, feeling the timbers shift and bend. Then we came out on the roof and the vast vault of the night sky opened out in glittering perfection. Last Heir But One led the way across to a rundown pavilion in the centre. I stopped to look over the parapet at the city, but there was nothing: the neighbourhood lights were just a few dim bulbs.

'My den,' he laughed. 'Peace and quiet, mmm? Not easy, but I have my reading and studies and so on.' He spoke as though he was a teenager rather than a middle-aged man. We climbed some steps to a door and he unlocked it and went inside.

It must have once been a comfortable hideaway on the roof but now it had fallen into disrepair. The nicotine-stained ceiling was coming away in huge sheets, hanging down in a parody of the punkahs that had once wafted the princely personages. There was a curtain shielding the iron bed, piles of dusty old books and a couple of car seats beside a table. He put his papers down and fussed around.

'Coffee? Yes, we must. I'll round up a couple of cups. Do you take milk and sugar – because I'm afraid I'm right out of them.'

I sat on the car seat and looked out his window, a small peephole that gave a view down to the front archway. No one could enter or leave without being observed from up here. The wall next to the window had been covered in newspaper and there was a single photograph of an aristocratic man in Achkan coat and turban.

'My father,' he said, returning with a flask and two glasses, 'You see what great dignity he had.' And his voice was so filled with regret and sadness that I was suddenly and acutely aware of the pain he felt. Perhaps their circumstances were the result of foolish business agreements but, nevertheless, to be so low after such heights, unable even to find milk and sugar for a guest's coffee.

He sat down and opened the file of papers. 'This is our case,' he said. 'Look, you read and you will see. There is some land and you see it was given, freely given, but this fellow is saying it is his. Now we will get this land and sell it. It's down by the old city wall. The money will be useful, we can do some repairs and so on.'

I tried to make sense of what I was reading: a judgement from the Privy Council dated 1847. Even Dickens, in his bleakest moments, cannot have contemplated a case dragging on as long as this in the Victorian courts of Chancery. The judgement had awarded the family eight villages and some lands around Junagadh State as compensation for the rejection of their claim to the throne. It was their refusal to accept the finality of this that had held them back, always hoping that some quirk of fate would restore their position. The case was obviously of fiendish complexity, not only beyond my powers of comprehension but perhaps anyone's.

'I have my father's books,' he said, pushing his glasses back into his hair with a rather feminine gesture. 'I am reading the *History of Persia* – of course, he spoke Persian very nice.'

He began on a long monologue about the land dispute and how their family had come so low. Words of Urdu crept in and the obsessive tone of a man consumed by one ambition – to restore this last fragment of the family land and so the family fortunes. I had no grasp of the case but could see from the man that it was a lost cause. His talk moved on to the CIA and KGB plots, of corruption and spies. He went back through the curtain, still talking, rummaging around for a book.

'You want to know about the Nawab? His things? Most were left behind and stolen, or sold off. They held auctions of it. Look, here it is.'

He came back with a book which he read to me in a stage voice.

'The Banesinghji of Wankaner was present when Bhutto turned away V.P. Menom, Sardar Patel and Jam Singhji. He was wearing a green coat and smoking a cigar and Patel told him, "This state will go to the dogs."' He broke off, smiling. 'The Nawab had over 800 dogs and each with a human attendant.'

'Was he eccentric?'

'Oh no, nothing like that!'

I had a fair idea of what he thought I had implied.

'Bhutto held the Nawab a virtual prisoner in the palace.'

'Then did Bhutto steal the treasures?'

'Who knows? He had opportunity, just as many did. They took truckloads of things away which were never seen again. My own brother saw seven go off to Bombay.'

'What were the treasures? Were there diamonds?'

'Yes, everything was there. We ruling families had everything in those days.'

'So who took the diamonds?'

But he was not interested in treasures that could be carted away. Land was surely more difficult to steal. Another Privy Council judgement, this time from 1922, was put under my nose. I guessed that this was the source of friction between the brothers' father and the Nawab. No sooner had this document confused me than he presented me with a letter from a zoologist commending his work with the lions of the Girnar.

'Yes, I did much fieldwork with the foreign scientists. Mating behaviour.' His eyes twinkled mischievously. 'No one had studied it before, especially the frequency of having sex.'

If diamonds were the jewel that rulers coveted, then big cats were the animals they admired; in Junagadh that meant lions. Every notable had to shoot one. Now they were reduced to studying the remnants, counting their copulations for foreign scientists.

'Have you been attacked by a lion?'

'I was charged three times by leopards. You keep still, but if it keeps coming, you stand aside. Did you know the lion's penis is very small? For sperm collection, they have a new method where an electrode is put up the lion's rectum and his penis comes up immediately. It's true!'

I moved nervously. 'What was it you were saying about the Nawab?'

'I don't remember.'

'Was he superstitious? Did he have astrologers?'

I was keen to keep off the subject of lions' rectums.

'All of them were superstitious. When were you born?'

I told him and he began to write out the numbers, adding digits together. 'You see. Nine here. Nine is important. One ruler had a bed that played nine tunes. I think 1975 to 79 was bad for you. You know the male doesn't eat when he is having sex – not for eight days.' He leaned forward, his long, oiled hair gleaming and glasses pushed back on his forehead.

'So are there good years to come?'

'It is that small.' He held out a finger, the nail was very long and curved.

I stood up. 'I have to go now.'

'No, no. Take more coffee.'

'Thank you but I arranged to meet Bilkha. Is that him down there?'

He sprang forward to look out the little window. 'There is no one.'

'He went around the corner.' Then I started for the door and clattered out onto the roof, where I stood gazing at the stars and waiting for him to follow. Eventually he emerged.

'I was just tidying those papers away,' he said, padlocking the door which a small child could have reduced to matchwood in a few seconds. 'Very important papers.'

We returned via the rickety stairs, edging past the snoring kitchen table, and then pausing to shake hands and say goodbye under the front archway.

'If we get our lands back, we will make some money and knock this old palace down to build a concrete block,' he said, revealing the family habit of misjudgement. In other parts of India, former nobles were refurbishing old houses into fashionable hotels and, with some investment, this house could have been beautiful, too. Even at the last, Junagadh seemed blighted, destined to destroy the very last traces of its past.

I left him in the dark archway and walked past the grotesque grave-yard for the last time. When I glanced up at the domes, I saw a figure on the parapet, a young lad, naked but for a scrap of loincloth, standing with his arms by his sides and staring down at me. I stopped. The boy did not move, just stared, never blinking. The image of the god on Palitana hill was in my mind: that stone idol who stared back. After a few moments, I turned my head away and walked briskly down towards the light.

Two days later, Bilkha brought me to the station in the jeep in time for the night express train to Ahmedabad. As we walked onto the plat-form a youth slipped in alongside me and started talking: 'Hey man, are you US. Male?'

I saw Bilkha smiling. A door had closed: I was on the outside, on my own again.

'English! Wow! My eyes have popped off! Can I practising my idioms on you? No skin off your nose? I love English idioms. Maybe if the cookie crumbles, we can be strapping friends.'

'A mate worse than death,' I thought, but he was not travelling, just seeing a friend off.

Ahmedabad next morning was an insufferable filthy mess after the birdsong and peace of Bilkha. I spent only one night and set off to Udaipur in Rajasthan, heading north towards the fort at Chittor where I would pick up the thread of the Koh-i-Noor story.

On the bus to the fort, I was interrogated by an old man who intro-duced himself as a historian.

'Who were the eleven great men of the twentieth century?'

I failed miserably in my guesses, so he reminded me.

'Churchill, Russell, Montgomery, Maynard Keynes, Shaw, Huxley, Toynbee, Askey . . .'

'Askey? Arthur Askey?!'

'Laski: L-A-S-K-I. Then Wells and Bonar Law.'

The man's head was enormous, and when he turned to me it seemed to be not a face at all, but an ambiguous collection of rheumy crevices and crinkles, disintegrating as the bus bounced. Only the sticking plaster on his glasses held it all together.

'CAPITAL OF SUDAN?' he barked.

'Khartoum. I was there in . . .'

'FASHODA INCIDENT – YEAR AND SIGNIFICANCE?'

'1890s, was it? The division of colonial Africa.'

He was impressed and his voice dropped to a whisper. 'Capital of Chad?'

'Ndjamena.'

Louder. 'Formerly?'

'Fort Lamy.'

Louder still. 'And Lamy was?'

'Er . . . a French general?'

'CAPITAL OF MAURETANIA? MAIN PRODUCTS, ETHNIC GROUPS, LAN-GUAGES, AND COLONIAL POWER?'

I faltered. 'Spain, was it? They might speak Berber.'

The rheumy wrinkles rearranged themselves into a smile. 'Spiffing. Absolutely spiffing. All completely wrong.' He had won. 'Do they say that still – in England? Mr Hardcastle used to.'

'They do,' I assured him.

The smile deepened. 'Good, good,' he said. 'You see, I am the last of my kind. Born and bred under the British. The new generation know nothing and have no dignity. Look at this.' He pulled his pom-pom hat back up his head to reveal an impressively smooth and shiny pate, a bizarre contrast to the rest of his face.

'That is the mirror of the soul where a man's life is written. I judge all men by what I see here.'

I pushed my hair back.

'A noble forehead.'

I warmed to the old curmudgeon. 'Do you study Indian history?'

He pointed downwards. 'This very place. This soil that has OUR BLOOD, our Rajput blood soaked through it so many times. What other study is necessary?' His hand grasped my knee; like synchron-ised caterpillars, the wrinkles on his face reassembled themselves into a frown. 'TWELVE GREAT HISTORIANS?'

'Tacitus?'

'No, no. Apart from Tacitus, there was one great historian and the other eleven are forgotten.'

'Marx.'

'And Marx.'

'Gibbon.'

'Apart from Tacitus, Marx and Gibbon – who was the only great historian?'

'Toynbee?'

He shook his jowls. 'The first historian – is Colonel James Tod. He is remembered because his prose is better than poetry.' He began to quote from memory. '"Historic truth has, in all countries, been sacrificed to national vanity: to its gratification every obstacle is made to give way; fictions become facts, and even religious prejudices vanish in this mirage of the imagination."'

He grinned. 'Got it? *Annals and Antiquities of Rajas'than* – the finest history book. Right. Tod was born in Scotland in 1782 and came to India with the Company in 1800. In 1818 he came here to Rajasthan and made peace between the rulers.'

As he spoke I realised that this stooped and broken old man was the possessor of an astonishing memory. Every detail of Tod's life with exact dates and names was set before me. 'Tod came here, to Chittor, and he was so absorbed by what he saw that he forgot to eat all day, then asked his servant why his shadow was long. He couldn't believe it was sunset!'

The place itself had now appeared on the horizon, a long flat-topped mountain with vertical crags all around. It was immediately obvious why this impressive natural site had been a critical stronghold throughout history.

'Alauddin Khilji had to take Chittor because it was the home of Rajput valour,' he declared.

I tried to ask a question and he held up his hand to silence me. 'WAIT! In 1303 Khilji came here when the king was Radan Sen whose wife was Padmini. Radan Sen called on the sons of one Laxman Singh to fight and six of them died. Thirty years later the grandson of Laxman Singh, Hamir, retook Chittor for the Rajputs and proved the Turk was not invincible – that was a great service performed BY MY ANCESTOR.'

He sat back smiling.

Alauddin Khilji had come at the start of a series of conquests that would make the first Indian empire. Legend has it that the attack on Chittor was motivated by a desire to seize Radan Sen's wife, Padmini, a noted beauty. During the siege Alauddin is said to have been allowed up into the fort to see Padmini for a second, her beauty revealed by a system of mirrors.

'My dear friend,' said the old man when I asked about this, 'that is all pure humbug got up by the poet Jaisi, 200 years later. Khilji was after loot. He sent his eunuch Malik Kafur to the Deccan again and again – more and more loot till he got the diamond.'

'Which diamond?'

'The Koh-i-Noor. Have you read Khusraw? He is our great poet – *Nuh Siphir* – the Nine Skies?'

He shook his rheumy wrinkles in despair at my headshake. 'Pah! Education. Khusraw was living in Alauddin's time. Let me remember.' He thought for a moment, then quoted. '"Rai Ladhar Deo shut himself inside the fort, like a snake over buried treasure but the Emperor's prestige overawed him. All his courage melted away and he was left a broken man."'

'That was at Warangal. Kafur took the jewel north and presented it to Alauddin at Delhi.'

As the name Koh-i-Noor only came into existence in 1739, the old man's account was speculative. However, given the almost magnetic attraction that great Indian rulers had for large diamonds, it seems highly probable that Alauddin Khilji did possess the stone. Like many who would follow, his ambitions had grown wilder in the hot and humid south: al-Barani says he wanted to found a new religion with himself as prophet. His was the first Indian empire, but his success was fleeting: his trusted eunuch Malik Kafur seized power in 1315 and Alauddin died, helpless as his empire disintegrated.

The bus was entering the modern town and the historian gave me his address. 'Come and see me. I am old and will not be here much longer. India is changing,' he added sadly. 'There are no giants now, only mediocrity.'

At the bus station his relatives were waiting to collect him and we said goodbye. As I moved away, he called after me: 'Capital of Mauretania is Nouakchott! Main products: iron, copper and fish! Learn it by heart and that will be SPIFFING!'

I walked through the modern town to the foot of the hill and the first gate – the gate of the sun. After a long steady climb up the zig-zagging road, I reached the top and wandered around the magnificent ruins. Scattered in the long dry grass were fragments of exquisite carvings and friezes. In one temple I noticed the central column had four capitols of naked devadasis to hold the roof aloft, but one was missing – I had seen it lying in the grass half a mile away. Walls blazed with suns, dancers and lines of fat ducks; then there was Padmini's palace with its windows to sit and sigh in and a mirror, placed so the tourists could pretend to be Alauddin.

The princess herself is said to have led the Rajput women to the funeral pyre when defeat was certain. 'The fair Pudmani closed the throng,' wrote Tod, 'which was augmented by whatever of female beauty or youth could be tainted by the Tatar lust. They were conveyed to the cavern, and the opening closed upon them, leaving them to find security from dishonour in the devouring element.'

In the troubled times that followed Alauddin's own death, the diamond fell into the hands of a Rajput dynasty whose stronghold was the fortress of Gwalior, south of Agra. It was there that I travelled next, spending a morning admiring the vast stone statues cut into the cliff face by Jain masons, then walking up to the fort with a party of sports teachers from Ladakh. In the mid-afternoon, the town all asleep, I took a train on to Agra. The great diamond that Alauddin had brought from the south had come this way too: on a fateful day in the spring of 1526, the ruler of Gwalior, Maharaja Bikramajit, had placed his family and his jewels for safe-keeping in Agra, then headed north with the army of the Delhi Sultan, Ibrahim Lodi. Neither of them ever came back. A new and decisive force had marched forward to take its place in Indian history, and the great diamond would move again, flying with ruthless speed to its new masters.

It was getting late in the afternoon when I arrived in Agra, and by the time I had found a hotel the light was fading fast. I pulled on my jacket against the cold air and took a bicycle rickshaw down to the Yamuna River. To our right was Agra Fort with its white marble terraces and balconies looking downriver to the Taj Mahal, but we turned upstream, fighting across the bridge against a flood of bullock carts, motorbikes and poisonous buses. The sun was a deep red disc sinking behind the city while shoppers hurried home. We passed the tomb of Itimad-ud-Daula and some nurseries, then stopped at a crossroads. I paid off the driver and crossed over. There was a factory on the corner belching thick black fumes from a metal chimney, and a few hundred yards past it, I saw a turning to the left, down towards the river.

There was a shack on the street where a thin elderly man was brewing tea on a charcoal stove.

'*Aram Bagh?*' I asked. '*Babur bagh?*'

He waved down the side street and I noticed that there was a gate at the end with a kiosk. Behind it were trees and the dusty purple shadows of night. A man was locking up, and I ran down to him.

'Excuse me! Is this Aram Bagh? Babur's garden?'

'Most certainly,' he said, smiling. He was dressed in a home-knit sweater with grey trousers, his moustache flecked with grey. One of those Indian men who, by dint of early hardships, seem to reach middle age at thirty. 'Are you wishing to see it?'

'Yes, please.'

He delved inside his kiosk and brought out a torch. 'We are closing, but since you are Englishman and the number one to visit for some long times, I take you.'

We set out across the grass, passing the tamarind and ashok trees. I could feel the dampness of the river ahead. In the grass were sandstone channels cutting the area into exact squares. One of these we followed, up some steps to a square white marble pool. In the centre of this was a dais, accessible by a marble bridge.

Everything was dry. A hundred yards or so to the right I could see a ruined well-tower where the water would have been lifted to set all this alive, running and gurgling with dancing shallow waters.

The caretaker went off to check something, and I stepped across the marble bridge onto the dais, then sat cross-legged facing the river. The sun had set and there was only a faint warm glow to the open spaces, as though the dust, pressed by the shadows, had now begun to ooze a veiled and secretive phosphorescence. Bats cut the sky between dark masses of trees. I felt the cold stone under me.

This was a garden, but not one of plants, rather of water. And now it was dead, the channels kept clear and dry like a mummified body drained of its blood. In my mind I saw the water rising from the well, pulled by oxen, then come surging along the channel parallel to the river below, picking up fallen leaves and sticks that boys had thrown. Then it turned, pouring into the pool around me, then onwards, down notched inclines that made the water dance away into the garden.

When the first Mughal, Babur, had arrived in India, he had come to this spot and ordered a garden to be laid out. He was thinking of the eight-fold gardens of Paradise, the Char-bagh, in Kabul, and wondering how he could survive in this pestilential land. 'We crossed the Jun-water [Yamuna] to look at garden-grounds a few days after entering Agra. Those grounds were so bad and unattractive that we traversed them with a hundred disgusts and repulsions. So ugly and displeasing were they, that the idea of making a Char-bagh in them passed from my mind, but needs must! as there was no other land near Agra, that same ground was taken in hand a few days later.'

His cushion would have been put on the cold stone on the very spot where I sat, and he passed many hours here, pining for the mountain air and composing poetry.

> My heart, like the bud of the red, red rose,
>   Lies fold within fold aflame;
> Would the breath of even a myriad Springs
>   Blow my heart's bud to a rose?

India, understandably expecting the worst of its invaders, had hooked a very different fish to Babur's ancestor Tamurlane.

Babur had reached Panipat to the north of Delhi in April, 1526. Facing his men were the armies of Sultan Ibrahim Lodi, 100,000 soldiers stiffened by one thousand war elephants, and these were terrifying armoured beasts trained to gore and trample. Babur had only 10,000 men but he had the latest in military kit – guns. With his mounted archers raining arrows from both sides and cannonballs tearing into the ranks, Babur won the day. The Sultan was killed and later found in a heap of his own dead numbering 6,000 men. A further 10,000, some chroniclers said 45,000, lay all around.

Immediately the battle was won, Babur's son Humayun was sent to ride on Agra and throw a ring of soldiers around the city to prevent any escape. Babur records what happened. 'In Sultan Ibrahim's defeat the Raja of Gualiar Bikramajit the Hindu had gone to hell. Bikramajit's children and family were in Agra at the time of Ibrahim's defeat. When Humayun reached Agra, they must have been planning to flee, but his postings of men (to watch the roads) prevented this and guard was kept over them. Humayun himself did not let them go. They made him voluntary offering of a mass of jewels and valuables amongst which was the famous diamond which Alau'u'd-din must have brought. Its reputation is that every appraiser has estimated its value at two and a half days' food for the whole world. Apparently it weighs 8 misquals.'

Babur kept very little of the wealth he had liberated, preferring to shower gifts on those around him. 'The treasure of five kings fell into his hands,' wrote his daughter, Gulbadan, 'He just gave it away.' Even his family in Kabul were not forgotten, each receiving, 'One special dancing girl of the dancing girls of Sultan Ibrahim, one gold plate full of jewels, ruby and pearls, diamonds and carnelian, emerald and turquoise, topaz and cat's eye.' Of diamonds he cared little, and when his son offered him the greatest diamond in the world, Babur recollected, 'I just gave it him back.'

Like Krishna before him, Babur was ennobled by his own generosity, though the diamond did not bring good fortune to Humayun. Longing to return to the Afghan homelands, he drifted into the habit of using opium and in mid-1530 he fell seriously ill. When all medical advice failed, Babur decided to offer his own life in place of his son's. Those around the emperor begged him to offer the great diamond, but Babur refused; besides, he had already given it away – the sacrifice had to be something of value to him. He began to walk around Humayun's bed, praying, 'I, who am Babur, give my life and my being for Humayun.'

According to the memoirs of Princess Gulbadan, the effect was instant: Babur took to his bed while Humayun began to recover. Within a few weeks, the emperor was dead. His body was taken to the garden in Agra, then to Kabul where he was buried in one of the ten terraced gardens he had laid out. There was no building over his grave – as he had requested – so he could be closer to the snow-capped peaks and the sound of the twelve waterfalls.

After Babur's demise, Humayun ruled fitfully, perhaps because of his opium habit. Within ten years he was defeated and put to flight. Together with a small band of followers and his immediate family, he rode into the deserts of Rajasthan. The danger of betrayal and death was all around them: local warlords gathered like vultures at the kill, waiting to see what spoils might be served up. It was well-known that Humayun possessed the great diamond and one raja, Rao Maldeo of Jodhpur, is said to have ridden into the Mughal camp, posing as a merchant who wanted to buy the jewel.

He found Humayun counting amber beads and in optimistic mood: an eagle had shaded him with its wings while he slept in the sun – a good omen. It was then that Maldeo's offer to buy the stone drew the famous response: 'Such precious gems cannot be bought; either they fall to one by the arbitrament of the flashing sword which is an expression of the divine will, or else they come through the grace of mighty monarchs.'

Soon after this a son was born and named Akbar. The astrologers predicted a great future for him, but things were to get considerably worse for the father. Abandoned by all his allies, he was forced to ride towards Persia with little more in his pocket than the diamond and a few Badakshan spinels, rare ruby-like gemstones.

It was a desperate gamble: the ruler of Persia, Shah Tahmasp, had fought Babur for Samarkand, and the reception Humayun would receive was uncertain. In fact, the Shah treated him like a visiting emperor, showering gifts and honours. His plan was to get Humayun to convert to his own Shi'ite branch of Islam, then support a reconquest of India – for the Shi'ites. After several months of negotiation, Humayun agreed. However, to be so much in the debt of the Shah was not to his liking and he offered a gift: a small decorated box; inside were the spinels and Babur's diamond.

With the support of the Shah's cavalry, Humayun did recover his kingdom. In July 1555 he sat on the throne at Delhi once again, but only six months later he was dead, fatally injured in a fall. A lifelong student of astrology, he had been on the roof of the octagonal tower he used as a library, observing the rising of Venus – the planet, as he would have known, that corresponded to the diamond in Hindu cosmology.

*

The caretaker returned, banging his torch which worked only inter-mittently. I followed him along the riverbank and then back into the garden. At a certain place I stopped, noticing a flight of stone steps that led down through a tangle of thorn bushes.

'What is down here?'

The caretaker turned. 'It is too dark.'

'But what is it?'

At my insistence he began pulling the thorn bushes aside. 'Babur is sleeping down here,' he said, as though we were about to stumble on the emperor himself, snoozing after a boozing session with his favourite nobles. 'He likes this place too much.' The caretaker's ignor-ance of the past tense was weaving a subtle magic, as though the distant events were somehow trapped by his lack of language, con-demned to haunt the present.

I followed the sickly yellow torchlight down, then turned right into a subterranean room. There was the squeaking of some creatures, bats probably, and the sudden, alarming clatter of a trapped pigeon fighting to escape. All I could see was the dusty floor covered in broken masonry.

'Look,' said the caretaker and passed the light across the floor. In that slow sweep of light I saw a central pool with fountain, all red stone, long since whitened by dust and droppings. To the rear of the room was a niche with a second pool and into this came a steep stone runnel, scalloped and shaped to make the water shimmer as it fell in from the roof.

'Babooor,' murmured the caretaker, 'Babooor!'

His words ran through the shadows like an invocation, and I felt the chill of the river air coming through some unseen stone duct. The pigeon struggled out and disappeared into the night, leaving a sudden silence which I felt must be filled. An epiphany was about to happen: a figure shading a lamp with his hand, or the sound of laughter. But the scrape of shoe on stone was only the caretaker pushing a rock to one side, and the distant roar in my ears was my own blood set racing with adrenaline.

'Babooor is sleeping here and he dream of his mountains.'

To escape from the heat, they had dug down. Then brought water to fall from the ceiling in cooling sprays and form delicious baths where they would laze away the hours of the hot season. We walked through more rooms, but the torch was fading, powerless to penetrate the gloomy depths, scarcely able to reveal the floor in front of our feet.

We climbed out of the cave palace and walked along by the river to the well. There was a stone tower which we climbed up and the care-taker showed me how the water would have been lifted. Although the ropes and tackle were long gone, it would have been simplicity itself to set the whole thing ticking once again.

'Come,' he said, and led me to the other side. Below us was a dim sunken lane and on either side of it ruined stalls. 'Here Babur is keeping his horses and soldiers. Always ready for war. Always ready.' It was as though he was out there in the gloom, waiting to be called, like King Arthur with his knights under the hill at Glastonbury.

The great diamond had left India, perhaps for the first time, and though it would return, it would never adorn the greatest Mughal of them all. The son born to Humayun while the family were on the run would indeed have a glorious future, doing more than any other to unify his disparate kingdom, but it was Akbar who would never own the great symbol of unity itself.

At the capital he built thirty miles from Agra, Akbar surrounded himself with the nine wittiest and cleverest companions he could find – his human navaratna. Outside this select group was an ever-increasing crowd of philosophers and thinkers, an army of knowledge brought to bear on the issues that absorbed the emperor. Any new-comer was roped in: Zoroastrians from Surat, Sufis, Jews, Jains, even Portuguese Jesuits, who were disappointed to find themselves cosseted and cared for – they had hoped to be martyred.

Behind the mosque at Fatehpur Sikri was the Ibadat Khana, House of Worship, where philosophers and savants were encouraged to debate. Akbar firmly believed that knowledge of other religions was important, ordering the first translations of both the *Mahabharata* and *Ramayana* into Persian. The approach of the Islamic millennium during his reign focussed the mystical aspects of his character, and in 1582 the Divine Faith was promulgated.

The Ibadat Khana where his ideas were formed no longer exists, but a similar debating chamber, the Diwan-i-Khas, survives in the centre of the palace complex. It is constructed in the same red sandstone as all Akbar's other buildings, but the effect is not a warm one: the shade is too liverish and the carving seems unnaturally perfect, as though cut by machines not men. Compared to the lacy white vivacity of Shah Jehan's Taj Mahal, Akbar's city has all the stiff precision of a school-ma'am's pleated skirt.

Inside the building, a single central column rises from the floor to support four bridges that come from each corner of the room. The capital of the column broadens into a lotus and Akbar would sit in this, listening to the debates below. This was not mere idle adornment and structure: in Hindu mythology the lotus springs from the belly of Vishnu and in the blossom is Rama. Akbar was directly associating himself with the god and, whether he knew it or not, with a lineage that went back five thousand years to the beginning of human civilisa-tion and the birth of the Sun god Ra: the diamond in the lotus.

Although Akbar's Divine Faith died with him, and he never became the god he wanted to be, echoes of his reign still linger. When I stood in the debating hall the day after I had found his grandfather's garden, an Indian family came solemnly up to the threshold. The three chubby sons were smartly dressed as little mirror images of their father in his sleeveless sweater and slacks. They were waiting for a party of American tourists to move on, and stood at the door in a line, like a row of Russian dolls waiting to be popped inside one another. When the Americans had gone, the family stepped inside and scattered marigolds along the ledges; then, pressing their palms together, they bowed towards the column.

I left Agra at sunset, taking the Delhi train north, following the trail of the Koh-i-Noor along the route that Alauddin's general Malik Kafur would have taken on his return from plundering the Deccan. Later too, long after Humayun had died, when his great grandson Shah Jehan was emperor, the jewel would come this way once more, drawn back to the centre of power as if by some magical force. Delhi was the place where the Koh-i-Noor had been named and the place where it would be finally lost to the Mughals, in the greatest robbery ever seen. The diamond, symbolically, was there at the beginning of their empire and it would be there at the end.

Gently lulled into sleep, I woke suddenly to find a hideous female face shoved close to mine.

'Baksheesh!' It screeched, then cackled with laughter. A gang of transvestites were moving down the train, cursing anyone who refused to tip them. I fobbed them off with some small coins, then bought some tea in a terracotta cup.

The approach to Delhi was long and slow with many halts. The other travellers had come from the south and were exhausted, long past conversation. Outside lights came and went, then we passed through a long darkness.

Up ahead I could see a lamp swinging along the track. The air brakes checked us to walking pace. I had my elbow up on the bar and face pressed close to catch sight of the city. Then I saw the lamp stop and shadows of men bent over something lying in the middle of the adjacent track. We came alongside and I saw a human head, severed at the neck, the eyes open and mouth convulsed into a grotesque smile. On the far side was a pathetic bundle of green rags.

Then we were back in the night, the rails squealing in protest as New Delhi Station approached. The image of that bloodied head would haunt me for some days, another suicide amongst the impoverished and desperate street people. It was the horrible smile on the face as it gazed up at the stars that I could not shake from my mind. A vague sense of unease gripped me and persisted, as though somehow I knew that my own luck was about to take a turn for the worse.

CHAPTER 9

Pale hands I loved beside the Shalimar,
Where are you now? Who lies beneath your spell? . . .
Pale hands, pink-tipped, like lotus buds that float
On those cool waters where we used to dwell,
I would have rather felt you round my throat
Crushing out life; than waving me farewell!

Laurence Hope, 'The Garden of Kama'

[Laurence Hope was a pseudonym for Adela Florence
Nicolson, née Cory, who disguised herself as a Pathan
boy and ran away to the North-West Frontier to be with
her husband. She wrote a number of passionate poems
about the romance of India, and when her husband died
in 1904, committed suicide.]

O N that first night in Delhi, I went out of my hotel to escape a
power cut and wandered, moth-like, towards the kerosene
lamps set up by the traders in Karol Bagh market. Women were
wrapped in Kashmiri shawls, beautiful autumnal shades of ochre. Street
urchins clustered around a man who was warming peanuts in a skillet
over an open fire, and pomegranates were piled up on wooden barrows.
At the entrance to the clothing market there was an army checkpoint:
the road blocked with barriers and a mocked-up metal detector to walk
through. There was no attempt to pretend this was a real detector; the
frame was wood and there were no wires or generators. But to pass you
had to step up a ramp and through the frame and each time someone
did that, it looked like a gibbet with an invisible rope.

'Has there been a bomb?' I asked, and the policeman nodded. 'One person is dead and more than fifty injured.'

'Where?'

'It is not known.'

'Who did it?'

'It is not known.'

The hotel receptionist was better informed. 'Pakistan did it,' he told me, to general agreement from the various ne'er-do-wells who hovered around the counter. 'They do not say so, but we know. They try to cause panics. There is one master bomber here now in Delhi but he cannot be nabbed. Next time, they say, he will attack a shopping area.'

A friend in England who had studied Persian had given me the name of a scholar living in Old Delhi, Dr Yunus Jaffery, and it was this man I set out to find on my first morning in the city.

It promised to be a fine day. The air had the crisp chill of an English autumn, that first September day when all the trees are still standing green and leafy, but the air temperature has dropped. The Delhi roads seemed longer as they stretched away into chilly mists, and distance added mystery to the far-off pavilions of former rulers. Fragments of red sandstone wall prickled with crenellations and creeping thorns; a whitish dome floated in the green, and even the concrete blocks seemed less ugly – the grubby fingerprints of monsoon seasons just the wrinkles of time, from a distance, at least.

Delhi is a city containing many cities: the modern town stands on the right bank of the Yamuna River and encloses, amongst others, British Delhi, Shah Jehan's Delhi and Alauddin's Delhi. And as it spreads, it swallows yet more previous incarnations: the vast and eerily beautiful fourteenth-century Delhi of the Tughluqs is now slowly being absorbed on the southern fringe, while to the north the relentless development is curling around the Ridge where early British residents had their country houses.

I was heading for Shah Jehan's Delhi which from the Mughals' time until Independence was the real Delhi – despite the claims of Edwin Lutyens and his grand boulevards fit for King Emperor George. At the Ajmeri Gate I got off the bus and looked around. The transition into

Shah Jehan's city is not always easy to spot: the wall has largely gone and the grubby, cable-festooned buildings are more or less equally dilapidated on either side. But the gate itself survives as a traffic island, permanently marooned in a sea of cyclo rickshaws, honking buses and clapped-out cars. Opposite this was Sheikh Zakar Hussain College, a handsome red sandstone building of Mughal design, its walls scooped and scaled by the wind, its ridges bristling with defensive battlements; from behind the blackened hoardings, pylons and poles, it rose like a stegosaurus emerging from the swamp.

The gatekeeper directed me through an archway and tunnel into a large courtyard. Ahead was a Mughal mosque with double white domes, while the other three sides were taken up by the two-storey college buildings. A gardener was tending the neat hedges that quartered the courtyard into pleasant strolls. He directed me up some steps and along a first-floor colonnade. There were stacks of yellowing newspapers to squeeze past and sagging rope charpoys leaning against the stone balustrade. At the end was a bamboo screen, or chick, hung over a door. I pulled it aside and knocked.

There was the scrape of a chair then a voice, slightly raised: 'Please enter!'

I opened the door into a small square room with arched ceiling. On the left were cupboards full of books, on the right a bed with a map of Persia above it. Dr Jaffery was sitting at the desk under the small window, a slightly built man with bright eyes. He came to shake hands, his manner alert and friendly – that of a retired alchemist, I decided, the one who has a last great experiment up his sleeve.

'Welcome, welcome, please sit down.'

He indicated the low coffee table with two chairs in the centre of the room, then went to pull a second curtain over the door.

'The weather is unseasonably cold,' he said, tucking his ears inside his knitted grey skullcap. 'Snow in Kashmir I believe. Will you take tea?'

'Yes, please.'

He began the laborious process of brewing a cuppa, one I would come to know quite well though not always relish. Dr Jaffery's tea was invariably strong.

'Have you visited Iran?' I asked, looking at the map and noting the

[189]

position of Shiraz and New Julfa where the Madras Armenians had come from.

'I was there,' he said. 'I am Persian-speaking, you know. Indian-Persian speaking I should say. There are very few of us remaining.'

'You teach Persian here?'

'I am retired now, but yes, I did. My family were Persian tutors to the Mughals from Shah Jehan's time. Are you a scholar?'

'I'm here to write a book,' I explained. 'On diamonds – particularly the large old stones like the Koh-i-Noor.'

'Oh, fascinating,' he said, setting a saucer of biscuits before me. 'Nadir Shah, Shah Jehan, Aurangzeb – he built this place you know, Aurangzeb. This room and the rest.'

He brought the tea over, then went to his bookshelves. I could hear the gentle sigh of the covers as he removed volumes and his murmured pleasure at the sight of each one as it appeared: 'Mmmm, fascinating.' Finally he chose one, smoothing the pages with his palm. 'Oh yes, look. "Sometimes for pleasing his mind." That is Shah Jehan, you know. Well, I am studying this man for some years.' He was translating directly from the Persian chronicles.

'Where was I? No, not pleasing, pleasuring is better. "Sometimes for pleasuring his mind and the purification of his thoughts, he was listening to sweet melodies. And for glorifying the mirror of illumination, he was giving brightness with his eyes to the jewels." There! "He was enjoying the rarities of precious gems of the oceans and the mines." In other words, you can say, he would gaze at his diamonds and gloat!'

I sipped my tea, noticing he had not poured himself one. Not having spent much time in Muslim areas, I had completely forgotten that it was Ramadhan.

'So Shah Jehan made the jewels shine? Did he believe he was something greater than a man? That sounds very un-Islamic.'

Dr Jaffery sat down, though not for long. He seemed restless, and I wondered if I had disturbed his Ramadhan routine.

'I'll tell you something funny. A Jew converted to Islam and gave a speech. Afterwards everyone in the audience was saying "How wonderful he made Islam sound!" So the ex-Jew said, "Remember, I was talking of Islam, not Muslims!"'

He got up, muttering something in Persian. 'So what I mean is, Islam and Muslims are not the same thing. He did believe it. Akbar thought he was The Reviver – the Appointed One who will be sent to revive Islam. But Shah Jehan was born in the year of the Islamic Millennium and he certainly believed *he* was the one. At his birth two planets were said to have conjoined and so he called himself Sahib Qiran, Lord of the Conjunction. In other words, the heavens marked his arrival.'

Dr Jaffery pushed the biscuits towards me. 'Would you like a biscuit? Here, it is our custom to offer.'

I took one, a delicate Ramadhan shortbread with an almond on top.

Dr Jaffery smiled. 'Ah! English – very direct. Very refreshing.' He began to pace the room again. 'In some places, like in Iran, when they offer tea, they want you to say No. And sometimes they want you to say Yes.'

My biscuit stopped in mid-air as I went for a second bite. 'So how do you know if they are truly offering tea, or not?'

He made a face. 'You do not know, so you refuse, and they insist, and you refuse. And somehow you may discover if they are offering only to be polite – and they will discover if you are refusing because you are not thirsty.'

He turned his hands over, eyes wide, and shook his chin, a lovely gesture of puzzlement and disbelief.

'Accepting a cup of tea can be very complex.'

'Oh, it is very dangerous to accept, almost as dangerous as to refuse!'

Perhaps the superficial Englishness of Delhi had fooled me, but Dr Jaffery's words reminded me to be on guard. This was the east. Once, in an Arab house in Sudan, I had shown interest in a rug and the owner had ripped it off the wall and given it to me. Then, when I refused, he became hurt, I accepted, felt guilty, tried to return it – the simplest of remarks had become a nightmare of suspicion between host and hosted. When I left the rug behind, the owner took it as a slight on his hospitality and sent it round to me. Which is how I came to own a rug depicting six dogs playing pool in an English pub. An invaluable lesson.

'Another biscuit?' Dr Jaffery pushed the saucer towards me.

'Er..no, thank you.'

He pushed his woolly cap back and scratched his scalp. 'But it is our custom to offer such biscuits. You must have one more.'

'Oh, okay.' I took one.

'Shah Jehan was a very greedy man,' he said, eying me as I nibbled the biscuit. 'The greediest of men. Do you know Shadad – the legend of Shadad, a Persian hero? He built Paradise only to lose it to the Angel of Death. Shah Jehan thought he was divine, and so he should live in Paradise.' He twitched the curtain at the door, then opened it and looked outside.

'The wind perhaps. Are you cold?'

'It is quite cold, isn't it?' Once out of the sun, the chill of the shadows soon reached my hands and feet.

'Here take my coat!' He closed the door and fetched it from the chair. But I was on full alert now: ready for the intricacies of Persian courtesy. Quite likely he was cold and wanted to wear the coat.

'No, no, I'm okay. I like the cold. I'm used to it.'

'So you are not cold?'

'Only a little – I mean no, not really. Are you?'

He put it down quickly. 'No. Me? No.'

'I'm sorry,' I said. 'It's Ramadhan and I've called at the wrong time.'

'Not a bit!' He went to the cupboard and took out a scarf. 'I will put this on.' So he had been cold.

'Would it be better if I came back tonight?' I asked. 'I think after you have broken your fast – that would be more convenient.'

'We can talk now – a little more,' he said. 'It is only that there is one man who is causing me much anxiety at the moment.'

'Not me, I hope.'

He laughed. 'You? No, no. Another man, and there are other factors.'

He left this hanging mysteriously.

'So Shah Jehan wanted to build Paradise.'

'He did.'

'Where?'

'Here, Shahjehanabad.'

Such is the filth and delapidation of the old town that it had simply never occured to me that Shah Jehan's Paradise might have been under our very feet.

'Alauddin Khilji really started it,' he continued, 'because he began to build a canal to bring fresh water.'

'But there is the river.'

'They wanted clear cold water, pure water, like they remembered from Afghanistan. Alauddin's canal comes from the north and Shah Jehan used it to supply his new city. Every house had clear running water. Then a canal passed to the Red Fort along Chandni Chowk.' This was the main thoroughfare of Old Delhi. 'In the Red Fort it was pulled up and sent down the canal they call the Nahar Bihisht – the River of Paradise – through the pavilions and hammams. I can show you one day, we will walk around the old city.'

'I'd like that – are the canals still there?'

'No, only outside the city – if you go to Shalimar Gardens. That is the place Shah Jehan built as a first stop on the Great Royal Road to Lahore. When Nadir Shah came, he made it his base.'

This alerted me. Nadir Shah had invaded India in 1739 and looted the Mughal treasury, including the Koh-i-Noor.

'Are the gardens still there?'

He made a face. 'I don't know. There may be something left. I think they have built over it.'

I got my map of the city out and asked him to mark approximately where the gardens should be. The spot appeared to be in the middle of a vast housing estate on the north-west corner of the city, but the canal was there, marked as a thin blue line coming in from the north.

'I'll go and look today,' I said. 'Leave you in peace.'

'Come tonight.' He got up quite readily. But I had slipped into double-guessing every move and so wondered if his quickness to rise meant I had indeed imposed on him.

He came down to the courtyard with me. 'Look, this is the stream.' There was a dry channel, about nine inches deep running across the quartered yard. 'It would have brought clean cold water to the college and mosque. Not any more though. Can you see how that archway is not having nice dimensions? They have lifted the floor of the courtyard and destroyed the symmetry. But there, what can we do? Come at nine tonight. Goodbye.'

I watched him shuffle back towards the stairs, then turned and went out through the archway – into Paradise.

*

It took some time to find a taxi driver who could speak English and understand the map. He had never heard of Shalimar Bagh, the Mughal garden, but knew the housing estate of that name. Once we were there, an old man gave us directions down a side road to the rear of some apartment blocks. At the very end was a turning place for cars and a high wall; beyond that were some trees.

We got out, and searching along the wall, found a padlocked gate. I could see neatly trimmed grass and the fat white trunks of royal palms planted in lines. I put my bag on the wall and climbed up. Shani, the driver, waited. 'What you are doing is most irregular,' he said. I jumped down. After a moment, his grinning face appeared and he scrambled over.

Further down the path we came across an aged gardener, reclining amongst the fallen leaves. There was very little left of Shah Jehan's garden, he told Shani in Hindi. The trees had been planted by the British, but there was a ruin we could look at, just behind the *behr* trees. He pointed to a thicket of scrubby fruit trees and knotted under-growth.

Someone had recently repaired the plasterwork on the back wall of the building, a rough and ready covering that left it looking like any other quick-build shanty shack – albeit of rather larger dimensions. Rounding the corner, I found myself facing a large open pavilion with a twenty-foot high arch in the centre flanked by colonnades, bricked up on one side to prevent a collapse. It was built on a pediment about six feet high, but there were no steps up at the centre where I would have expected. I went and peeped over the lip into the room beyond, a large airy space with traces of once magnificent scalloped plasterwork in the corners of a flat dome. The outer stonework was of red sand-stone which had been licked and hollowed by the wind.

Shani was poking around in the dirt behind me. There was a fallen tree and piles of leaves swept up by the gardeners, but Shani was brushing the debris away from something.

'Look.' It was a brick-lined hole about one foot across and a yard in depth. He glanced around. 'And here is something.'

It was a lip in the earth that ran in a line away from the building; a second line ran parallel to it. Now I saw that what had appeared to be some random division of land was actually a shallow channel about three paces wide. Shani had uncovered more of the brick-lined pits within the channel and was getting quite excited. Two alternating rows of them, like large round footprints, heading down the gardens towards a wall and a pair of scrappy pavilions.

'They were planting something here,' he said. 'Many of them.'

I glanced back at the main building. The floor was badly churned up, but the shallow channel appeared to continue on through the pavilion.

'Lotus,' I said. 'I bet they were lotus flowers.' Now I saw why there were no steps at the front of the building: it had been a waterfall and they planted the lotuses in the deep pits so the flower would appear to be floating on the water, magical blossoms unattached to anything but the shimmering waters.

Shani was nodding. 'For Mughal only lotus – they love only lotus.'

We set off down the path and came to a dry pond about thirty feet square with its bed dotted with twenty-five similar pots. I walked across and climbed up on the far side. The wall had a break in it, possibly the original gateway; beyond I could see across a long desolate flat to smoking factories and scraps of half-finished shacks. According to my map the low line away to my left was the Western Yamuna Canal – Alauddin's waterway – the artery that had once brought the water of life to this paradise.

I turned and headed back towards the pavilion. Shani was ahead of me, strolling along with his hands clasped behind his back: 'I think Shah Jehan is walking with free mind along here. Nice lady next to him.'

At the pavilion he found a doorway on the left. Inside we stood in the main hall. 'The water came in here,' he said, pointing to three narrow slits at the base of the rear wall.

The notables would have sat in the main hall, admiring the north-facing view and enjoying the cool breezes which they cherished. At night, servants filled the place with candles and lined the edges of the lotus pools, too. With mirrors on the walls, the light generated would have been quite powerful. Would it have been sufficient, I wondered, to trick the poor lotuses into opening at the Mughal's bidding, rather than that of the Sun god?

Shani disappeared, looking for the gardener to give him a beedi. I sat on the edge of the channel and sketched the scene.

It was water that had best expressed Shah Jehan's love of beauty: baths with rosewater fountains, candlelit waterfalls and pools dappled by the golden backs of fish, each with a jewelled ring in its mouth. Water channels cut the gardens and terraces into perfect geometrical forms, like a skilled glyptician cleaving the diamond. Purity and perfection were the ideals, and if water embodied them, then so too did jewels.

Shah Jehan loved his treasures passionately, enjoying the magic bottle that was India more than any other before him. Indications of the wealth were given by many travellers: Tavernier personally examined the contents of the treasury, but it was an earlier visitor, the Englishman William Hawkins, who catalogued the imperial wealth in terms comprehensible to non-jewellers: diamonds – 82½ lbs, pearls – 660 lbs, rubies – 110lbs, emeralds – 275 lbs, jade – 55 lbs, spinels – 2,000, jewelled swords – 2,200, and on and on through the jewelled saddles and war elephants to the 4,000 singing birds.

Rather surprisingly, the diamond with which Humayun had bought the favour of the Persian king had returned to India quite quickly. Shah Tahmasp, still eager to convert Sunnis to Shi'ism, sent the jewel to one of the five Deccan kingdoms that were ranged along the Mughal Empire's southern border. But then it disappears from the records, possibly sold by the envoy. Portuguese sources claim sightings of large diamonds, but nothing is certain. Legend has it that it came into the possession of Mir Jumla, Prime Minister to the Sultan of Golconda, and he gave it to Shah Jehan. But this diamond and that given by Babur to Humayun are not known to be the same – a fog of dubious weights and other uncertainties obscures the truth. All we know is that Shah Jehan, Humayun's grandson, received a large and fabulous diamond which he placed, along with the rest, in the ever-burgeoning treasury at his new capital at Delhi. There, along with the Peacock Throne, it was examined by the indefatigable Tavernier, and there it lay through the long years of Aurangzeb's bigotry and his successors' incompetence. By 1739, the Mughal empire under Muhammad Shah was a decrepit shadow of its former self, a soft target for any enterprising young blood who cared to empty its treasure chests. And the young blood was not long in coming.

On the night of 7th March, 1739, Shalimar Gardens received unexpected visitors: a body of armed men arriving after dark, bloodied but jubilant. Like the Mughals, they spoke Persian and would have made themselves quite at home in such surroundings, recognising the gardens from similar sites in Persia.

Although the city of Delhi was only a short ride away and panic-stricken at the news of a Mughal defeat, the men chose to rest the night in Shalimar. Having ridden so far and battled their way across the Sind, the delicate perfection of the garden must have seemed all the greater: water moving in shimmering symmetry, pools patterned with lotuses, the clarity and purity of it all – it may have reminded their leader, Nadir Shah, of one particular item, a jewel of the first water that he had come to retrieve.

Nadir Shah was an extraordinary individual by the standards of his own time and any other. Born into a shepherding family in eastern Persia, he had risen inexorably to the throne, driven by the desire to recreate the glories of ancient Persia. His objective in attacking Mughal India was not to govern, but to exact tribute and, failing that, to plunder.

After the night in Shalimar, Nadir went to the Red Fort to meet the defeated Muhammad Shah. According to Mirza Zuman, Nadir's chronicler, the Mughal congratulated the Persian on his victory and Nadir behaved 'with the greatest Complaisance and seeming Affection to him'.

But this was all part of the game, the endless courtesies of refusing tea when you were thirsty, or clothing when cold. The truth was that Nadir wanted to leave the Mughal on his throne and take his jewels, but how much tribute to demand was a tricky question. And then there was the famous diamond: such a jewel, though large, was easily hidden or smuggled away. Nadir's 'seeming Affection' was no more loving than the embrace of the snake.

This first contact must have convinced Nadir Shah that he had to be at the centre of power because he gave the order to move from Shalimar Gardens to the Red Fort. And with his departure the gardens stepped back from the historical limelight, never to return. The Persian came and went as swiftly as a late summer frost: he did not topple walls or break stones, but when he had gone, the garden was dead, and there would be no recovery for these stately pleasure domes.

Within a few years the walls were breached, the gardeners fled and the pavilions colonised by bats. In 1801, an East India Company officer called William Franklin rode out to survey the ruins, recording: 'These gardens were laid out with admirable taste, and cost the enormous sum of a million sterling.' He searched, but there was no sign of the 'pearl-scattering' fountains inside the hall, the marble throne or the white and gold borders; these had all gone. 'The prospect to the southward of Shalimar towards Delhi, as far as the eye can reach,' wrote Franklin, 'is covered with the remains of extensive gardens, pavilions, mosques, and burying places, all desolate and in ruins. The environs of this once magnificent and celebrated city appear now no more than a shapeless heap of ruins; and the country round about is equally forlorn.'

These days the prospect is no less desolate and forlorn. The garden Shah Jehan had built as the first outpost of Paradise, where Aurangzeb had crowned himself, and where the sword of Nadir Shah had waited, was quietly disappearing under a tidal wave of cheap family apartments.

When the sunlight was low and golden, Shani returned with the gardener and they led me around the back of the pavilion. In the undergrowth was a broad, deep well, perhaps a back-up source of water in case the canal ran dry. The dirty green disc of the water seemed a long long way away. On one side, a few feet down, was a little niche containing a white figurine.

'I wonder how many years it will be,' I said, 'Before they build on this.'

'No, no,' said Shani. 'It cannot happen. That is the goddess – she is watching the eye of the water and will not let it die.'

Shani dropped me after dark near the Old City's Jama Mosque, a building which narrowly survived the post-Mutiny madness of the British in 1857. Below its vast towers and domes, the narrow twisting lanes were swarming with life. Evening prayers had finished and the Muslim population were rushing out to break their fast. There were bright displays of lamps and fairy lights, stalls stacked with sweets and biscuits and dates. Men were cooking samosas in cauldrons of oil, while boys rushed past with orders of tea, heading out to little hole-in-the-wall shops where merchants sold brassware, taps, perfumes, ready to wear holy eye spots, wedding invitations, books – always an eclectic selection, my favourite being *Astrology for the Amateur Aquarium Keeper*.

Entering this maelstrom was like diving down into smaller and smaller worlds: streets became lanes became alleys became paths became gunnels became fatman's agony, and yet there was always a motorbike coming the other way; and the shops started as healthy rooms stuffed with bolts of cloth that shrank until there was no room inside the emporium for the emporiast – tiny toeholds on the capitalist ladder, or desperate means of survival. The street restaurants with space for two diners were lifting their veils – dropped in the day to conceal Muslim diners. A goat was being petted by the kite-seller. Older women wore the burka, a silky grey or blue head-to-toe sheet with a latticework screen for the eyes, like a little harem window on legs. Younger girls prefer the all-black veil which is far less attractive, as the old ladies embroider their burkas with flowing arabesques of blossom and leaf.

Outside an engineering factory no bigger than a telephone kiosk, I was assailed by the scent of attar of roses – a perfume invented, they say, by Nur Jehan, Jehangir's wife.

Two youths, one a speaker of English, the other of Indian English, engaged me in conversation: the former translating for the latter.

'Brother! Where are you coming from?'

'From England.'

He turned to his friend and translated. 'Proper England he is coming from.' Once that was clear, he asked me, 'Are you only or having family?'

'I'm married but here alone.'

The second youth frowned and waited for clarification, which came. 'Auntie is there.'

Smile of understanding.

'Children?'

'Two boys and one girl.'

Translated: 'He is having two kids and one daughter.'

Smiles all round. Britisher. Family man, very trustworthy. Speaks a little English.

The people of the old city were once largely Muslim, but Partition dealt a deadly blow to the Urdu-speaking culture inside the walls. Those who left for Pakistan or were killed had their property seized by incomers, many of them Punjabis who had lost everything in their homelands. It was this tragic changeover in population that tore the heart out of Shahjehanabad. The incomers had neither the time nor the money to worry over the niceties of architecture or historical importance: tin, concrete and breeze block were the new democratic materials of the common man, filling up useless arches and balconies, dividing rooms and buildings. The process has not stopped – Shahjehanabad's limited stock of historical buildings is being destroyed even now. I watched while builders divided one beautiful old house in two, not floor by floor into apartments, but down the middle like a cake. The front door now had a wall up the centre, cutting it into two completely impractical entrances, each a foot wide. This same shoddy, breeze block partition continued up through the entire house.

Eventually, my wandering along a vague compass line brought me out onto a main street which was choked with cycle rickshaws, their drivers yelling at each other: '*Chaloo! Bachke!*'. The cause of the delay was a wedding procession: a young man dressed as a maharaja in white tunic and red and gold spangled turban was riding a white horse towards Ajmeri Gate. Behind were the guests, equally colourful, and flanked on either side by a dozen ragamuffins with chandeliers on their heads. These lamp-bearers would once have carried candles, but the modern wedding requires something more extravagant – in this case, electric chandeliers on brass poles, all connected to each other by yards and yards of heavy cable. The poor boys were struggling, tugged first forward then back by their colleagues, only to stagger sideways and be run over by irate cyclo drivers: '*Chalooo! Chalooo!*' At the back of the procession were the unsung heroes: two filthy urchins shoving a gigantic thumping generator on cast iron wheels through the filth and dangers of the Delhi gutter.

Out at the front were some of the young groom's mates, and one dropped off the lead to whisper to me. 'Are you a friendly boy?'

'Sorry?'

'A friendly boy?' He leaned closer. 'Are you interested in gayism?'

The groom was passing in a clatter of drums and a wail of pipes. He looked rather frightened but managed a wan smile.

At Ajmeri Gate there was a further delay: police were searching passers-by; a tip-off had suggested the bombers were using addresses in the Old City to remain hidden. Everyone I spoke to had a different rumour to peddle: some said the bombers had Semtex, others that they were on a suicide mission, some blamed the Tamils, others the Americans or the Assamese. The only certainty was that everything was uncertain.

The courtyard of Zakar Hussain College seemed blessedly quiet and dark after the noise and light of the street. I went up the steps to the balcony and stumbled past the charpoys and piles of newspaper, feeling the sharp cold wind from the north. The bamboo chicks swung and slapped at the walls and windows. At Dr Jaffery's door, I raised my hand to knock then stopped: there were voices from inside – Dr Jaffery's no more than a murmur, but the other a big booming bass.

I knocked. There was a sudden silence, then the scraping of the door opening. Dr Jaffery looked pleased to see me. Inside he introduced me to a fellow scholar from Iran who was a very large man indeed, dressed in double-breasted blue suit with a neatly trimmed black beard.

'He is doing a PhD on Akbar,' explained Dr Jaffery as we sat down. 'And he is the Imam – prayer-leader for Iranians in Delhi.'

The Imam coughed modestly. He seemed very young to be a religious leader.

'What is the subject of your thesis?' I asked, but this proved to be an alarmingly direct question and the Imam sensibly ignored it to avoid embarrassment.

'First,' he said, smoothing his pink hands together, 'first I would like to introduce my friend Dr Jaffery, a man whose scholarship and learning have spread his fame to the four corners of Iran.' A lengthy encomium followed, extolling the virtues of Dr Jaffery who sat through it all smiling, before launching into one of his own for the Imam. Then I discovered the answer to my question: the Imam was reading original Persian texts of Akbar's time and had dug out some facts ignored by previous scholars.

Example?

'Yes, I can give you,' said the Imam. 'During Mughal times a group came from Persia to India and in the books they are called Sufis. They were very important men because one of them was Abu Fasl, Akbar's chronicler.'

One of Akbar's nine jewels, I recalled, the navaratna of the imperial courtiers.

'For example,' interrupted Dr Jaffery. 'If you are calling me names and say to me 2-0-4 or 4-0-2, what are you doing?'

He flipped his hands over, lips pursed. 'Nothing! It means nothing. But now you call me 4-2-0, it is different. I jump up and will fight with you because it is the number police use for cheaters.'

The Imam took over. 'You see number has power. One number and we do nothing, another we are fighting. Maybe you die.'

'And how does that connect with Abu Fasl?'

'He was Persian and Sufi, but if we read the books more carefully we find he is Nuktawi. Those are people who believed in the mystical power of certain numbers and letters.'

It was as if a brick had slotted into place, completing a building: Akbar's chief friend and advisor had been a numerologist, a man imbued with the signifiance of numbers who brought the scholarship of the Arab renaissance to bear on the Indian cosmologies. The Nuktawids were Muslims who believed in reincarnation and, according to the *Encyclopedia of Islam*, had a fixation on the number 19. Suppressed by Shah Ismail I of Persia, they fled east, diplomatically adjusting their calendar to make Akbar a saint. So it was that the ancient lore of the Hindus had been mingled with the insight and intelligence of Islam, and the diamond in the lotus became Akbar, presiding over his Divine Faith from his eight-fold flower of red sandstone. As for the Nuktawids they died out, appropriately, in the nineteenth century.

The Imam had gone into his praise of Dr Jaffery routine – a routine of which the recipient seemed to be a little tired.

'Kevin went to search for Shalimar Bagh today,' he said, putting an end to the flattery. 'Did you find the place?'

I explained what had happened and mentioned Nadir Shah. The Imam became quite excited. 'Nadir is a great hero for all Iranians,' he said. 'In Meshed they have his statue and people go there to pay respect to him. Then the children are dressing up as Nadir, too.'

'Would you like tea?' asked Dr Jaffery.

'No,' said the Imam, 'No really, I took tea already.'

'Please,' said Dr Jaffery.

'No, no my good friend – really – really.' He was waving his hands in front of him. For a big man they were tiny and perfectly manicured: the hands of a twenty-stone tenor, made for holding scented hankerchiefs during big arias.

'I usually take one cup at this time myself.'

'It is late.'

'No, it is early.'

'It is so much trouble, so many problems for you.'

'It is no problem.'

'You are very kind but I . . .'

'Just for company – keep us company.' He had not actually asked me yet.

'Oh! You are . . . but no . . .'

The cup was laid before him. 'Ah! Doctor, really, it is too much.'

'Kevin?'

'Er, yes please.'

The Imam's face registered all the profound astonishment of a Phrygian watching Alexander slice through the Gordian knot. He could not be persuaded to a biscuit, but feeling a little scandalous, I was.

'You will visit me,' he declared, 'at our Embassy and Cultural Centre. Please, my card.'

I took it from the outstretched hand, wondering what he wanted from me. His wrist was hairy.

'We have books on Nadir Shah, I am sure of it. And I have a photograph of my son dressed like the king – at Meshed. Really.' I agreed to meet him there.

About half an hour later I set off back to Karol Bagh, taking an autorickshaw from outside the college. The streets around my hotel were dark and I couldn't find the right place. In the end I abandoned the rickshaw and finished my search on foot.

'You must not do that,' said the hotel receptionist when I eventually arrived. 'There are too many thieves.'

'There were police everywhere – these bombings.'

'The police are thieves, too.'

'And the bombs?'

'Maybe.'

'You think the police planted the bombs?'

'Why not?'

I went to my room, wondering if anything was as it seemed.

The Iranian Cultural Centre was in New Delhi, the Delhi of Edwin
Lutyens, of long straight boulevards and red brick. Most Indian politicians of stature live here and so, with the election looming, there were
banners and stands outside some houses, the largest of them at the
headquarters of the BJP, the eventual winners.

The Imam's office was in an annexe behind the gravel car park and
well-trimmed gardens, a spotless room filled with sombre books and
two portrait photographs: the president and Ayatollah Khomeini.
There was a neat desk under the window and a coffee table with some
learned monographs for guests to peruse. People came in and out.
Some were taken outside for whispered conversations.

'You will be my guest in Iran,' said the Imam when we were alone,
'You will treat my house as your house. You will eat our traditional
food and see our traditional sights. You will visit all the places and stay
with my relatives who are there. I will get your visa and meet you at
the airport in my car which will be your car.'

I steered the conversation away from my Iranian holiday to Nadir
Shah.

'Yes, here is a picture of his idol in Meshed.'

There was a statue of a large, long-bearded man, frowning under
the weight of an immense hat.

'He is our great hero. He defeated all his enemies. He made Persia
strong like before.'

I admired the Imam's son dressed in cardboard armour and wield-
ing a scimitar with formidable nonchalance.

'Nadir took a lot of jewels with him from India,' I said, coaxingly.
'Theft really, wasn't it?'

But the Imam had no time for the decadent western disease of hero-
reassessment. 'It was his right as victor. You read the chronicles: Nadir

waited and waited for them to hand over the tribute which was his by right. Then the Delhi mob were insulting his men and causing so many problems. Nadir is our great hero. He made Persia strong like before.'

'Do you think he knew about the Koh-i-Noor before he came?'

'Yes, of course he knew. The gift of this wonderful jewel from Humayun to Shah Tahmasp was well known in Persia, a famous occasion. Then the return of it to India – he would know. He came for that diamond. It was his by right.'

As I passed the photograph of his son back across the desk, I glanced down at my feet. Something had caught my attention: a yellow mark on my shoe. I lifted my foot.

'Is good?' asked the Imam. 'You have some problem?'

It was then I realised that my right shoe was caked, absolutely caked, in buffalo faeces. In that dour, colourless office, the brilliant shade of yellow seemed to throb and glow with a sulphuric intensity. I could practically see the steam rising. I put my foot hurriedly under the table.

'Sorry?'

'I am saying: you will enjoy every hospitality. You will see Persepolis and you will see Susa and you will invite me for visiting your own home country.'

He was warming to his thesis, leaving his desk to pace around the room. Desperately I tried to keep my foot out of sight, twisting my leg out from the desk and under the coffee table. 'Of course, no problem.'

'I will be no trouble for you. I will stay in hotel. I will invite you to hotel for dinner. I will make some studies in some libraries. I will spend twenty-five pounds sterling per day. Can you write me a letter? Maybe a nice paper – University of Oxford – what is your institution?'

I spun on my chair and, with a superhuman flexibility, got my foot under his desk before he turned, praying that my mutant toecap would not fall off. 'University paper – yes, much better.'

He smiled, came over to clap me on the shoulder. This time a gentle, slow sweep of the leg kept my body between him and the foot.

'The bureaucrats are liking this paper too much.'

I could only think of getting out fast, and now he was back behind his desk, I saw a chance.

'No problem.'

'I will write you and you will write me. Here is my address.'

I jumped up. 'Yes, good – well, must be getting along.'

He smoothed past me, massaging his hands while I prayed. In the lower extreme of my peripheral vision, I could see my foot, like a blur of mustard gas drifting towards the enemy.

We left the office and reached the gravel car park. A limousine was pulling up and an aide-de-camp dressed in a dark suit leapt out and hurried around to open the rear door. A venerable Islamic cleric emerged. He was dressed in immaculate robes with a maroon turban tied tightly in the Khomeini manner. His shoes, I couldn't help but notice, were superbly clean, while his face was full of weighty matters and the burdens of responsibility placed upon him.

'Oh, excusing me,' said the Imam, 'I must make greeting.'

I smiled and stepped back. Despite my calm demeanour, I was panicking. My knowledge of diplomatic courtesies was limited, but I was reasonably certain that greeting a leading representative of one of the major Islamic nations on earth, heirs to the lands of Darius and Alexander, successors to the Shah of Shahs, and guardians of the Holy City of Qom, greeting such a man could not be done while shod with a good half pound of fluorescent buffalo cack.

The gravel path would create a noise if I scraped my shoe vigorously, but there was a plant pot by the door. As stealthily as possible, I ran the edge of my shoe across the rim of the pot. The aide was watching me. I feigned nonchalance and he looked away. The cowpat was stuck fast. It must have dried there over a period of hours. I scraped harder, but this only unbalanced the plant pot which now toppled forwards with a crash, spilling a geranium and some soil. The Imam and Ayatollah were exchanging warm embraces and murmuring sweet nothings to each other, hands clasped. I bent down, grabbed a piece of geranium and wiped the cowpat off. Scarlet petals were scattered over the path.

That was when I discovered that it had dried only on the exterior. My hand broke through the crust and slurped across the offending substance. I dropped the geranium and stood up in renewed horror: My right hand! My right hand was lathered in vivid yellow.

'Yes, my friend.'

The Imam was coming towards me with the Ayatollah, both

bearing gravely dignified smiles. I whipped around and managed one swift wipe of my palm on the seat of my trousers before, smiling, I reached out to grasp the Ayatollah's extended hand.

'And upon thee be peace,' I murmured. 'And the blessings of God, the compassionate and the merciful.'

The aide-de camp was carefully removing a speck of dirt from the car windscreen with a damp chamois leather. The Ayatollah gave a gentle bow of acknowledgement and releasing my hand, turned to enter the offices. And as he did so, he stepped squarely on the cowpat.

The Imam did not notice: he was too busy opening the door. The Ayatollah never flinched. With the regal command becoming of his position, he passed through the door and disappeared into the building. It was a performance worthy of his illustrious compatriots, the men who had so patiently born the insults of the Delhi mob while awaiting the end to negotiations on the tricky issue of tribute for Nadir Shah.

As I passed the limousine on my way out, the aide was folding the chamois into a neat square and watching me with a stony face.

For the next few days I adopted a routine of breakfasting at the hotel (they specialised in omelettes cooked without eggs which reminded me of Harish Desai in Junagadh and his tales of family food feuds), then walking to the Hardinge Library on the edge of Shahjehanabad. No matter how early I arrived or how late I left, the cavernous reference library was always full of students, many of them asleep. Pigeons gently fluttered around the ceiling, sending down white feathers to rest on the heads of the sleepers – avian do-not-disturb markers.

The library gave up its secrets slowly: each book painstakingly requested, noted, searched for in the dingy labyrinths beyond the counter, then swapped for my passport. The result was that I always seemed to be walking through the city at night, heading towards Dr Jaffery's college, then my hotel in Karol Bagh. I would walk along compass lines, cutting back and forth through the alleyways and lanes. Some became familiar, but then I would try a different route, trusting that I would eventually recognise where I was. When I did not, there would be a momentary tremor of fear and uncertainty before another couple of twists and I'd be out by a gateway that I knew.

[207]

The city was feverish with Ramadhan and the bombings. Tales of secret agents seen crossing the borders appeared in the newspapers; descriptions of the 'master bomber' – dark hair, brown eyes, moustache. Some Muslims told me they tried not to speak Urdu in public: the fear of the mob is never far below the surface in India. Any Pakistani associations, even the suspicion of such, could be a fatal liability in a crisis.

At Dr Jaffery's one windy night, he leapt across the room and threw open the door. There was only the night sky and the bamboo chicks flapping.

'There was someone there,' he said.

'Are you being watched?'

'It was only the wind.'

His experiences at Partition were never far from his mind and he spoke of it often: the memory of past persecution always ready to fill up the shadows of the present. A move to evict him from the study he had occupied for so long had unsettled him. Although the case had been dropped, it obviously caused him anxiety. He was just a scholar, a man interested in the past, and one without the protection of any august institution. All he desired was to be left alone to translate the chronicles of Shah Jehan, but even in that there was no respite: the son killing the brothers, the father imprisoned; no one able to trust anyone at all. In India the past is never far behind.

I had given up reminding him of our planned walk through the Old City, but one evening he asked me to come next morning at ten. When I arrived he was dressed to go out.

'I will show you where Nadir Shah stood during the massacre,' he said. 'And a few other things too.'

We went in through the Ajmeri Gate and, with his eyes to help me, I began to see things I had missed: the cobras' heads over doors to mark the houses of Shiva followers; the Christian angels gathered around a Hindu demon – 'That began with the Jesuits and Akbar'; then the high arched doorways that once allowed elephants to enter. 'I remember them as a boy. There were old families here who still kept them – this house belonged to a nobleman and he went shopping on his elephant. I can still recall the sight of it!'

The last of the elephants was gone, however, and with it the Delhi of Dr Jaffery's childhood, a city where the echoes of the Mughal presence still lingered.

We took a rickshaw to the front of the Jama Mosque, built across a wide empty expanse from the Red Fort. 'It was the British who cleared all the buildings here,' Dr Jaffery explained. 'After 1857.'

We walked past a gang of pigeon-sellers and turned the corner into Chandni Chowk. In Mughal times this had been the premier street of the capital with water running down a canal in the centre and shady trees to cool the shoppers. Dr Jaffery could remember the trees surviving until the 1950s, but then the road took over and became what it is today: a choked up mess of cyclos, ox-carts, lorries, cars and jay-walkers. Waving his arm across the scene, as though wiping a murky window, Dr Jaffery pointed out the Mughal elements that survived and the British additions.

There was a Sikh gurdwara, or temple, occupying what was once the Kot Wali or Town Hall, and next to it an archway was being built. We walked past this to the start of the shops and took a narrow flight of steps up onto the roof of a leather goods shop, also the courtyard of the Roshan-e-Daula Mosque. Though it has three golden domes and four small minarets, the mosque is easily missed as it stands back a little, aloof from the forward-pressing, loud-shouting shop-fronts. We found a few of the faithful, whiling away the afternoon asleep on the tiles.

'Here, we can see,' said Dr Jaffery, and took off his shoes to lead me to the parapet. Below was the grand thoroughfare where Shah Jehan would have paraded, to the left the place where Begum Serai once stood – a Mughal garden with pavilions for important visitors – the five star accommodation of its day. Now all was cheap advertising hoardings, black cables and endless grime. The barks of pavement clothes-sellers and the honking autorickshaws had long since replaced the sigh of the breeze in the trees and the gurgle of running water.

The mosque itself had closed its doors, but there was a small office built on the end, overlooking the road. Dr Jaffery took me to the window and I glanced inside. There was an iron bed, some old books, and a bricked-up window piled high with dark bottles of patent medicine.

'That was the window,' said my guide, 'where the caretaker is keeping his medicines. Nadir Shah came up here and stood there. In fact, he stayed some time there, watching.'

The story is well-documented by contemporaries. Nadir had come from the Red Fort with the idea of quelling the growing insurrection over food prices, but as he stood in the window of the mosque, a shot rang out and killed the officer next to him. Nadir's fury was instant and terrible: he ordered 'a general slaughter to be commenced'. Men, women and children were put to the sword, houses burnt to the ground and everything of value looted. People went crazy with fear, and several are said to have killed their own families rather than let the troops near them. Corpses were piled up and burned, one account put the number of dead at 120,000, others at 150,000. Of Nadir's men only 400 died. The jewellery market, cotton bazaar and all the quarters around the Jama Mosque were plundered.

'You see those shops,' said Dr Jaffery, pointing across the mayhem of the street below. 'In that time some were jewellers and they were all plundered. Only after seven hours did Nadir agree to stop it.' His eyes were bright, face animated. He was seeing it all there in front of him: the terror and the carnage, the implacable dictator glowering down from the very position we occupied. In his eyes, the skinny street porters with long barrows piled high with boxes might have been Persian plunderers making off to Shalimar Gardens.

'Nadir Shah was so feared,' he went on, 'that when his order was given to stop, some soldiers were in the middle of cutting victims' throats.' He held his hand like a blade at his own Adam's apple. 'And stopped. Halfway!'

The Persian had then demanded 20 crore of rupees (an incredible 25 million sterling even at that time), plus jewels, gold plate, precious ornaments and the marriage of his son to a Mughal princess. Consequently, with bodies still piled up in the streets, a wedding procession took place, happily uniting the two royal families, one of whom was in the process of stripping the other of its wealth.

Collection of the tribute took some time. 'Nothing was done or thought of,' wrote the chronicler, 'but gathering in this Money, in which no Barbarities were left unpractised.' But at last, Nadir Shah was content – or almost.

Dr Jaffery took a last look in the caretaker's office. 'That very window! To think he was here.' We sat on the step and put our shoes back on.

'According to legend,' he said, 'a concubine of Muhammad Shah told Nadir that the great diamond, the Koh-i-Noor, was hidden in her master's turban. It was the final thing he desired.'

For weeks Nadir Shah had played the guessing games of oriental politics with Muhammad Shah, rather than simply take the whole lot by force. Perhaps he thought that force would not necessarily reveal the greatest prize of them all – the diamond which he regarded as the rightful property of the Persian King of Kings. That reward would fall to the subtler but no less powerful forces of guile and good manners.

The two leaders held a last farewell breakfast and presented each other with various gifts. Muhammad Shah got some trinkets and Nadir Shah got a large slice of the known world. Then, with much aplomb and generosity, Nadir announced that the throne would remain Mughal. They were indeed both kings and, according to the dictates of oriental protocol, should exchange headwear. Muhammad Shah, no doubt seething with fury, was obliged to comply.

Once out of the durbar and in his private chambers, Nadir unrolled the cloth and out fell the glittering stone whose provenance was said to go back to the Sun god himself. As the light kindled that strange fire within the crystal, Nadir exclaimed: 'Koh-i-Noor! Mountain of Light!' It was then that the name was born.

Whether that diamond was the stone of Babur and Krishna, or one mined a century before and given to Shah Jehan, the truth scarcely mattered because, from that moment on, the Koh-i-Noor was destined to be the most famous, and most fought over, diamond of all time.

On 6th May, 1739, Nadir Shah and his army departed. The vast wagon train is said to have included more than a thousand heavily laden elephants, 7,000 horses and 10,000 camels. It is almost impossible to assess the value of what was taken by today's standards; perhaps the best analogy is to imagine the present City of London stripped of its wealth, every bank vault empty, the headquarters of De Beers totally bare, and, of course, the galleries containing the Crown Jewels in the Tower of London empty.

That the city recovered at all was a miracle: by all the traditions of Indian history, Shahjehanabad should have become an overgrown pile of rubble in the jungle. But it did survive, as did the Mughal dynasty, much reduced. The final blow for the descendants of Babur had yet to be delivered, and by some twist of fate, it would be on almost the same spot where Dr Jaffery and I now stood.

He took my arm and led me to the edge of the parapet. Between the mosque and the Sikh gurdwara was an empty space which he pointed out.

'This area was the place of execution, under both the Mughal and British rulers. You will go next to Punjab?'

I nodded.

'The Sikhs were the last Indian owners of the Koh-i-Noor before you British got it,' he said. 'This is their place in Delhi where some of their early martyrs died. Now they are building an arch.'

The workmen were putting the finishing touches to the white construction, the last pieces of wooden scaffold about to come down.

'You see, Nadir Shah was only the beginning of the end for the Mughals,' said Dr Jaffery. 'Despite everything, they survived as a dynasty, eventually ruling no further than the walls of the Red Fort, but still alive. It was the British who finished it – here, in 1857. The same place.'

Following the Mutiny, Delhi had been retaken by the British after a ferocious battle. On 24th September, 1857, a young officer called Hodson captured the old Emperor, Bahadur Shah, and brought him back to Shahjehanabad, passing down Chandni Chowk and depositing him at the Begum Serai. It had been a calamitous decision to join the mutineers for the aging Mughal, but he had been provoked by Marquis Dalhousie, Governor-General of India, who had told him that his title and position would die with him.

Charles Griffiths, a British officer, saw the Emperor after Hodson brought him to the Serai. 'Sitting cross-legged on a cushion placed on a common native charpoy, or bed, in his veranda or courtyard, was the last representative of the Great Mogul dynasty. There was nothing imposing in his appearance, save a long white beard which reached to his girdle. About middle height, and upwards of seventy years old, he was dressed in white, with a conical-shaped turban of the same colour and material, while at his back two attendants stood, waving over his head large fans of peacocks' feathers, the emblem of sovereignty – a pitiable farce in the case of one who was already shorn of his regal attributes.'

Hodson then secured the surrender of the Emperor's two sons and grandson, heirs to what remained of the Mughal throne. The exact circumstances of what happened next are unknown but Hodson, acting with characteristic impetuosity, took out his rifle and shot all three captives dead. The bodies were then dragged to the place of execution and left there for all to see, just a few feet from the window where Nadir Shah had stood over a century before.

There is no monument or plaque to commemorate the place where the murdered Mughal princes lay. Sikhs hurry in and out of their gurdwara, dodging through the porters and the salesmen with their piles of socks. They honour their own dead: martyrs made by Aurangzeb, and it would be odd if they mourned the passing of the dynasty from which he came. If Akbar's Divine Faith had taken root, it might have been different, but that grandiose folly died with him. The last Mughal emperor, found guilty on every charge at his trial, was exiled to Rangoon where the climate and hardships soon claimed him.

Hodson became a hero of sorts to the more jingoistic British imperialists. It was, after all, the year of the grisly Cawnpore massacre and tales of dreadful atrocities, some genuine, were fanning the flames of hatred. 'In twenty-four hours, therefore,' he wrote, 'I disposed of the principal members of the house of Timur the Tartar. I am not cruel, but I confess I did rejoice at the opportunity of ridding the earth of these wretches . . . I expect no reward,' he added, 'perhaps not even thanks.' What he did get was justice – shot dead at Lucknow a few months later. In his pocket was a list of sites worth looting.

CHAPTER 10

O Sun of the World! Cast your splendours here,
A strange time, like a shadow, has come upon us.

Ghalib, nineteenth-century Delhi poet

THE following evening I had arranged to visit Dr Jaffery. He was preparing a lecture on the architecture of Shah Jehan, and I spent the afternoon proof-reading the text for him at the Hardinge Library, brushing the occasional fallen pigeon feather from the pages.

It was late when I set off across the town, almost dark. The back road that leads onto Chandni Chowk is a parking lot for trucks, buses and carts, the drivers enjoying tea from cracked cups and some gossip. There are fragments of the old Mughal gardens, the Begum Serai, and there are families who live against the fences in blackened spaces around a hearth with a few fragments of possessions most of us would call rubbish: bits of rag, sticks, a sheet of torn blue polythene. It was this area, between the Kashmiri Gate and Chandni Chowk where some of the most ferocious fighting took place when the British stormed back into Delhi following the Mutiny. Perhaps for that reason it has a particularly woebegone appearance today. The inhabitants live like urban bushmen: scraping a living from the impoverished environment. On the lane that leads up to Chandni Chowk, I stopped to give an old beggar a few small coins and straightening up from his tin on the ground, I saw a man looking back at me from fifty yards away. It was only a momentary glimpse, but I recognised him.

Then a lorry came between us. I set off up the street after him, hurrying out onto Chandni Chowk. Darkness was falling and the hawkers were unwrapping their bundles of cheap clothes along the pavements: saris and gentlemen's hankerchiefs, woolly Pathan caps and collared waistcoats. I dodged around a bull wearing a raincoat and across the road, weaving through the porters – *Chaloo! Chaloo!* – their trolleys piled impossibly high with boxes.

I caught one more glimpse of the man as he hurried on ahead of me. The grey hair was hidden under a cap but the pointed moustaches were unmistakeable. I was even close enough to see the glint of rubies in his ear. Then he was gone. I dived up the alleyway after him but the flood of humanity held me up.

There was only one turning and I couldn't think where else he might have gone. It was an alleyway no wider than a cow that still managed to have a few shops: a cubby-hole where a boy was sorting machine parts, a tiny office containing a red telephone and finally an old man asleep beside a grubby display of tap washers. After these the walls closed in. I glanced up. There was a narrow strip of night sky far above. A barefoot, snotty-nosed boy pushed past. I came to a gate and opened it. A woman let out a little yelp; there was a flurry of red sari and the gate slammed back at me. A shutter creaked above my head.

'Malik,' I called, 'Malik from Hyderabad?'

No one answered. The shutter slammed. I returned to the main street and on the corner stopped to buy a couple of samosas with a blob of green chutney. I was almost certain that it had been the man I had met in Surat, the man on the run from fourteen life sentences, but why had he avoided me? By the time I made it to Ajmeri Gate, I had convinced myself it was a mistake.

Dr Jaffery was pacing his room with a book in his hand. 'Come, come, listen.'

I sat under the dome and listened.

'"A wonderful necklace of pearls costing 3 lakhs of rupees, a heart-ravishing necklace costing 2 lakhs of rupees, an eye-soothing necklace costing 2 lakhs and 50,000 rupees, a pleasure-giving necklace . . ." Have you got it yet?'

I shook my head.

'"A yellow ruby called Guli Aftar – sunflower – a diamond called Koh-i-Noor."'

'Ah! It's the list of Nadir's booty!'

'Exactly. Listen: "A ruby of Badakhshan – the ring of Jamshed."
Remember? Jamshed was the Persian hero who tried to build Paradise
on earth – the city of Iram – which was lost forever.' He tapped the page
and went back to his list, a head-spinning array of treasure. 'Nadir's
men did not know the value of the jewels and so sold them back to the
Indians. If one had the price of 50,000 rupees, he sold it for a 100.'

He went on through the description, an account of the raid written
by a Persian in 1739. There was no mention of the turban-swapping
story which, we decided, was probably a later addition. Even the
mention of the Koh-i-Noor halfway through an immense list of rings
and stones, seemed to suggest the author had little regard for any
special significance attached to it. '"They plundered in half a day what
had been gathered in a thousand years."'

He set the book down. 'Our Iranian friend sent it for me to read to
you.'

Outside I could hear the bamboo chick tapping on the door like a
blind man's stick on a kerbstone. Dr Jaffery pulled the curtain across
and began to make tea.

About an hour later, around nine o'clock, I came out of the room
and went down into the courtyard. The wind was bitingly cold and the
few people around outside were muffled up in shawls and blankets.
There was normally a rank of autorickshaws opposite the college, but
on this occasion the kerbside was deserted. Feeling a little annoyed, I
turned the corner and set off walking in the direction of Karol Bagh.
After a hundred yards I crossed over in order to hail any passing taxi
but, as it happened, I didn't need to.

A rickshaw pulled alongside me, the driver peering out from his cab.
In the back there were already two men with suitcases, but that was
nothing unusual: Delhiites often share transport when necessary.
These two were wrapped in Kashmiri shawls and looked frozen.

'Where you going?' asked the driver.

'Karol Bagh.'

The man nearer to me nodded. 'We are going there – our hotel is
there.' He had a likeable face: thin with a neat beard. The other was
chubby, smooth-shaven, and smiling. 'We can share the cost of our
journeying.'

I had heard that one before and it rarely resulted in any savings, but I climbed in.

The driver yanked at a cable and managed to slam the engine into gear. We set off.

'Where have you come from?' I asked. There was a side entrance to New Delhi Railway Station near Ajmeri Gate and I assumed they had come out from there. If I had considered only for a second, I would have realised that anyone staying in Karol Bagh would use the Paharganj entrance, but the thought never occured to me.

'We are from Himachal Pradesh,' said the chubby one. 'But we came from Bombay – our brother is there.'

The elder one next to me, manoeuvred the suitcase onto his knee and opened it. I caught a glimpse of some clothes. He took out a packet of beedis and offered me one. I refused. He shook the packet. 'It is our custom.'

Persian politesse, I thought, reluctantly accepting. No sooner had we got them lit than the rickshaw broke down. The driver got out, muttering to himself. We had only covered about 400 yards and I was ready to ditch the machine for another, but my fellow passengers wouldn't hear of it.

'Always hurry – you westerners,' laughed the older man. 'Hurry, worry, curry. In India you must slow down. Relax.'

It went through my mind: it must be a known catchphrase. Then: how strange he should repeat one of Malik's little rhymes only a couple of hours after I had spotted him.

I shrugged. It felt wrong to leave while I was still smoking their beedis. Besides, it was a shrewdly persuasive comment – appealing to that side of any traveller who likes to think he has settled into the local pace of things.

The driver spent some time fiddling with pliers then took to smacking at the handlebar with a monkey wrench. There was no anger in what he was doing, no frustration. In all India, with all the broken-down machines I had encountered, I had never seen anyone get angry with any of them. He was simpy whacking it like he would whack a lazy donkey. And the rickshaw obviously understood and appreciated his attitude because it started first time when he tried. Patience, I told myself. We set off again.

Our conversation, as I remember it, was fairly innocuous. Places in India. Family.

The rickshaw broke down again. This time in a dark section of road where the sparse traffic sped past, oblivious to pedestrians. There were fires burning on the ground and several bundles of rags next to them: sleeping street people, lying like corpses stretched out after a massacre. Here and there a foot or hand stuck out, the flesh black and crusty. We warmed ourselves for a few minutes. None of them moved.

The driver was attempting to rig the gear cable to the windscreen where he could then yank it to change. It didn't look hopeful. I went over and thrust ten rupees towards him. 'Here, I'm going to get another rickshaw – take this.'

He waved it away. 'No, no. One minute only!'

The others climbed back inside. 'Come on – he is finished. Come on.'

I dithered. There was no sign of a rickshaw approaching – the usual sickly yellow headlamp wobbling through the darkness. In either direction was a long walk.

'Now he is ready – come on!'

I took my seat. The elder man grinned. 'I think India will teach you many things – like our hospitality, yes?'

He opened the suitcase and took out a packet of biscuits, the ginger snaps you can buy on railway stations. He opened it and offered me one.

'No thanks.'

He shook the packet. 'Come. It is our custom.'

'I really don't want one.'

'Is our Indian food not good enough? We are not rich men, but we offer you freely, as friends.'

It was the bind of courtesy, a silken trap stronger than steel, the same trap that Nadir Shah had worked his victim into. I took the biscuit.

The engine gunned to life and the driver, grinning happily took a ginger snap himself. I bit off half and ate.

As we jerked into movement, I remember thinking, there is a soft bit here under my fingertip which doesn't seem right, but the first morsel was already sliding down my throat. There was no warning. Perhaps a momentary shutdown in peripheral vision. A twist of darkness. I saw the elder man's face smiling at me from the side, looking vaguely like Haile Selassie. Hurry, worry, curry. My head suddenly fell back and hit the metal support of the hood. Then I was unconscious.

At some point during that long night, I woke. I was lying on my back on a concrete floor gazing at the ceiling. I have no idea how long I stared, trying to make sense of a fluorescent tube. My shirt was off and I was covered in dirt and blood, but I had no knowledge of that at the time. All I wanted was to understand that line of light, how the sun could be so stretched and cold.

Later, I had turned my head to the right and could see a group of men squatting on the floor a few feet away from me. Their faces were laughing and hands busy. Behind was a window covered by shutters – light blue slats, darkness between them. I could not move but did not feel any pain.

One of the men turned and looked at me, said something. They all looked. Chubby and Haile Selassie were both there, with heavy coats across their shoulders against the cold and me half-naked but not cold at all.

I was struggling to get up, at least mentally I was struggling because there was no reaction at all from my limbs. It was as though that gigantic line of light was lying across my chest, pinning me to the ground. Then a shadow came in from above my head and blotted out the light and I saw, as though it were happening to someone else, a syringe come to my arm and the needle slipping inside me. I saw the hands squeeze the plunger and the liquid going in and I saw the side of that grizzled head close to mine, the greying flourish of a moustache, and in the ear, a lotus flower of eight rubies with a diamond in the centre.

A light came on and I sat up. A shattering pain split across the back of my head. I reached up and found blood caked with dirt. A door was open and a man there with a cup of tea in his hand.

'Drink this,' he said.

I watched him walk to the bedside and scintillating tracers of light came shooting off the top of his head and the rim of the teacup. The carpet pattern wriggled into life around his footfalls.

'What time is it?' I asked.

'Ten o'clock.'

I struggled to sit up. 'I have to go. I'm meeting someone at ten-thirty.'

He put the tea down. 'It is better you rest. It is night.'

I looked at the window and saw he was right. But I had arranged to go back to see Dr Jaffrey one last time at ten-thirty in the morning.

'What day is it?'

He smiled. 'Today is Thursday.'

I lay back and he left the room. The robbery had been on Tuesday night so, apart from that one waking moment and the syringe . . . I sat up. The room swayed. I searched down my forearm to the little red dot. That memory was true.

Drinking the tea, I felt stronger and stood up. My bag was there with the others. Inside I found my money pouch that rested in a sling under my arm. It had been carefully slit open along the seams, but there were still some travellers cheques inside – and my passport and air ticket. Puzzled, I began to rummage through my bag.

Memory is such an unreliable mirror of the past. I had two books with me that day: *Koh-i-Noor Diamond* by Iradj Amini and *Delhi: Its Monuments and History* by Percival Spear. On the back cover of the Spear in a wavering hand, recognisably mine, I found the words 'Pool, Camera, Auros, Gods, Camera.' Inside the back cover was another note: 'dragged down steps/ head hurt'. When I wrote these things, I have no recollection. In a moment of semi-lucidity during that night, I had been moved to record the events, a brief noctuary, concealing more than it reveals. If I wrote anything on the other book I do not know, it has gone. This was the second curious aspect of the robbery: they had taken the diamond book and left the guide to Delhi.

Like my money holster, the bag had been thoroughly examined: seams split and cut, every flap and corner opened and searched. My cameras were gone, so too was the exposed film and an 1837 East India Company half-anna found on the Isle of Diu. I sat back on the bed and tried to understand what had happened: they had stolen film but only exposed rolls; they had stolen money but only cash; they had searched my bags minutely but not taken my passport. Finally in the bottom of the bag I found a twenty dollar bill, and rolled up inside it all the lucky charms I had amassed over the years: the rainforest seeds from Borneo, the cowrie from Socotra, the stone cross from Ethiopia on its three-stranded black thread – all scrunched up inside the face of President Andrew Jackson. The only one missing was the ring from Hyderabad, the nine-stoned ring that had cost so little, with the diamond in the centre.

Had the charms worked, I wondered, by frightening a gang of superstitious thieves into mercy. But the careful examination of the seams suggested they had been looking for something, and that, I decided, could only have been diamonds.

It was true that I had become careless about mentioning my interest. India, like England, is a place where people will happily chat but not necessarily open up their hearts. In order to reap, I had sown: nonchalantly mentioning my diamond project in order to get a response. But in Delhi, I had been more circumspect, and I could not recall telling any casual acquaintances. Certainly I did not recognise Chubby and Haile Selassie from previous meetings and, of the others, only the ruby ear-ring of the man who had injected me was clear in my mind. Could it have been Malik from the Surat teashop? The possibility that he had followed me through Gujarat and Rajasthan was so remote: it must have been a chance encounter turned to good advantage. Then I remembered the business card: Malik had given me a business card. I could try the number.

Over the months I had been in India I had been handed dozens of business cards, all of which I had shoved in a side pocket of the camera bag. Now they were in the bottom of the main compartment. I tipped them all out and began scrabbling through them. After several searches, I gave up. I could not find Malik's. Every card I had kept was there: the irrigation engineer on the train one night, the printer-cum-lay preacher, the astrogemologist, the jewellers and diamond dealers – all of them except Malik. Someone had sorted through the cards and removed that one.

Exhausted by all this activity, I lay down and fell instantly asleep.

*

In the morning the manager of the hotel personally brought me one of his eggless omelettes and some tea.

'You very lucky man!' he said. 'Some fellow is finding you in drain by the road. If you are spending one night there, you will die for sure.'

'Where was that – and when?' The tea was thick with milk and sugar. It tasted wonderful.

'Not far from here. This fellow saw you and pulled you up and then is searching your pockets.'

'Umph!' To see if there was anything left, I thought, rather uncharitably considering he had saved me from the rats and roaches.

'In your pocket you were very wise to be keeping a business card of this hotel, so he gave us a tinkle.'

'Did he see anyone throw me there?'

'Nothing. He put you in a taxi to this place and you arrived here yesterday at seven in the morning.' So I was missing for about thirty-six hours.

The manager was quite proud of his part in the drama. 'We tried to wake you. Really, we tried very hard – and you were walking and talking – I think you have no memory of these events – Ha! Then you were eating very large quantities of food. Really, stupendous quantities. Miraculous! I have the bills here.'

He rooted around in his pocket and produced a large wadge of receipts for various dishes: fried rice, tea, omelette, chicken curry with nan and popadom, tea, bhajis, mashed potato with an egg on top and baked beans, tea. I had to admit they were all the sorts of foods I might have chosen from his rich and varied menu. Apparently, in the hours at the hotel that had dropped from my memory, all I had done was stuff prodigious quantities of food inside me. Strange then, that I had been quite hungry soon after coming round.

'I had better go to the police,' I said.

He didn't look very impressed. 'They will do nothing.'

'I'll go anyway.'

After eating, I had a shower and discovered that my hair was full of dried blood from a gash behind my left ear. My hands, too, had been grazed and dirt rubbed in, perhaps from being dragged. There was no hot water and the cold affected me badly, the tiles at my feet began to zoom up and down. I had to sit down on the wet toilet seat and promptly got an electric shock. That roused me.

The police initially tried to send me away, claiming the crime had not occurred in their area. I took three attempts at writing a statement, the first of which I kept and reads as though written in Indian English by a man with only a rudimentary grasp of English spelling: 'Ther ricksha was very faulty,' I wrote. 'Stopping every few yards and driver was rigging up gear wire to windscreen.' Any decent lawyer would have proved such a statement to be a fabrication of the police officer.

Later, I went to see Dr Jaffery who looked concerned. 'What has happened to you? I was surprised when you did not come – an Englishman – we expect them to arrive on time. But look, you cannot understand what I am saying can you?'

It was true. Pink rings from around his eyes had detached themselves and were spinning away into the gathering gloom. I could hear a rushing noise in my ears and sweat was dripping from my nose despite the chilly air. I went back to Karol Bagh but, as the rickshaw approached the street, I felt a rising fear of being there after dark. I simply could not face that claustrophobic back street again. My plan had been to travel up to the Punjab and so I rang my contact there, a lawyer named Mehtab, who was interested in the case of the Koh-i-Noor. He promised to meet me at Chandigarh station if I could get on the 4 p.m. Shatabdi Express. 'I'll be wearing a blue turban,' he said.

The hotel manager tried to prevent me leaving. 'You are a very sick man,' he shouted. 'You must take your rest. Here are some more bills.'

I paid the lot without question. By this time I was shaking with fever, but I had to leave. I even suspected the manager of being in league with the robbers. At every corner I saw the leering face of Haile Selassie, the elder thief, and Malik with his hand crawling like a tarantula along the back of the seat towards my shoulder. Hurry, worry, curry.

I was late getting to New Delhi Railway Station and the train was already crowded. When I found a seat, there was a worried-looking youth next to it, peering out of the window at the passing people.

'Excuse me,' I said. 'Is that seat free?'

He jumped to his feet, startled, and pushed past me into the aisle.

[223]

'No, no!' he cried, 'My uncle's neck is swelling!' Then he bolted up the carriage and disappeared. I did not see him again and, given my own confused mental state, it was just as well. Of the journey itself, I can remember nothing. Probably I slept.

Nadir Shah's own magnificent withdrawal from Delhi began at a stately pace but soon took on the aspect of a flight. Bands of marauders picked off stragglers – looting the looters. Nadir Shah himself began to suffer from bouts of vomiting and constipation. Once back in Persia he withdrew to his mountain fortress near Mashad with his jewels. His severe temperament now turned cruel: any dissension was met with execution. A French Jesuit, Father Bazin, who accompanied him on a punitive expedition, saw pyramids of heads thirty feet high along their route. A rumour that his much-loved son was implicated in an assassination attempt threw him into a fury. The Prince's eyes were gouged out with a red-hot wire. The malevolent influence of the great diamond was suspected.

In June 1747, the Shah's family and officers, sick of his tyranny, broke into his tent at night and hacked off his head. Nadir's troops contained a group of Afghans, among them one Ahmad Khan Abdali who had joined Nadir at Kandahar the year before the capture of Delhi. Hearing the commotion, he rushed into Nadir's tent, took the imperial seal from his finger and the Koh-i-Noor diamond, then fled for Kandahar.

The stone had moved yet again, much to the discomfort of Nadir's grandson, Shah Rukh Mirza, who everyone believed still possessed the diamond. In a chaotic forty years, he was made child king, deposed and blinded, restored, then deposed once more. His replacement, Agha Muhammad, was a eunuch with appalling table manners – disembowelling servants on a whim during dinner – and a taste for building monuments in human eyes. At Kerman he had trays of them brought to him: 40,000 in all, with his officer trembling because any shortfall was to be made up from his own account.

The vicious despot was convinced Shah Rukh Mirza had the Koh-i-Noor and ordered torture sessions. The blind man revealed the hiding place of every jewel he possessed, the last a great ruby taken by

Nadir from Delhi. Unable however to reveal the famous diamond, he provoked Agha Muhammad to crown him – with molten lead.

Meanwhile the actual possessor of the diamond, Ahmad Khan Abdali, had changed his name to Durrani – pearls – and carved out an Afghan empire, the forerunner of the modern state. The Koh-i-Noor came down to his grandson, Zaman, who was deposed and blinded but sufficiently quick-witted to hide the world's greatest treasure inside a crack in his prison wall. There it remained for two years while the passion for blinding rivals raged all around. Kings and would-be kings dug out eyes at every opportunity: it was as though, unable to possess that great symbol of clarity and divinity, they would make certain no rival would ever gaze upon its glory.

Eventually, Zaman's brother, Shuja, seized the throne and recovered the diamond. In 1809 he wore it as a bracelet while meeting a British representative, Mountstuart Elphinstone, in Peshawar. The Englishman was impressed and sent back the first of several reports that would alert certain ambitious British officers to the jewel's whereabouts. They were not alone: Shuja's ostentatious love of jewels had also aroused the cupidity of the governor of Peshawar. Taking advantage of an uprising in Kabul, the governor imprisoned Shuja and made his demands. But he was too late. Shuja had passed the stone to his wife, who had then fled to Lahore and thrown herself on the mercies of Maharaja Ranjit Singh, the Lion of the Punjab. The diamond had entered on the last phase of its Indian existence.

At Chandigarh I climbed down to find a station full of blue turbans, hundreds of them. But one smiling face came towards me: 'Mister Kevin?'

My brain was still reeling from the chemical attack it had sustained, but, by great good fortune, I had gone from the worst of Indians to the best.

Mehtab was with his uncle, a formal and reserved gentleman who took us to his little Fiat car and drove outrageously fast to his club. There we met an ex-army man (almost every other man in the Punjab is) who told me his son had foretold in a dream that he would be attacked by a black cobra and next day he was. Then on to a Chinese restaurant where the waitress was dressed as Suzie Wong and came from Assam. Uncle was wearing a mauve shirt with yellow knitted tie, brown checked sports jacket, black trousers and blue turban, his beard tucked up in a fishnet suspended from his ears. Mehtab wore a blue windcheater, tartan shirt with knitted tie and jeans. Small objects, like runaway fondue chunks, were floating across my vision. If I leaned back in my chair, I seemed to go on forever. If I leaned forward, I wanted to fall in my plate. When no one was looking, I held my head in my hands and muttered, 'This is bonkers.' Suzie Wong chided me for not touching my sweet and sour chicken. I hadn't even noticed it. Mehtab said that four or five Sikhs were claiming that the Koh-i-Noor was theirs by right and that he wanted to be a sculptor and painter not a lawyer. He wrote down my name and address. 'In case we are stopped by the police. Men in blue turbans do get stopped.'

'Are you a Sikh nationalist?'

'The blue turban is worn by the Akali Party usually – but for me it is personal reasons.'

We drove back, unchecked at the roadblocks, to Mehtab's aunt's house. Looking out of the car window, I got the impression that I had left India: the headlights swept across straight well-made roads, trees, concrete, space, empty space. After Old Delhi it felt as though I had fallen through a hole into nothingness, no points of reference, no idea what this was – just the men dressed in oddly matched colours, as though they chose randomly each day from a communal pile, only the turbans holding them together as a race.

Mehtab's aunt's house was a concrete modern dwelling in suburbia – the future as seen by designers of the 1950s. She was away visiting relatives, but there were two servants; I never saw them, only heard their whispers from behind the kitchen door. The furniture was simple, solid woodwork with plain pastel covers. There were vases of glass tulips and occasional tables and coasters with pictures on them. I fell asleep shivering, in a room lined with fitted cupboards.

Next morning, I felt less confused and a bit better for it. Mehtab came and took me to his house for breakfast. Chandigarh was just as I had sensed the previous night: a vast campus of straight boulevards and concrete buildings. The human touch was the beaten paths cutting across the square lawns. People don't like walking in right-angles.

Mehtab's front room was lined with old masters. Behind the sofa was a Vermeer, opposite was a Russian Impressionist, and at the end a Constable – only half-finished. His careful preparations to convert to the life of an artist involved copying these paintings perfectly. He was also a gifted sculptor: on a small table stood the bust of a guru, a head of such calm and tranquillity that I could have gazed at it for the rest of the morning.

But Mehtab had plans.

'Here, take this.' He handed me a crash helmet and a thick coat. I was still shivering; Chandigarh was bitterly cold.

We took his motor scooter across town, past the shops and restaurants, the banks and jewellery stores. Chandigarh is a peculiar place: people shop in supermarkets, they follow road signs and speed limits, some even wear crash helmets while riding motor scooters; civic gardeners garden, and people go to admire the roses rather than feed them to their goats; concrete is regarded as an attractive building material, and there are no shabby cigarette and betel kiosks on every street corner. I was in a peculiar dream: a European vision of an Indian future that had become the present yet appeared dated. It took a shop sign to bring me back to earth: Anus Beauty Parlour. Hours later, I realised the apostrophe was missing.

We came to a terraced house in a suburb and, knocking on the door, were shown through to a concrete yard at the rear. In a deckchair an elderly man with a long white beard was sunning himself. He had a pink fluffy blanket around his shoulders, a bright saffron turban, a herringbone kurta, white jodhpurs and square-toed leather boots. He sprang up when he heard us. Straight-backed and six feet tall. 'Ha! An Englishman.'

Mehtab pressed his hands together in respect and bent to touch the man's knees. The man seized my hand like a terrier onto a rat and squeezed. 'Your good name? Rushby? From which part?'

He pulled me into the sunlight to get a better look.

'Rushby from Thirsk has come,' he bellowed to the surrounding houses. 'Your parents are still? Your mother lives with you? Why not? I will never understand you English. You are married? Children's names and ages?'

He pulled a pair of sunglasses from his pocket and donned them.

'You like them? Sikh dress begins here with the turban, then the kurta.' He continued on down. 'Finally, kechcha – underwear – and there we will leave the matter!' He threw back his leonine head and roared with laughter. 'Better not to mention the rest!'

I had met Professor Sher Singh: poet, mystic, scholar, broadcaster, lecturer and anthropologist. 'Have you written books?' he demanded as we sat down.

'Yes, I have – one book.'

'Good! I have written dozens of books and have thirty more planned. But you are young and I am not.'

Tea was brought and we sat in silence, sipping at the warm sweet liquid. There were distant noises of domestic routine from across the fences: pans clashing, children shouting, a motorbike starting. It felt like home.

Mehtab explained my interest in the Koh-i-Noor. The Professor nodded. 'When Ranjit Singh – you know the last great leader of our Sikh nation – when he was asked its value, he replied: "Two shoes." By which he meant two blows of a shoe – or rather, the strong man will have it. Might is right!'

He smoothed his beard thoughtfully. 'Now these people want to claim it back. You should ask yourself why. Digging up a skeleton – but the skeleton has no use but in a house of skeletons. What will they do with it? Walk around the Punjab with a crown on their head?' He roared with laughter.

'Wherever you go, people are the same. Is there anything wrong with plunder? Man living naked plundered nature. When I was in London, I looked around and saw that only the bricks and mortar were English. Yes, it's true, isn't it?'

'Now, the Koh-i-Noor was the property of kings, and kings are the state.' He held up a finger. 'The seer, the great soul, the prophet, he is always against the state. If he says he is not, he is a bastard and a liar. The king is always bound to oppress the people – definitely. That is how he rules – a bundle of orders to be willy or nilly obeyed by the people.'

His daughter-in-law appeared with more tea and he asked her to bring a book out. A slim maroon volume appeared and he opened it.

'Your Maharani, Queen Elizabeth came here recently and visited our holiest shrine, the Golden Temple. That is, the owner of the Koh-i-Noor came here and sat on the stage looking across at that beautiful temple – you will see – the most beautiful sight in all the world. And I sat there on the stage with her – Yes, I was there! This book was presented to her with a model of the temple.'

He looked down and read out loud. '"The divine currents of population separated us and now brought us back to our ancient separated brethren being consanguines."' He looked up. 'Do you see? We are Jats and we came from the Scythian race of central Asia who also peregrinated westwards. You know them as Jutes, or as in Jutland. The same! Vikings and Normans who settled in your Yark-shire and Lincoln-shire. Buddha, Odin, Wodin, Wednesday – the gods were the same. That is our peoples' common ancestry.'

He snapped the book shut and raised it aloft. 'At that holy place, with this book in her hand, she said not one word. She did not even walk all the way around the holy lake. Not one word!'

He shook his head. 'Then I began to hate kings and queens even more than before. So what is this wish for the return of the Koh-i-Noor? I will tell you: it is hue and cry without reply!'

His hand seized mine with a loud slap and he dissolved into a round of shoulder-shaking laughter: 'Hue and cry without reply!'

'Perhaps she was embarrassed,' I said. 'I mean about the massacre.' That particular one had taken place in the Golden Temple in 1919 at the orders of General Dyer.

The Professor shook his head. 'Did she do it? No. In England they think it important to apologise – but not here. What made me angry was she saw that holy place and said nothing.'

We sat back and drank the tea. Though I was in the warm sun, sweat was dripping off me, and I could feel my limbs beginning to shake uncontrollably. The Professor's pink fluffy blanket and saffron turban in the sunlight became almost painfully intense.

'I said: Are you sick?' The Professor was half-standing looking in my face.

'I think I've caught a bug,' I said. 'There was a robbery.' The story began to come out. The Professor stood up.

'Get this man to bed!' He ordered. Mehtab helped me into the house. The last thing I heard as my head touched the pillow was the Professor's booming voice echoing around the houses. 'Rushby of Thirsk has retired hurt!'

I slept from that morning until the next – almost twenty hours. Once I got up in the night to find myself at the barred window pulling at the rods, completely disoriented: I was in that shuttered room and someone was coming for me with a syringe. It took several minutes to work out where I was: which town, which house, which room; and the thought in my head was: 'I hope the needle was clean.'

I fell asleep again and dreamed of a body covered by a shroud which was slowly being pulled back from below the feet. And I waited and waited, watching the folds of cloth slide and ripple like water, waiting to see who it was that had died. But then, at the last moment, as the edge of the shroud finally appeared and began to lift up to uncover the hair and face, I grabbed it. A sudden and terrible fear seized me and I was thinking, 'What if it's me under the cloth?' So I held on grimly though someone was pulling hard. Then I couldn't hold it any longer, and just as the hair appeared, I woke, sweating profusely, to find a huge figure looming over me: an orange halo, a great white beard, moustaches curled into tusks and two hands clasping a gnarled shepherd's crook.

'Rushby of Thirsk,' his voice boomed. 'Are you alive?'

I nodded. 'I think so.'

'I have had my walk,' he said. 'Five o'clock every morning. But today is too cold.' He pulled the orange blanket closer around his head, then turned and disappeared from view. I slept again.

At nine in the morning I woke and looked around the icily cold room. There was a portrait of Guru Nanak looking down at me with a kindly smile, a glass-fronted cupboard full of knick-knacks and a steel filing cabinet. Next to the bed was an armchair and in it sat the Professor, dressed in white kurta, grey cardigan, jodhpurs, black pumps, saffron turban and an orange fluffy blanket.

'You are having bad dreams,' he said, seeing me awake. 'Many times I sat here and watched my wife in that bed as she lay sick and dying.'

[230]

He pulled the blanket closer around him. 'It is a very hard thing at my age to lose one's life partner – very hard.'

'When did it happen?'

'A year ago. Exactly one year. That is why I am feeling these things today.'

We remained in silence for a long time and I eventually nodded off back to sleep. When I woke again, he had gone.

There were sounds of pans clattering in the kitchen and a child's voice. I got up and dressed. The Professor's daughter-in-law smiled and waved me through towards his room. He slept in a back room lined with his books, thousands and thousands of them: they were stacked three deep on the shelves from floor to ceiling, they propped up his bed, they filled the drawers meant for clothes; his bedside table was made of books, on it were more books and under the bed were suitcases filled with books, sitting on a layer of books.

The Professor was lying full length on his bed under the blankets. He pulled them back when I entered and a book slid onto the floor. 'If you lick a diamond, you will die,' he said. 'I don't believe it, but that doesn't mean it isn't true.' He got up, already fully-clothed, and put on his boots. 'Let us sit in the sun.'

We went outside. The contrast between the stone-cold shade and hot sunlight was so great, I could bear neither and ended up sitting with my lower half in the sun, the rest in the shade.

'In Turkey on the train,' said the Professor. 'I woke to find my shirt cut open and everything gone – all my money, my bag, my passport – all of it. They had drugged me. When I went to the police they demanded a bribe. I said, "I have nothing left to give you." So they said they could not help.' He laughed. 'I tell you this to make you feel better!'

He tapped my knee. 'When Christ was being crucified, some were shedding tears and some were shedding his blood. But when events like your robbery happen, we can all see the hand of God and believe. God saved you for – how much did they take – $600! It would have been much easier for them to kill you – believe me – they usually do that. Why did they not? It was the divine. It is not your time. I can see it.'

It was my first intimation of the Professor's more esoteric powers.

His daughter-in-law called us to breakfast: parathas with various delicious curries. The Professor's son had already gone to work so it was just the two of us eating: his daughter-in-law and small grandson ate after we finished.

Thus began a number of dreamy days spent sitting and sleeping. Mehtab brought me a pair of longjohns to wear, and a sleeveless Punjabi jacket. My beard had grown and when I looked in the mirror I hardly recognised the dishevelled alien that I saw. In the daytime, the sunlight was so strong that I could barely look at the white walls of the yard, but the shadows of the rooms gathered themselves in thick, impenetrable clusters; only at night, in the glow of low bulbs and fluorescent tubes, did it seem possible to see clearly.

Each morning the Professor took his tea in the yard, wearing his Californian sunglasses: 'I was there in 1970. All the young people were hippies and living together peacefully. Good people – but not too fond of work. I gave some teachings to them, but I would not be their guru as they wished. That is forbidden to Sikhism.'

'And London – England?'

'Yes, I was in Glastonbury at dawn on midsummer's day, but I didn't see Arthur or Guinevere. Then at a dinner in London. It was very grand, given by a Scotsman who came dressed in a skirt – but otherwise he was a good fellow.'

Later, I found out the host had been Lord Mountbatten. By dint of his childlike curiosity, imposing appearance and autodidactic knowledge, the Professor had turned into some sort of spokesman for the Sikhs. He had found himself at a Tory Party Conference delivering a petition on turbans and motorcycles to the Prime Minister, Edward Heath. He had broadcast to the Soviet peoples on the socialism inherent in the teachings of the ten Sikh gurus. He had strolled with Nehru in the Prime Minister's garden in Delhi. Nehru had encouraged him to join the Congress Party, promising a great career. The Professor declined the offer: 'I have seen the reality of politicians, devoid of the intrinsic values of human life.'

'Who have you seen?' asked Nehru.

'I have seen you,' said the Professor.

He opened a Pentecostal Church on Highway 101 in California. In the aftermath of Indira Gandhi's assassination and the brutal killings of Sikhs, he had stood up in a television debate and asked a question which left the Governor of Punjab tight-lipped and trembling. 'Why have murderers and their accomplices belonging to Congress not been arrested and duly punished?' The television show, a vehicle for the government's views, was closed down. Always he had been a thorn in the side of the establishment and vested interests.

That evening, sitting by his bed where he was examining books, he said to me, 'For the past month I have been reading only predictions and prophecies. A great meteor will pierce the oceans and steam will be created. Cold will descend on the earth for three years. If it survives, America will rule the twenty-first century.'

He pulled the blankets over his head. 'It is very cold now. You must ask Mehtab to arrange meetings with the men who claim the Koh-i-Noor. Then you will ask them why they want that stone. Then ask yourself why. Man is very low in spite of his high ideals. It is better that you do not tell them who told you to ask such questions. It may be better not to mention that we have met because, if you do, then they will assume you know something, or I have told you something.'

I went to bed and dreamed of crossing a bamboo bridge and stopping halfway to feed fish with rings of ruby and pearl in their mouths.

The following morning I walked out onto the veranda to find Mehtab hunched forward in his chair while the Professor leaned back, eyes closed, breathing deeply.

'Yes,' he said, eventually. 'It is the right decision.'

There was a large copy of the Koran open on the spare chair. The Professor lifted it onto his knee. They had been discussing Mehtab's future but now moved on to the question of whether Islam specifically excludes non-believers from its holy places.

'Sikhism is open to all,' said the Professor. 'Without exclusion. The temple has a door on every side. All may enter. Food may be eaten with anyone – rich, poor, sick, men and women – there is no caste restriction.'

His words reminded me of my hostless lunch in Bombay, and of the servants who refused to eat with Bilkha. I had thought then: 'How can people live together when they cannot eat together?' And yet the ironic thing about the openness of Sikhism is that it has not resulted in converts from diverse walks of life. Despite all the outsiders who come to India in search of spiritual fulfilment, few head north to the Punjab. Sikhism has remained a religion based on a single community. The Professor's son showed me a newspaper cutting about the one foreign convert – a Frenchman who had been baptised in the Golden Temple.

Mehtab and I drove across the town to his house where we had breakfast. It was a second-floor flat with a closed-in atmosphere: the smell of oil paints and curry, sketch pads full of beautiful drawings of faces.

'The Lieutenant-Colonel will come later,' said Mehtab. 'He is one claimant to the diamond.'

A list of things that I should not mention followed. My head was beginning to spin with all the various things I was not to let slip, lest anyone think I had been told what I should not. The atmosphere of intrigue and suspicion was palpable: names of clans and leaders whose shifts of allegiance dated back a hundred years or more were to be weighed on scales of antique origin, until what was simple became complex. There was a parallel with the Koh-i-Noor's own history, in which measurement and authenticity are so closely intertwined. The diamond was 'two and a half days' food for the whole world', 8 misqals, 319 ratis, 9 tanks, 216 surkhs, 268 English carats, or was it 360? – so many numbers claiming to be true, until the weight itself was forgotten and you delved down deeper and deeper into a morass of doubt, questioning the motives of each claim against the rest, doubting the very validity of all measurements.

'The line of Ranjit Singh has died out with only collaterals remaining,' Mehtab explained. 'It is these people. Some have strong claims, others weak.'

Ranjit Singh's own claim might be said to be weak, being based purely on extortion – but then if legality and fair play were the rules of business, the Koh-i-Noor would have to be put back in the ground.

The Lion of the Punjab was actually a one-eyed, pock-marked fox who had carved out his kingdom by the age of twenty. He had been born in 1780, just over seventy years after the death of the last Sikh guru, Govind Singh, who had given the Sikhs the militaristic attitudes that helped Ranjit achieve his aims. The Maharaja delighted in the trappings of power, and when he heard that the great stone was in the possession of the imprisoned Shah Shuja, he took the opportunity to secure his release. He had come to an understanding with Shuja's wife, Wafa Begum, that she would hand over the diamond, if he could rescue her husband.

Once safely in Lahore, however, the deposed Shuja saw things differently, steadfastly maintaining the diamond had been pawned to pay for military campaigns. Only when Ranjit Singh put Shuja in fear of his life was it handed over on 1st June, 1813. The Afghan survived the ordeal and went on to become a puppet leader for the British invasion of Afghanistan in 1842 – a fiasco that ended with Shah Shuja and all the British, bar one, dead.

Ranjit Singh loved the diamond dearly. When he went out riding, he had it mounted on the bridle so he could always watch it. European visitors reported on the magnificence of the jewel, further spreading its fame. One was William Godolphin Osborne, the British Governor-General's nephew. He wrote: 'The jewel rivalled, if not surpassed, in brilliancy the glance of fire which every now and then shot from his single eye as it wandered restlessly round the circle.'

Ranjit Singh's death in 1839, however, led to a chaotic period of internecine strife, culminating in the First Anglo-Sikh War of 1845. The British, led by the one-handed Waterloo-veteran Sir Henry Hardinge, were the eventual winners and confirmed the seven-year-old Dulip Singh as Maharaja. Hardinge was rewarded with a peerage by the British and a view of the Koh-i-Noor by Dulip Singh.

The peace held until 1848 when a rebellion broke out against the growing British influence. Hardinge had been replaced by the thirty-five-year-old Marquis Dalhousie, a man whose arrogant and imperialistic views were to do incalculable damage. The Sikhs were defeated and Dalhousie arranged an ignominious peace. 'The task before me is the utter destruction and prostration of the Sikh power,' he wrote, 'the subversion of its dynasty, and the subjection of its people. This must be done promptly, fully and finally.'

On the 29th March, 1849 the Maharaja Dulip Singh, still only twelve, sat on the golden throne of his father for the last time and signed away his kingdom. Just to make sure, the British took the throne too. It is now in the Victoria and Albert Museum in London.

There is no doubt that Dalhousie saw the Punjab as a cornerstone in the the newly invigorated British Indian Empire, and the Koh-i-Noor as the crowning glory, the diamond that proved their imperial right. 'It is not every day that an officer of their Government adds four millions of subjects to the British Empire,' he wrote, 'And places the historical jewel of the Mughal Emperors in the crown of his Sovereign. This I have done.'

But that was the problem. Dalhousie actually had no legal right to give the diamond to anyone, as East India Company directors were quick to point out. All Indian treaties were with them, not the Crown.

Dalhousie ignored their protests; the transfer to the British Queen of the Koh-i-Noor would be a valuable symbol. The stone was entrusted to John Lawrence, a dour Scottish presbyterian, who had as much liking for jewels as idolators. He put it in his waistcoat pocket and forgot about it, until Dalhousie decided to take it himself to Bombay. When Lawrence delved in his pocket, he found to his horror that the jewel was gone. Fortunately, a servant had put it to one side after Lawrence had absent-mindedly misplaced it in the bathroom.

The diamond reached England safely and was presented to Victoria at Buckingham Palace on 3rd July, 1850. Even before its arrival, tales of the curse attached to the stone had been circulating, some even claimed that Victoria's recent run of bad luck was caused by it. During that May the Queen had been attacked twice: first by an Irishman who shot a pistol at her, then by a retired officer who stepped out of a crowd and smacked her sharply on the head with his brass-tipped walking stick. A hastily-concocted story that the diamond was only fatal to men was put about, but Victoria never wore it in a crown.

The claims of the various parties in Punjab today are based on those distant events. The diamond was not state property, they argue, and not legitimate booty. Rather than being stolen from the boy, Dulip Singh, it should have passed down the generations – to them.

The front door bell rang and Mehtab went out. I could hear voices passing into the front room, then several minutes of close discussions. No doubt the Lieutenant-Colonel was being coached in what I knew and what not to say to me.

After some time, Mehtab appeared and led me through. The curtains were drawn and in the dim light I saw a large, genial man with doctor's half-rim glasses and his beard in a hair net. He wore a red tartan shirt, brown suit, red turban and blue trainers. In front of the carefully controlled and subdued shades of Mehtab's Old Masters, he appeared like a particularly shocking blast of modernist colour.

We shook hands and sat next to each other on the sofa. The neat room, the subdued lighting, the hushed atmosphere: it seemed we were a match-made couple on a first date or, I decided, they really thought I was someone – someone who had a say – someone worth convincing.

From his face I guessed the Lieutenant-Colonel was a man with a good sense of humour; I pushed my hand in my jacket pocket and pretended to get hold of something. 'By the Powers vested in me by Her Majesty's Government – I am hereby instructed to restore to its rightful owner the jewel known as the Koh-i-Noor.'

The Lieutenant-Colonel's eyes widened and flicked over to Mehtab and back to me, watching as I drew my hand from my pocket, fist closed around something.

'What will you do with it, Colonel?'

He broke into a good-natured laugh and pressed his hands together between his knees. 'Greed is always there. If someone says I'm not afraid in battle, he's a liar. I've seen it – I've been there – you take control of yourself and take the right decision.'

'Which is?'

'It should be given to my family to then be given to the Golden Temple.'

I turned my fist over and opened the fingers. All three of us stared at the empty hand, then the Colonel chuckled.

'I am optimistic that it will really come.'

'It was just a joke – sorry. But aren't you afraid of the curse?'

'All just stories.'

He began to explain the origin of his claim. A small fort close to the border with Pakistan had been in his family for generations, but because of the proximity of the border, it had been uninhabited. Recently, he had gone back and opened a locked room to find a roll of antique carpet. When it was unrolled, out popped a small bag containing documents and letters.

He delved in his briefcase and pulled out some faint photocopies.

'These were the documents we sent to Switzerland,' he said. I looked puzzled. 'For the safe deposit box.'

'Which deposit box?'

He began to explain. 'In Switzerland they had certain safe deposit boxes which had not been touched since the Second World War. Then some people said the contents belonged to Jewish families and the Swiss were recently forced to publish a list of names – account holders who had not come forward or made any transactions since 1945.' He chuckled. 'Some sharp-eyed person spotted an Indian name among them – Dulip Singh's daughter.'

'So whoever proves their claim to inheritance – and the Koh-i-Noor – will get the contents of the box?'

'Probably there is nothing inside of value.'

'So why claim it?'

'A drowning man clutches at straws!' He didn't look like a desperate man, just a jovial middle-aged Sikh who had done reasonably well for himself. 'Besides, if it is a family possession, we have a right to it. There may be some jewellery of Dulip Singh.'

I sorted through the paperwork, hand-worn and dog-eared sheets, much like those I had examined at the house of the Nawab's relatives in Junagadh. But despite my attempts to make sense of it, I failed. Each Maharaja had taken several wives, and with the various half-brothers and step-uncles, the situation was complex enough. But added to this were rumours of illegitimacy: Dulip Singh was said to be the offspring of a water carrier and one of Ranjit Singh's dancing girls. In British eyes at the time, this might have been damning, but adoption was considered quite normal in much of Asia – distant relatives being favourites to bolster the male line when necessary. One Indian ruling family had failed to produce a son for eight generations and so adopted on each occasion – the failure, it was said, could be traced to an ancient curse.

The Lieutenant-Colonel was claiming as part of a group, all cousins, and any benefits would be spread thinly. Given the costs of a case – and the extraordinary length of time they can take in India – I found myself questioning if there could be some other benefit, not monetary.

'Whoever proves their case,' I said, watching him carefully, 'they may not get the diamond, they may not find any jewels in the deposit box, there may be no actual financial benefit at all, but their status here in Punjab would be very high, wouldn't it?'

He laughed. 'Oh, it . . . depends.'

'They would have great power, wouldn't they?'

Mehtab was staring at me.

The Lieutenant-Colonel shrugged. 'Well, it . . . who can say?'

There was no denial, and Mehtab's face told me I was onto something. But the Lieutenant-Colonel played a steadfast straight bat and our conversation drifted onto his own past and role in the 1965 Indo-Pakistani War. After ten minutes Mehtab interrupted. 'I think maybe we can finish?'

I shook hands with the Lieutenant-Colonel and Mehtab showed him out. When he returned, he was smiling, 'It's very good – I have the Koh-i-Noor in my pocket – what will you do? – I like it.'

We sat under Constable's Salisbury Cathedral. 'If that diamond came back to the Punjab, it would be a powerful symbol of the Sikh nation,' I said. 'Perhaps even dangerous.'

I could see the chanting mob carrying the diamond on a palanquin through the streets, their heads full of Ranjit Singh, the Lion of the Punjab, the glorious Sikh nation, owners of the greatest diamond on earth. Then it would be placed in the Golden Temple, a few miles from a border region disputed by two nuclear powers. The old Punjab kingdom of Ranjit Singh, of course, was divided by Partition.

Mehtab thought before answering. 'Some say that way. But if it belongs here rightfully, shouldn't it come?'

'And whoever was chosen as the legitimate heir of Dulip Singh would have power.'

'Possibly. The politicians would certainly take notice of them, perhaps try to use them. Even now they are courting these people, in case they succeed. There is one claimant, a strong one, called Beant Singh Sandhanwalia. He is in Amritsar. You can ask him – but don't say I told you so.'

After lunch we drove back to sit with the Professor. He was feeling the cold. Although the sky was blue and the sun blazing, there seemed to be no heat in it. The shadows remained icy, the houses never warming. So he sat in the yard, mulling over his prophecies and predictions, reading from Revelation and Nostradamus.

I told him of my dream of crossing the bridge and feeding the fish.

'The Jains have their thirthankars,' he said, 'ford-crossers. What they mean is that a spiritual journey must end with the crossing of water.'

Later in the day, his son Amerjeet took me on a tour of the city, zipping up and down the long straight boulevards on a motor scooter. There was little traffic but plenty of well-kept verges and islands. Beyond the trees were the sterile concrete hoppers of Le Corbusier, the French architect behind the city's design. With the golden light fading on their streaked, featureless slabs, they appeared like any other shabby ruins – lost forts and palaces of some forgotten kingdom. At the lake families watched an open-air play about tax evasion, ate candy floss, and rode on pedaloes. There was a jogging track, golf club and swimming pool; there were no beggars, betel stains or discarded cigarette ends. Beautiful girls with profiles straight from a Mughal painting wore jeans and designer tee-shirts. 'Once you live in Chandigarh,' said Amerjeet, 'you will never want to live anywhere else. If you live here and go to London, it is not a shock to the system.'

I began to pine for the chaotic vibrancy of Old Delhi. The India that I wanted seemed to have been erased from the picture, and perhaps this was the fate of the rest – Chandigarh was merely in the vanguard.

We were standing by the wall looking down at the boats when he asked me to hold on to his young son and ran down to the boatman. They had a brief but energetic conversation, then he returned, shaking his head.

'What's wrong?'

'I wanted him to sell me a nail.'

'A nail?'

'Yes, an iron nail from a boat.' He looked a bit sheepish.

'Why do you want an iron nail from a boat?'

'An astrologer told me to wear one as a ring for forty days.'

I wondered if this was somehow a surrogate for doing a journey: carry something that has crossed the water. Amerjeet was keen to tell me of other remedies. 'Sometimes they tell you to feed fish or a black dog every morning.'

'But the boatman refused?'

'He said many people come and ask to buy a nail but he always refuses and sends them away.'

'He doesn't believe in that nonsense?'

'No! He believes it. The problem is that his boats are made of plastic.'

The modern world, it seemed, had got ahead of its people.

When we returned to the house, the Professor had gone to bed feeling unwell, and my fever came back, too. That night was the worst I had had, waking up confused and disoriented, dreaming of violent attacks and fish with rings in their noses being caught and force-fed. Then I was in an open-topped car with some religious maniacs who were holding a pad of chloroform over my nose and mouth and I was trying to hold my breath and play dead but they only pressed the pad down harder and harder and I just had to breathe.

At dawn there was the Professor sitting in the armchair, stroking his white beard.

'You are dreaming again, Rushby of Thirsk. I, too, had bad dreams and went for my walk but could not complete it this morning. Are you really leaving us today?'

'Yes, I will take the bus to Amritsar.'

'There is no need for hurrying. In our tradition you may stay for weeks, even months, and still we will only be happy.'

'Thank you – I can't think how I would have managed without your help.'

Later in the morning, having dissuaded Mehtab from accompanying me to Amritsar, I bought a ticket on the coach and set off.

The bus journey was six hours of rattle and bounce. We crossed the Sutlej, a green glacial rush of water from the Himalayas, bound for the Indus and the Arabian Sea. Twice we stopped at thatched wayside halts and drank freshly squeezed oranges with a sprinkling of salt and spices. There were canals full of water and big mansions: the Punjab is the richest state in India.

The newspaper that day reported three men arrested with guns in Chandigarh, a reminder that, though the rebellion has died down, it has not gone away. A young Sikh in the seat next to me told me that after 1990 the militants had either gone into exile or been hunted down. 'The police would report two men dead in an "encounter" and then these men were assumed to be militants,' he said in a low voice. 'Thousands died, but usually these encounters were created by the police. They were just shooting people at will.'

The chief of police at that time had just been convicted of sexual harassment and had fled to Delhi. 'He is on the list,' said the young man ominously.

'Have you heard of the Koh-i-Noor diamond?' I asked.

He looked at me curiously. 'Of course. It is a rallying point for us. We want it back from your Queen, then we can unite the Sikhs.'

'Do you think the British will give it back?'

'Yes,' he said firmly. 'At the end of Victoria's reign it could not be imagined that the British would leave India, but they did – within fifty years. So who knows?'

We reached the outskirts of Amritsar, a normal Indian city after Chandigarh: streets choked with people and vehicles, piles of refuse, and a dull smog cloaking the red disc of the setting sun. I took a cycle rickshaw to a cheap hotel. My money was almost gone now and I was forced to stay in places full of fleas and cockroaches. This one was no exception: a filthy room that shook when lorries thundered past and freezing cold. I ate in an empty restaurant, then went back and slept fully clothed under the blanket.

The hospitality of Mehtab and the Professor had helped disguise my reaction to the robbery: now I saw a thief in everyone who spoke to me. Attempts to overcharge me made me lose my temper instantly; when I stood up I felt faint; when I sat down my hip bones ached – I really was in pathetic shape.

For two days I hung about the dreary hotel, unable to summon the energy to get out of bed and visit the Golden Temple or to contact Beant Singh. The television churned out endless Hindi pop videos, Bombay Busby Berkeley extravaganzas of fizzing vitality and colour. I warmed my hands on the back of the set. In the mornings a boy would bring a plastic bucket of hot water – enough for a few delicious seconds of scooping. Then quickly dry and back into all my clothes: longjohns, tee-shirt, shirt, jumper, sleeveless rough wool waistcoat, jacket, shawl, scarf and Pathan cap, at all times. But still shivering.

On the third afternoon I forced myself out for a walk. Near the railway station I saw a sign for a homeopathic clinic. The doctor was closing up for lunch and took me with him. We ate chicken tikka and drank canned beer at his club, once the haunt of British officers. 'My family are from Burma,' he said. 'We went many many generations ago and built up a ferry business around Rangoon. It was very successful. Then World War Two came: my grandfather and father lost everything. They walked from Rangoon to Calcutta through the jungle. I can remember them talking about it when I was a small child – the horror of it. My father never lost his fear of the jungle after that; they saw such terrible things, such suffering. My father came to Amritsar and started this business twenty-five years ago. Now I carry it on.'

We ordered two more beers, the first alcohol I had drunk since leaving Diu almost two months before. 'Sikhs drink too much – that's a bad thing here,' he said. 'But the good thing is the sense of equality. All can eat together – even the leper can eat with the king. But everywhere in the world castes emerge – haves and have-nots – feudalism survives in Punjab. Big landlords call me and demand I go and see them at home, or they appear at the surgery and expect to jump the queue when fifty people are waiting. I refuse. So they don't like me.' He grinned. Like the Professor, I think he enjoyed pricking the egos of the high and mighty.

'So is it poor people who come to you?'

'All kinds – some rich VIPs do come. Do you know Operation Blue Star?' He was referring to the 1984 storming of the Golden Temple complex by Indira Gandhi's troops. 'The Army cut off Amritsar and attacked. But they were utterly unprepared for those defenders who kept them back. In the end the army had to bring up tanks and artillery against rifles.

'Well, it was a difficult time, but I kept the surgery open. One day an army general came – a Sikh himself but commanding the attack on the temple. He wanted some homeopathic medicine. He said to me: "If we had such fighters, we could take all Pakistan."'

He smiled and leaned back. The story was intended to illustrate the tenacity of the Sikh militants, but I was thinking of the Koh-i-Noor and the consequences if it unleashed such ferocious martial energy. Most of the former Sikh state is now in Pakistan. In fact, Pakistan claims the Koh-i-Noor itself on the grounds that its natural home is Lahore. The claim was presented in 1976 by Zulfikar Ali Bhutto, then Prime Minister and son of the Diwan of Junagadh, Shah Nawaz Bhutto. I was almost convinced that it would be better for all concerned if the stone lay, peacefully, in the Tower of London, whoever the rightful owner might be. But I had yet to meet Beant Singh.

Shortly before nightfall, the doctor drove me back to my hotel. 'Is there some medicine I could take?' I asked, feeling I ought to restore the doctor-patient boundaries – for his sake.

He waved the request away. 'Nothing for you. Just rest a little.' I said goodbye and got out of the car, hoping that one day, an Indian visitor to Britain might stumble into a doctor's surgery and be taken for lunch at the local golf club.

There was a small fire burning on the wasteland near the hotel and an old man warming his hands. I didn't want to go back to that cold room with its dripping tap and torn curtains. Instead I telephoned the number Mehtab had given me and arranged a meeting that night with the next claimant to the jewel of Krishna.

CHAPTER 11

Shadow-maker, shadow-slayer, arrowing
light from clime to clime,
Hear thy myriad laureates hail thee
monarch in their woodland rhyme.
Warble bird, and open flower, and,
men, below the dome of azure
Kneel adoring Him the Timeless in the
flame that measures Time!

Alfred, Lord Tennyson, 'Akbar's Dream'

THE car came for me after nine when the city was already settling down for the night. The street beggars had lit their scraps of cardboard for a moment's respite from the cold, or else taken shelter in the shanties that seem to grow like weeds on any unguarded verge. We sped out of town along a straight road lined with eucalyptus, the trunks ghostly white in the headlights. The wind had dropped and curls of mist were gathering in the hollows. We turned off and took a rough earth track for about half a mile, pulling up at a pair of black iron gates.

They opened before we knocked. I was led into a living room where three men were waiting: an interpreter, Beant Singh's son and Beant Singh himself, looking composed and venerable with a white beard and a cream Kashmiri shawl around his shoulders. There were armchairs with neat white anti-macassars, a pair of crossed brass swords, a picture of Guru Nanak and a wall carpet portraying Guru Gobind Singh.

Beant Singh looked the part, as Mehtab had told me: dignified and aloof. The interpreter spoke for him, answering my questions without even bothering to check with the man himself. Mehtab had warned me about this – 'He's a local journalist who has agreed to help with the case.'

Some nuts and biscuits were brought in with tea. 'Beant Singh's great grandfather, Thakur Singh was poisoned by British agents in Pondicherry in 1887,' said the interpreter. 'His grandfather was then held under house arrest in Delhi for ten years and during that time thousands of acres around here were confiscated and auctioned by the British. Beant Singh saw the light of day in 1926 in their ancestral village. During Japanese invasion and Partition more lands were lost. So he lived most his life, quietly farming the small lands left to him.'

'What changed that?'

'In 1976 the Indian government claimed Dulip Singh's remains from Britain. Then Beant Singh announced he was the rightful heir, but the remains never came.'

I turned to the man himself. 'And since then you have been trying to recover your lost properties?'

But the journalist answered. 'That is correct. His claim is based on the fact that his father, Pratap Singh was adopted by Princess Sophia Alexandra Duleep Singh, His Highness's third daughter. His father was the Maharaja's cousin. It is written in a letter to your Queen.'

He spoke in Punjabi and there was a flurry of activity from all but Beant Singh: he had yet to speak or move, apart from the occasional gracious nod of his head.

A large buff file of correspondence was produced and lots of papers piled onto me, including a photocopy of the petition presented to Queen Elizabeth II. It began, 'With due deference and unflinching faith in your deep sense of justice and fairness, in the culture and polity your Excellency represents, I lay down the following lines for your kind perusal . . .' and ended:

. . . to restore to me the possession and venerable belongings i.e.
    a) Plume (Kalgi of Guru Gobind Singh)
    b) 'Kohinoor' diamond

c) The Gold Chair of Maharaja Ranjit Singh

d) Any other property in the name of the late Maharaja Duleep Singh.

> . . . with best regards,
> Truly yours,
> Beant Singh Sandhanwalia.

Next a vast genealogy was produced on a sheet of paper as big as a bedsheet. The Maharaja's ancestry was shown, reaching back to Chundar 'Founder of the Lunar Dynasty', and at the bottom, on the extreme right, someone had pencilled in Beant Singh.

All this was very unconvincing, but I felt my initial sceptical reaction to be wrong. The case was caught up in traditions and practices and language long forgotten elsewhere, but that was irrelevant. Like the wormholes in an antique piece of furniture, they even added authenticity. Beant Singh's case was as sound as any could be, given the time elapsed. A panel of professors at Amritsar University had investigated and concluded that he was the rightful heir.

In his letter to Tony Blair, Beant Singh had repeated the claim and ended, 'It is never too late to right a wrong, Your Excellency, Hoping for Justice and fair play. Yours faithfully . . .'

But the problem was, the Koh-i-Noor's history has no connection with justice and fair play; power is its guiding light. When India, or indeed Pakistan, Afghanistan and Iran (for all have claims) are so strong that Britain needs to curry favour, the Koh-i-Noor might find itself heading east, but not before.

'Do you really think you will get it?' I asked. 'A snake doesn't give back its dinner.'

'Yes, he does,' said the intepreter. 'I mean Beant Singh believes he will get it.'

'No, ask him, please.'

Beant Singh smiled gently and said in Punjabi, 'The British gave back Hong Kong, didn't they?'

'What would you do with the diamond?'

'Give it to the Golden Temple.'

'But that is a symbol of Sikh nationalism.'

Again I had to insist on a direct answer. 'The Golden Temple is for anyone, not only Sikhs, it has four doors and anyone can pray there. The Koh-i-Noor would be the property of all Indians. You know Ranjit Singh was a secular person – he had Persian as the court language and Hindu officials.'

A plate of cake was now brought in, a huge pink thing with lots of artificial cream. We were each handed a plate with cake forks and a fresh cup of tea. I had the impression this was not the first time they had gone through the ritual of entertaining a guest who needed convincing.

'Isn't the truth,' I asked between mouthfuls – Beant Singh had cleverly avoided having any. It's difficult to appear dignified with artificial cream on the tip of your nose, 'isn't the truth that ownership is not about money but about power? If you have the diamond, you become a very important man in the Punjab, a hugely important man. Politicians come to you, you get an office, your opinion is consulted, you decide things.'

Beant Singh listened carefully. I think he understood before he got the translation. I wondered how much he knew about what I knew before I even arrived. I had been told he was already fêted by local bigwigs and had an office, though no position.

'We want only that Dulip Singh and Thakur Singh's sacrifices are recognised – their suffering both economic and physical – we want recognition that they were heroes of Indian Independence.'

He would not accept the political influence motive.

'No! Only in respect of honour.'

'And if I had the diamond in my pocket now – sent to return it to you. Wouldn't you be tempted to keep it?'

The interpreter laughed, but Beant Singh drew himself up gravely and tutted dismissively.

I thought I heard his son whisper under his breath. 'But would you give it?' And we grinned at each other.

There was no way through this thicket of suspicion: no one would ever admit that the diamond held untapped reserves of political power; no one would even admit to knowing another man before the political advantage had been calculated.

It was almost eleven when I was driven back into town. The mist had thickened around the trees, sudden blank sheets of vapour that were thrown over the car then whipped away. The driver did not slow down: the streets were empty now except for the occasional rickshaw man trying to sleep on his passenger seat.

'You should visit the Golden Temple,' he said. 'But go early – around 4 a.m.'

'Why?'

'There is some ceremony – it may be interesting for you.'

The idea of leaving the bed in the bitter cold, before the sun was up or tea brewed, was not very attractive, but I assured him I would take his advice.

I didn't sleep much that night. My head was spinning with claims and counter-claims, with proofs and rebuttals, with what I was not to say and to whom, with the names of men who had claimed the diamond over the millennia and those who claimed it now; I saw all their greedy eyes and selfish motives, their tricks and subterfuges. The only men who came out well in the whole sorry story were those who gave the stone away without ever wanting it: Babur, the first Mughal, who simply handed it to his son and asked to be buried under the sky, not in some great, cold mausoleum; Krishna who only wanted it in order to prove himself innocent of theft, then gave it away again.

I got up several times and opened the door that led to a step-wide balcony over the road. The iron balustrade was thick with black smuts thrown up by lorries during the day. Across the road was a smart restaurant, one I might have treated myself to a meal in, had I not been relieved of my cash. In the gutter in front of it, an old rickshaw man huddled in a ragged brown blanket tried to warm himself on a few burning sticks. I was shaking with cold, too, and envied him his fire.

Some time around two o'clock I must have fallen asleep though not for long, I woke with a start at three, still shivering. That was the final irritation that snapped me: waking cold, though I was fully dressed and wrapped in a blanket with my face swathed in a headscarf. I paced around the room talking to myself, like a street lunatic, railing against the thieves who had robbed me and all the petty irritations that travel in India entails. Like some Jain ascetic, I was ready to be buried alive

[249]

inside a remote hermit's cave and left in peace: I wanted nothing more to do with human beings.

At 4 a.m I left the room only to find the hotel door padlocked and no one around. So I kicked at the metal until someone came, grunting and scratching. 'Where you go? You pay bill already?'

'I'm going to the temple,' I said, 'Then I'll come back and get my bag and leave.'

The old rickshaw man was pleased to have a fare, as his fire had burnt out. We set off slowly, weaving across the road while he hawked up great gobs of phlegm. There was a quarter moon hanging low over the rooftops which gave sufficient light to see. At the railway bridge we walked up to the top, then rode down and the wind was so sharp it whipped tears out of my eyes. The old man grunted and groaned. In the market, there were men and dogs standing immobile in the middle of the road, as though waiting for the sun to thaw their frozen blood. Behind them were the dark and dingy streets, buildings hard-used and uncared for, with rubbish piled at the doors and windows blackened. As we approached the temple, I heard singing, and there were people moving purposefully, stepping forward to reach their goal.

The first sight as we rounded a corner was not overwhelming: two hundred yards away stood a vast white building, worthy of a Victorian railway headquarters, with clocktower and classical flourishes, all floodlit. The singing, more a nasalised chanting with drums and reedy harmonium, was being relayed from inside.

I followed the crowd, depositing my shoes and socks in the cloak-room, then hurrying towards the archway guarded by two large Sikhs, brandishing spears.

'No tobaccos?' demanded one.

I shook my head.

'Keep hair covered.' I pulled my headscarf tighter around my head. He pointed at the footbath with his spear. 'Wash.'

The marble slabs underfoot were like ice and my feet were going numb. The footbath, by comparison, seemed almost warm.

Then the Golden Temple began to weave its spell. Entering through the arch, steps lead down and there is a pool, once a natural lake they say, about 250 yards by 150. To the right of its centre, connected by a long causeway to the bank, was the Golden Temple itself.

Every temple in India I had visited, every church in Europe, any-where that seeks to evoke the spiritual or appeal to man's religious side, all those places make the visitor look up. Your eyes are drawn heavenwards by the soaring columns, or the domes or the spires, but the Golden Temple does the opposite. At the entrance, you are twenty steps above the water and the light, clipping the wavetops, wriggles across the walls of gold in sinuous rhythms. If your head is empty of sleep and your feet freezing, while your head sweats a fever, those sinuous rhythms begin to weave and twitch to the chanted charms, the endless repetition of the sacred book, the *Granth Sahib*, read aloud and never stopped, like the sacred flame of the Zoroastrians, forever burning.

The temple is not large, a two-storey structure with a fine casement window looking out over the lake, gilded like the stern window on a great galleon. A sixty-yard causeway tethers it to the shore and this walkway continues all around the lower storey which is of white marble with a door on each side. Above this, all is gold. The windows are flanked by pilasters of gold and shaded by golden ledges. The cornice is lined with tiny golden domes and then at each corner is a chchatri, an octagonal pavilion with a golden dome. In the centre of the roof rises a segmented golden dome hedged all around with gilded spires and masts.

To see it, across the black water under black night sky, is the finest sight in India. I went down to the water with the other pilgrims, then set off along the white marble bank, moving quickly to keep warm. At the eastern steps men were stripping off to dip in the holy waters. Next to them, in a glass-fronted hermit's cell, was a venerable greybeard, sitting cross-legged and reciting the *Granth Sahib*, a huge leather-bound tome laid on tasselled silk cushions.

People moved quickly, without talking, and across the lake in the tall white building known as the Akal Takhat, a big drum began to pound, its reverberations echoing off the walls of the temple complex. At the end of the causeway coming through a large gateway I saw men lifting a golden palanquin onto their shoulders. Inside were gold cushions and garlands of marigolds. Some people threw flower petals over the crowned roof. Each of the palanquin-bearers staggered forward a few paces, then others would come and take on their burden, dozens of them, working together to carry the palanquin across the court-yard. When they reached the foot of a flight of steps at the side of the Akal Takhat, they set it down.

The Akal Takhat is the centre of Sikhism, the place where all deci-sions are taken and the weapons of the gurus are kept. In a first-floor room, under white marble arches, men in blue turbans were gathering and chanting. The heartbeat of the drum then paused. A man next to me blew on a long serpent of a horn, the cry of it fading into eerie silence as the people stood watching. There were hundreds of them now.

Suddenly the drum began again, this time an urgent rhythm, pounding along at battle speed. I saw an old man come across to the window and on his shoulders was the *Granth Sahib* in a silk brocade cover. He reappeared at the head of the stairs and descended. Men car-rying staffs guarded his precious cargo, another swept it with long flicks of a fly-whisk, and one more carried a saffron tasselled flag woven with the Sanskrit letter for OM – *Om Mani Padme Hum*, All Hail the Diamond in the Lotus. The book was laid in the palanquin, then hoisted onto a dozen shoulders. Around me the men surged forward to be in front, to take their turn. I stepped instinctively back, unsure if I was observer or participant, then I felt hands take my shoulders and looking around I saw a saffron turban and white beard.

'Take your place,' he said. 'You can take your place.'

He moved me forward into the throng by the gate and we waited with the rest, stepping backwards onto the causeway as the crowd pressed in. As the holy book approached, the firm hands took my shoulders again and directed me under the corner bar of the palan-quin. Then I took the golden rod in my hands and felt both the chill of the metal and the warmth where the hands of the previous man had been. The weight came down on my shoulder as he slipped out in front of me; a big weight bearing down, but only for an instant, a fraction of a second, when it flashed into my mind that perhaps I could not take this weight, it would be too much. Then I felt it lift as others took the strain too, and we surged forward, staggering slightly, across the dark water towards the glittering temple. I wanted to carry that weight all the way across the water. I felt a tremendous burst of adrenaline. The palanquin was rolling forward to its destination on a wave of humanity, surfing to the golden lotus in the lake.

At the west door of the temple itself, the palanquin was set down and the chief *giani*, or priest, took the book on his shoulders for the final few steps into the temple. Inside was a press of people and the book moved slowly to its place under a jewelled umbrella – like the fly-whisk, a traditional eastern sign of kingship. Everyone was chanting the opening words of the *Granth Sahib*, 'Sat nam wahe guru', 'The Lord is wonderful, Truth is his name!' Faces looked in from a first-floor balcony. The book was laid on a lectern and the cover opened. Now the *giani* began to sing alone, his voice deep and soft in the silence of hundreds of people. The pattering of the tabla joined him, then the wheeze of the harmonium.

For what seemed an age I had thought of nothing, just taken part, now I watched the old *giani* singing and the jewels above his head, and I thought: don't bring the diamond here, with its curse for those who covet it. No good would come of the Koh-i-Noor's presence in the Golden Temple: it was brought to the Punjab by extortion, and it left there by theft. This is one flower that needs no diamond inside it – none other than the *Granth Sahib*. Better that the last wish of Ranjit Singh, delivered on his deathbed and conveniently ignored by his courtiers, better that his wish is followed. 'Let the Koh-i-Noor be taken to the temple of Jagganath,' he is supposed to have said, 'as an offering to Krishna.'

His ministers refused to comply, claiming the stone was treasure of state and as such the property of the Maharaja's successors, not his to dispose of as he pleased. No one thought to remind them that great diamonds can only be the gift of kings or the spoils of the flashing sword. Ranjit Singh's last wish was set aside and the Sikhs lost the jewel regardless. The diamond moved, as it always had, and Queen Victoria, as Empress of India, had a claim that was logical, if not strictly legal. Her great great granddaughter, however, does not. What better fate than to return it to Krishna, the man-god who was there at the beginning, and let the diamond take its place in India where it belongs.

As the people began to sing with their priest, I stepped outside to let others in and found myself on the walkway around the side of the temple. Looking out over the water, the air was suddenly filled with birds, thousands of swallows swirling and diving around the temple.

It was still totally dark above and too cold for any insect to fly, so what had brought them was a mystery. But they came: thick clouds of scything wings, squealing in pleasure at the sheer joy of wheeling around and around the golden bud of the temple. Then, as fast as they had appeared, they were gone, settling onto the ledges and niches of the surrounding temple buildings.

I went to the low platform on the western door and touched the water of the lake. Hundreds of people were now moving back across the water and I joined them. At the gateway, attendants were spooning mounds of thick sweet porridge into the right hand of each pilgrim. Everyone stood on the marble banks eating together – no caste bar, no dietary restrictions, no exclusions, no food feuds.

I walked then, following many others around and around the lake, a half mile each time until the sun came up. Then I sat at last, exhausted, where I could soak up the rays. Only when I was warm was I ready to leave.

On the outside of the temple, at the perimeter gate, there were gangs of police in blue and red turbans, tapping their steel-tipped lathis on their boots. Hordes of souvenir shops had opened up, selling fairy-lit pictures of gurus and other worthless gaudy trinkets covered in plastic imitations of rubies, emeralds and diamonds. I collected my shoes. The chanting of the *Granth Sahib* over the loudspeaker was there in the background, but now I could hear the chuntering of tractor engines, the buzz of motorbikes, the cries of babies and the men driving animals out to forage – all the noise of an Indian city waking. Then came the shouts of the rickshaw-pullers as they spotted me: 'Hey You! Foreigner! Come here!'

The unity of mankind did not extend one inch beyond that gate, but at least such a precious jewel existed within the beauty of the white walls and golden centre. I pulled on my socks and shoes, then stood up and stepped out into India, taking with me a memory of that jewel.

EPILOGUE

A month later, on a brutally cold day in an English spring, I drove along the A11 towards Thetford, Suffolk. On the edge of the Elveden woods there is a turning up to the new holiday resort with its futuristic bubble and swimming pool full of slides and tropical plants. A little way further on stands a church and, if you look carefully, through the trees you can see a large stately home. It is now owned by the Guinness family and left unoccupied most of the time, but in Queen Victoria's day it was the residence of Maharaja Dulip Singh.

I pulled up in a lay-by just beyond the church and crossed over the road, between the thundering juggernauts (the word comes from the temple of Jagganath where they keep a fifteen-yard tall chariot for Krishna to ride in at the annual Rath Yatra festival). The churchyard is as peaceful as you could hope: a colonnade leads across from the nave to a tower where there is a chain fence and a sign that reads, 'Private Property'. You can see the house from there and sometimes a visiting Sikh gentleman, carried away by the occasion, tries to get a little nearer and a security man appears and leads him back.

Dulip Singh played at being an English country gentleman from the age of fifteen onwards, converting to Christianity and giving his children English names. Victoria took a kind interest in his welfare, advising warm underwear. Once she allowed him to examine the newly recut Koh-i-Noor which the specialists at Garrards had reduced from 186 carats to 108, thus improving its brilliance and destroying what had lasted for thousands of years. It was pure coincidence that they managed to hit on the numerical representation of the lotus, though a recent reweighing found it to be 105 – the old stone has not finished with its mysteries yet.

The Maharaja admired the jewel and presented it back to Victoria. Later on in life, when he had fallen out with the British, he would comment, 'She has no more right to that diamond than I have to Windsor Castle.'

He spent the last years of his life attempting to instigate a rebellion in the Punjab. In St Petersburg, he solicited revolutionary help in the unlikely disguise of an Irishman named Patrick Casey. The plan was foiled and he was arrested at Aden, then sent back to Paris. It was there that he died in 1893: rumours suggested that he had discovered his second wife, Ada, to be a British agent, and the shock brought on an epileptic fit. His body was returned to his old estate for burial next to his first wife, Bamba, and his son, Albert.

There were a few yellow tulips on the grave when I visited, yellow being the royal colour of the east. I walked across to the tower and looked at the house, all closed up and quiet. There was no need to step over the chain to alert the security guard because he came over anyway, an affable man doing his job and friendly when I explained myself.

'There's beautiful Indian archways inside,' he said, 'and a drawing room in the Indian style. The BBC used it when they filmed *The Moonstone*.'

We walked over to the graves again, the largest stones in the grave-yard, befitting the old lord of the manor.

He was no ordinary security man, I discovered, but the grandson of Dulip Singh's gamekeeper. 'He was very fond of His Highness,' he said. 'But there was no nonsense with him. One ghillie up in Scotland called him a black bugger for dropping his rod and His Highness sacked him on the spot.'

'Do you get many Sikhs coming to visit?'

'Oh, yes. They want to see inside the house, of course, but I can't let them. It's a shame really 'cos they come a long way. I believe they're putting a statue up in Thetford next year, so I imagine we'll see a lot more of them. Nice people, real gentlemen.'

We began to drift back towards the shelter of the colonnade. A bitter wind was gusting through, shaking the heads of a few early daffodils.

'Did your family keep any mementoes?' I asked. 'From the Maharja, I mean.'

He shook his head. 'Not that I know of . . . there was a painting when I was a boy, a portrait of His Highness. It used to hang on our sitting room wall above the fire.'

'It's gone?'

He nodded. 'As I remember, a Sikh gentleman came looking around. He was lost and my mother got chatting to him and invited him in. When he saw that portrait over our fire, his eyes filled up. My mother was a kind-hearted soul so she lifted it down and gave it to him. He didn't want to accept at first, of course, but she insisted – said it was his by rights.'

We reached the chain and stopped. 'Well, I best be getting back,' he said. 'Goodbye.'

We shook hands, then he stepped over the chain and set off towards the empty house.

CHRONOLOGY

Diamonds are easy to hide and difficult to trace – hence the uncertainties over the origins of the Koh-i-Noor. The name itself only appears in 1739 when Nadir Shah looted the great diamond from Delhi. Previously there had been Krishna's Syamantaka jewel, Babur's diamond, and many others. That these stones were all one – the same gem that sits in the Tower of London today – is possible but not proven. Perhaps what is important is that monarchs have wanted, so desperately, to believe in that strange and astonishing pedigree.

DATE	EVENTS	THE GREAT DIAMOND/ KOH-I-NOOR
C.1000 BC		Krishna rescues great diamond which has been given to man by the Sun god.
1296 AD	Alauddin Khilji takes the throne in Delhi and begins plundering the Deccan.	
1309		Alauddin's forces capture Warangal and take a great diamond from the Raja.
1316–1525		After Alauddin's death the great diamond finds its way into the hands of the Raja of Gwalior.

DATE	EVENTS	THE GREAT DIAMOND/ KOH-I-NOOR
1518	The diamond-rich area of Golconda becomes an independent kingdom.	
1525	Babur, the first Mughal, invades India.	His son Humayun captures the diamond in Agra and, though Babur allows him to keep it, the name 'Babur's diamond' is often used.
1544		Humayun, in exile, gives the diamond to Shah Tahmasp of Persia.
1547		Diamond sent to the Deccan and probably sold.
1556–1605	Akbar	
1605–1627	Jehangir	
1620	British factory established in Surat.	
1628–1658	Shah Jehan	
1656		Mir Jumla, Prime Minister of Golconda, gives a large diamond to Shah Jehan.
1658–1707	Aurangzeb	
1664	Sivaji's first sack of Surat.	
1687	Golconda and its treasure is seized by Aurangzeb.	
1719–1748	Muhammad Shah (the last independent Mughal).	
1739	Persian invader Nadir Shah sacks Delhi but leaves the Mughals as vassals.	Nadir Shah takes a large diamond in the invasion and names it 'Koh-i-Noor' – Mountain of Light.
1747	Nadir Shah assassinated.	Ahmad Khan Abdali takes Koh-i-Noor to Afghanistan and founds the Durrani dynasty. The Koh-i-Noor is passed down to the last of them, Shah Shuja.

DATE	EVENTS	THE GREAT DIAMOND/ KOH-I-NOOR
1799	Ranjit Singh founds a Sikh kingdom in the Punjab.	
1813		Ranjit Singh takes the Koh-i-Noor from the exiled Shah Shuja.
1839	Ranjit Singh dies.	
1843	Dulip Singh, his son, takes the throne but loses the Second Sikh War to the British.	
1846		Capture of the Koh-i-Noor from the Sikhs.
1850		Dalhousie gives the Koh-i-Noor to Queen Victoria, who has it recut.
1857	The Mutiny breaks out in Meerut on 10th May. Delhi is retaken by the British in September.	
1858	The Mutiny ends in Gwalior on 20th June.	
1862	Last Mughal, Bahadur Shah, dies in exile in Rangoon.	

BIBLIOGRAPHY

Many of the older works listed here are available in India as reprints.

EARLY WORKS IN TRANSLATION:

ABU-L-FAZL, *Akbar-nama*. Trans. Beveridge, H., 3 vols., Calcutta, 1907–1939.
BABUR, *Baburnama*. Trans. Beveridge, A., London, 1921.
DUTT, R. (trans.), *The Mahabharata*. Everyman, 1917.
ELLIOTT, H.M., AND DOWSON, J., *The History of India as told by its own historians*. 7 vols., London, 1867.
GULBADAN, *Humayun-nama*. Trans. Beveridge, A., London, 1902.
JEHANGIR, *Tuzuk-i-Jahangiri*. Trans. Rogers, A., London, 1909–1914.
KHUSRAU, A., *Khaza'inul Futuh*. Trans. Muhammad Habib, Madras, 1931.
WILSON, H.H. (trans.), *Vishnu Purana*. London, 1868.

EARLY TRAVELLERS:

BERNIER, F., *Travels in the Mogul Empire*. Constable, 1891.
FOSTER, W. (ed.), *Early Travels in India, 1583–1619*. London, 1921.
MARCO POLO, *The Travels*, Penguin, 1958.
MOSELEY, C.W.R.D., *The Travels of Sir John Mandeville*. Penguin, 1983.
TAVERNIER, J.B., *Travels in India*. (ed. V. Ball), 2 vols., London, 1889.

WORKS DEALING SPECIFICALLY WITH DIAMONDS:

ABDUL AZIZ, *The Imperial Treasury of the Indian Mughuls*. Lahore, 1942.
AMINI, IRADJ, *The Koh-i-Noor Diamond*. New Delhi, 1994.

[263]

BALFOUR, L., *Famous Diamonds*. Colchester, 1992.

CHRISTIE'S, *Important Indian Jewellery*. Sale catalogue. October, 1997.

EPSTEIN, E.J., *The Diamond Invention*. Hutchinson, 1982.

GILL, ARTAR SINGH, *Maharaja and the Koh-i-Noor*. Punjab, 1982.

HALL, CATHY, *Gems and Precious Stones*. Quintet, 1993.

HOWARTH, S., *Koh-i-Noor Diamond*. Quartet, 1980.

KANTILAL, C., *Diamonds from India*. Bombay, 1983.

SAHA, N.N., *Speaking and Healing through Gems*. New Delhi, 1984.

OTHER WORKS:

BINYON, L., *Akbar*. Constable, 1932.

BOSWORTH, (ed.), *Encyclopedia of Islam*. Vol. VIII, Leiden, 1995.

BROWN, H. (ed.), *The Sahibs*. Hodge, 1948.

BURTON, D., *The Raj at Table*. Faber and Faber, 1993.

DALTON, C., *The Life of Thomas Pitt*. C.U.P., 1915.

DASS, D.J., *Maharaja: lives, loves and intrigues of the Indian princes*. Bombay, 1969.

DESAI, S.H., *Saurashtra: a historical profile*. Junagadh, 1996.

ELLISON BANKS FINDLY, *Nur Jahan: Empress of Mughal India*. O.U.P., 1993.

FOSTER, W., *The English Factories in India*. Oxford, 1908.

GASCOIGNE, B., *The Great Moghuls*. Constable, 1998.

GOSSE, PHILIP, *The History of Piracy*. Longmans, 1932.

HANSEN, W., *The Peacock Throne*. B.S.B., 1982.

HOEY, B., *Mountbatten, the Private Story*. Sidgwick and Jackson, 1994.

KEAY, J., *India Discovered*. Collins, 1981.

KEAY, J., *The Honourable Company*. HarperCollins, 1991.

LOCKHART, L., *Nadir Shah*. Luzac, 1938.

LUTHER, NARENDRA, *Prince, Poet, Lover, Builder: Muhammad Qult Qutb Shah, the Founder of Hyderabad*. Ministry of Information, New Delhi, 1991.

MEISAMI, J.S., *Sea of Precious Virtues: bahr al-fava'id*. University of Utah Press, 1991

MENOM, V.P., *The Integration of the Indian States*. Princeton, 1956.

MESROUB, J.S., *Armenians in India*. New Delhi, 1937.

MICHELL, G., *The Penguin Guide to the Monuments of India*. Vol I, 1989.

NEZHAD, M.H.M., *Zindaqiyeh pur Majraye Nadir Shah*. Tehran, 1966.

PATNAIK, NAVEEN, *A Second Paradise: Indian Courtly Life 1590–1947*. Sidgwick and Jackson, 1985.

RIZVI, S.A.A., *The Wonder that was India*. Sidgwick and Jackson, 1987.

SHARMA, Y.D., *Delhi and its Neighbourhood*. Archaeological Survey of India, 1990.

SPEAR, P., *Delhi: its monuments and history.* Oxford India, 1943. Reprinted 1994.

SPEAR, P., *A History of India.* Vol II. Pelican, 1965.

TALBOYS WHEELER, J., *Early Records of British India.* London, 1878.

TOD, J., *Annals and Antiquities of Rajas'than.* 2 Vols., 1829. Reprinted Calcutta, 1997.

TROTTOR, CAPT. L.J., *A Leader of Light Horse: Life of Hodson of Hodson's Horse.* 1901.

VILLIERS STUART, C.M., *Gardens of the Great Mughals.* A.C. Black, 1913.

YULE, H. AND BURNELL, A., *Hobson-Jobson.* London, 1886. Reprinted Calcutta, 1986.

INDEX